Cushions & Curtains

Ann Openshaw

The Art of Crafts

First published in 2001 by
The Crowood Press Ltd
Ramsbury, Marlborough
Wiltshire SN8 2HR

British Library Cataloguing-in-Publication Data
A catalogue record for this book is available from the British Library.

ISBN 1 86126 351 1

Photographs by Phil Chambers.

Line artwork by Graham Kent.

Computer work for the author by Alex Pickering.

Typefaces used: Melior (*main text and headings*), Helvetica (*captions*).

Designed by D & N Publishing
Baydon, Marlborough, Wiltshire.

Printed in Hong Kong

DEDICATION

For 'Arthur', my children, grandchildren, loyal friends and my students past and present.

ACKNOWLEDGEMENTS

I have received the most enormous support from so many kind friends and students in the course of writing this book. For each of their special contributions I am very grateful to Moira and Stuart Jennings, Eldig Luke, Sue Hart, Geoffrey and Thyra Harrison, Pat Dixon, Rod and Val Haymer, Alan Reeves, Paul Knight, Kim White, Karen Sheehy, Bernice and Michael Streule, and particularly Alex Pickering, Phil Chambers and Graham Kent. Many thanks to the whole team for their generous support and friendship, which has made writing this book so meaningful and worthwhile.

The fabrics and accessories in this book have been purchased from or provided by the John Lewis Partnership. The Crowood Press and the author would like to thank the Partnership at High Wycombe for their generous advice and assistance.

The author acknowledges the use of *The Illustrated Book of Fabrics* by Martin Hardingham as a reference.

Contents

Introduction

For many years my students have been urging me to write a book along the lines of the courses I have given them. From personal experience I know the importance of not assuming the reader understands certain techniques, which can then make it difficult to follow the instructions, particularly as the tasks become more complex, but rather to work through the steps in a steady and structured way.

In this book I have used the same approach as in my courses to give you the help and instruction, which my students have enjoyed. I have started at the very beginning with fabrics and equipment, guiding you through and explaining the range of products available – this can be as daunting as making the first stitch.

The projects themselves start with a simple cushion to help you learn some initial techniques, and then progress by introducing new skills as we work through more advanced cushions and footstools before moving on to curtains. Don't be discouraged if something goes wrong; remember to work slowly through the steps and use the diagrams and photographs to follow the project.

Gradually, with the new skills and confidence that is gained from completed projects, the world of soft furnishings will open up to you and you will be able to try your own ideas tailored to your own homes and tastes with professional and exciting results. This is where the fun starts – when you know you can do it too and you have a sense of pride in what you have achieved.

Please bear in mind that this book has been written as a course in soft furnishings. It is important, particularly if you are a complete beginner, that you start at the beginning and progressively work through the book, rather than reading only specific sections of it.

METRIC AND IMPERIAL MEASUREMENT

Before beginning the worked projects of this book, make up your mind whether you will work in metric or imperial measurements. Do not change direction.

The worked projects in this book are in both metric and imperial to make it easier for you to follow.

I still find many of my students, both young and old, prefer to use imperial measurements. I do try to encourage use of the metric system because I think you will find it very much easier to make calculations for fabrics, and in particular for curtains, if you work in metric measurements.

1 Fabrics for Soft Furnishings

Today, at the start of the twenty-first century, there are so many different fabrics on the market that it can be quite overwhelming when you first enter the soft-furnishing department of departmental stores or fabric shops. The labels attached to the rolls (bolts) can be equally daunting. I do not intend to go into great detail in this extensive subject, but it would help considerably for you to understand a little about fabrics and their make up.

You must also be aware of colour, another subject in its own right and, like fabrics, with a long and interesting history. One of the purposes of this book is to help you choose fabrics with understanding and confidence. Therefore a very basic knowledge of awareness of colour will help you to use it to advantage in your soft furnishings. You may become increasingly interested in fabrics and colour yourself and, if so, there are many good books available on these subjects which make interesting reading.

COLOUR

Each of us have our own taste and know what colours we like. Some find it difficult to blend their ideas with colours they might favour; others are lucky and are born with *natural colour* sense. But most of us need a little guidance and if we look at nature, she will provide the basics. Look at the sky, the sea and the fields. The bright yellow in the sunshine giving you warmth; the sunny yellow daffodils in the spring; the cool blues of the sky and sea; and the green refreshing fields.

The next time you see a rainbow look and observe the deep reds and oranges on one side that will immediately jump out and hold your eye. These are termed the *hot colours* and they give you the impression of advancing towards you. These advancing colours appear to be closer than they really are. On the other side there are blue, indigo and violet, which appear to fade away, and these are termed the *cold colours*. These receding cool colours give you the feeling of distance.

THE COLOUR WHEEL

Many of you will, of course, be familiar with the Colour Wheel and it can be most helpful when considering a choice of colour for your soft furnishing.

The Primary Colours

Red, yellow and blue are the primary colours of dyes and paints, so called because none of these colours can be made by mixing other colours together. These colours sit at equal intervals from each other round the wheel. It is from a combination of these that all other colours are made.

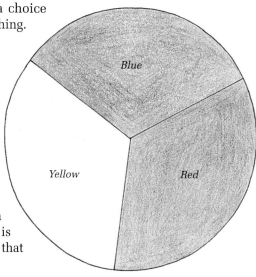

Fig 1 The primary colours.

Fig 2 The secondary colours.

The Secondary Colours

These are formed by mixing two primary (P) colours.

Red	and	*Yellow*	=	*Orange*
Yellow	and	*Blue*	=	*Green*
Blue	and	*Red*	=	*Purple*

Orange, green and purple are known as secondary (S) colours.

The Tertiary Colours

Between each primary and secondary colour is a third colour, the tertiary (T) colour. This is produced by mixing a primary colour with two secondary colours:

Red	and	*Orange*	=	*Flame*
Orange	and	*Yellow*	=	*Tangerine*
Yellow	and	*Green*	=	*Lime*
Green	and	*Blue*	=	*Turquoise*
Blue	and	*Violet*	=	*Lilac*
Violet	and	*Red*	=	*Mauve*

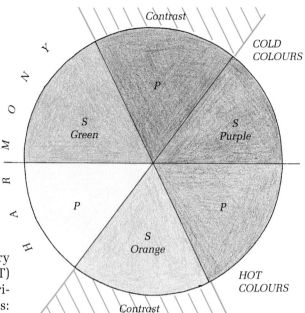

Fig 3 The tertiary colours.

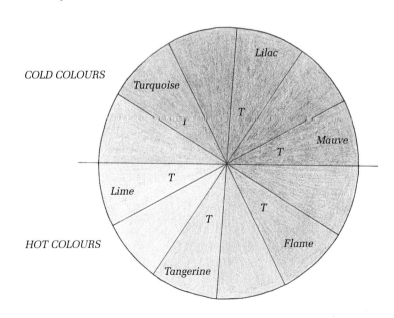

Look again at the colour wheel. The two halves of the circle divide more or less into warm colours and cool colours.

The Colour Wheel (Fig 3) is made up of twelve colours mixed from the three primary colours: red, yellow and blue. Between, there are hundreds of shades of every colour. Paint manufacturers provide colour charts of every imaginable colour.

There will be words that you will meet often when reading about colour. Some we have met already:

Colour is, for example, red, brown, green etc. *Tone* is darkness or lightness of a colour and *shade* small variations of colours and tones. A *tint* is a colour that has been weakened to some extent by the addition of white, for example, pink is a tint produced by weakening red with white. Look at the colour wheel again.

Harmonizing colours are colours that sit next to one another on the colour wheel, for example, green/yellow and yellow lime. This is a harmonizing colour scheme: where colours adjacent or close to each other on the circle work together.

Monochromatic. By using one colour only (often black or sepia), various tones are possible. This is a monochromatic colour scheme. Some of the most successful colour schemes are based on tones of the same colour or by using a textured fabric to add interest.

Complementary colours are colours that sit opposite each other on the colour wheel, for example, yellow/violet, orange/blue. This is a 'Complementary Colour Scheme'. These opposite colours give maximum contrast.

Discordant colours have been taken out of the natural colour order and do not harmonize and do not normally work well together.

The *Neutrals* such as grey, cream, beige and brown. Black and white being the two extremes, are once again seen in nature's colours of slate, stone, wood and earth.

Colour can give the appearance of making a room look warmer or cooler or larger or smaller. The cool colours appearing to recede, whereas warm colours appear to advance.

How do we make all this work for us?

Consider the aspect of the room and establish the direction that the room faces – is it north, south, east or west? Colour varies according to the time of day and whether the light is natural or artificial.

Remember, the sun rises in the east and sets in the west.

ASPECT

- If a room faces east towards the morning sun, it will tend to become cooler during the day with less light.

- If a room faces south it will be bright and sunny all day.

- If a room faces west the best of the sunshine and light will be towards the end of the day.

- If a room faces north it will have no direct sunshine. This will be a room that is devoid of direct sunlight and you must use colour to its advantage to give it warmth and colour.

- The effect of artificial light will change the appearance and colour of the room. When choosing your fabrics and colour-matching fabrics with floor coverings, wallpapers and paints you must see the colour in both artificial and natural light.

- It is important to know the effect light has in the northern hemisphere compared to the southern hemisphere. The sun always rises in the east and sets in the west.

In the northern hemisphere the sun appears to move from left to right across the sky. In the southern hemisphere it appears to do the opposite. These features will affect the way the sun penetrates the room.

The direction of your window is important but you must not forget the view – if any – that you have from the window, and your curtains or any window dressing should be chosen to embrace both direction and outlook.

Even from this brief introduction, you will have gained some understanding and awareness of colour and have realized that it can be used to great advantage in planning a room and choosing your fabrics. To summarize then:

◆ We know yellow is generally a bright, sunny colour and would normally lighten a dark room or one that faces away from the passage of light.

◆ Blue we think of as a cold or cooling colour. We might choose a light blue to give a feeling of space, or a dark blue for a feeling of relaxation.

◆ Green has a fresh feeling that is soothing and restful. A pale green used in a warm, sunny room gives a restful, soothing feeling, whereas a darker olive green is warmer.

◆ Red is a very strong, hot colour. You will see from the colour wheel that red is complemented by green, which has the effect of cooling it down.

◆ Pink is a colour very often used in bedrooms where it gives a feeling of warmth, particularly in a room not facing the sun. The addition of deeper pink, such as rose, can add to this warmth. Dusky pinks make a contrast to green tones.

◆ Peach, apricot and terracotta will bring warmth to an otherwise cold, blue room.

The colour wheel makes it easy. Remember, opposite colours on the wheel offer maximum contrast and colours adjacent harmonize.

FABRICS

Fabric Construction and Weaves

Fabrics are woven, or in some cases knitted or felted materials from either natural or man-made fibres. Fibres are derived from animals or vegetable, or man-made substances. Fibres are spun into threads and then woven on a loom to form a fabric by interlacing the threads. These threads are known as warp threads, which run lengthways on the loom and are crossed by the weft threads into the warp to make a web, i.e. a weave. Many of the fabrics used in soft furnishings are a simple, plain weave of one colour or with the pattern printed on the surface, most of these being printed by machine. Textured weaves using a plain weave are also used to produce a woven pattern where colour is evident on both sides of the fabric, for example, checks and stripes. Fancy weaves are also used where the fabric is woven to produce a textured surface with self-coloured motifs as un-raised designs or with an arrangement of threads to produce a raised surface.

These fabrics can be natural or man-made or blended as a combination of two or more different fibres in the same fabric with manufacturers adding extra properties such as shrink resistance, moth proofing, non-iron or fire proofing etc.

Natural Fabrics

Cotton, linen, silk and wool. These natural fabrics, derived from vegetable and animal sources, have existed long in history and are still widely used today and in many cases still remain 'the best'.

Cotton is a vegetable fibre from a soft, white, fluffy, fibrous substance covering the seeds of cotton flower, a tropical plant. In the main cotton is a cheap fabric to produce. It is strong and dyes well and can be blended with man-made fibres such as polyester.

Linen is a vegetable fibre from the bark of a flax plant. It is not as widely grown as cotton and is much more expensive to produce. It is a strong, hard-wearing fabric but it does crease very badly and for this reason it is often blended with other fibres such as cotton, silk and wool. When it is blended with cotton it is known as *linen union*. Crease-resistant finishes can be added to overcome the strong tendency for this fabric to crease easily.

Silk is an animal fibre from the fine, soft, strong fibre produced by the silkworm, spinning its cocoon of silk. Although silk is a delicate fabric it is the strongest and finest of the natural fabrics, but it must be handled with great care and protected from sunlight, which will cause it to rot.

Wool is an animal fibre, which comes from the fine soft hair that forms the fleece of sheep and goats. It is warm and absorbs moisture. Its biggest disadvantage is that it shrinks easily and is attacked by moths. Wool is often pre-shrunk or treated by manufacturers to be shrink resistant and moth proof.

Man-Made (Synthetic) Fabrics

Man-made fibres are either manufactured entirely by chemical processes or by chemical treatment of natural materials such as wood pulp or cotton waste. Manufacturers are constantly producing new and exciting fibres and treatments for fibres, which allow the man-made fabrics to emulate and, in some cases,

improve on the performance and properties of natural fibre fabrics.

Rayon was the first man-made fabric to be produced from a cellulose fibre. *Cellulose* is the main structural material from plant cell walls. This was produced from wood pulp. In its original form it is little used today and has been modified to produce many new fabrics.

Nylon was the first totally chemical man-made fibre to be developed from minerals from a petroleum base. Like rayon, these fibres have now been modified and mixed with other fibres to produce improved fabrics with added properties.

Polyester made from petroleum chemicals, first made by ICI Imperial Chemical Company under the trade mark *Terylene* and produced in America under the trade name *Dacron*.

Man-made fabrics are many in number and appear under many trade names, which need not be listed here. Suffice it to say if a fabric is not one of those listed under the heading of the natural fabrics – cotton, linen, silk or wool – then it is *man-made*.

FABRICS USED IN SOFT FURNISHINGS

Furnishing fabrics are manufactured with a consideration towards durability, resistance to fading and treated in such a way to enhance the drape and may have extra properties added. It is for these reasons that dress fabrics, which are manufactured with the accent on comfort, should not be used for soft furnishings.

Soft furnishing fabrics are manufactured in 122cm (48in) or 137cm to 140cm (54in to 56in) widths.

Bolts of Material. These are produced in batches, so make sure that if you require more than the amount on one bolt you do have the remaining fabric from the same batch of bolts as different batches of fabric may have slight variations in colour. Bolts of material range from 120–150m. *If possible ask the shop to roll your fabric.*

Fabrics can be grouped into three weights: light, medium and heavy. It is important when using two or more fabrics together in one piece of work that they should be of equal weight otherwise the heavier fabric can distort the lighter.

Light-Weight Fabrics

Sheers, voiles, lace and nets including lightweight cottons and silks. Sheers are fine, translucent or semi-transparent, and many of these are now made with man-made or mixed fibres. The natural fibres are more delicate and less crease resistant but they do drape and hang in softer lines.

Some of these fabrics can be difficult to work with.

Medium-Weight Fabrics

These medium-weight fabrics, mostly used for soft furnishings, cover a range of natural fabrics (cottons, linens and wools) or man-made fabrics or a mixture or both. These fabrics are easy to handle and are used for cushions, curtains and other soft furnishings. Some are suitable for upholstery.

Heavy-Weight Fabrics

These are hard wearing and often used for upholstery. They include cotton, linen union, wool, velvets, tapestry and heavy-weight Damasks. These heavy-weight fabrics can be difficult to work with.

Lining Materials

The addition of a curtain lining considerably adds to the overall appearance of a curtain, adding body and improving the drape of your fabric. At the same time it protects the curtain from dirt and dust and, more important, from the sunlight which both fades and rots the curtain fabric. This is particularly so for silk fabrics.

Linings help to exclude light and add some insulation, as well as giving a neater appearance to the reverse side of the curtain by hiding the turnings and hems.

A variety of different curtain linings are on the market today and it would be an advantage to have a little understanding of these linings before going into the fabric department.

Cotton lining sateen is the most commonly used as this cotton sateen has a

Fig 4 Sateen lining.

slightly shiny surface with an uneven weave to give it a firm finish. It is manufactured in white and in neutral shades of cream or ecru and beige and a range of plain colours. Traditionally, cream or ecru is the most used in making curtains and in the main the most suitable. The white tends to look too white and can discolour quite quickly in sunlight, and the beige is too dark and can change the colour of your face fabric.

You should consider that once a curtain hangs against the daylight, the colour of the lining can change the colour of your face fabric. You must always hold up a piece of your face fabric against the light, backed by a piece of lining of your choice, and see the effect. This is particularly important if you are choosing a face fabric with a white or very pale background.

The other important consideration is the look of your curtains from outside. Do you want a unified appearance to your curtains and blinds as you approach the house?

The same problem will arise if you decide to choose one of the many coloured linings available. They look wonderful in the shop but against the light they can completely change the colour of your fabric. Added to this coloured linings do not always have good dyes and they can fade quickly with the sunlight against them. You must check this before buying as there are certain manufacturers who do guarantee against this and you can return the fabric if this happens. Alternatively, a cheaper, plain coloured chintz fabric is a very suitable choice as a lining fabric as this is less likely to fade.

Lining fabrics are sold in 120cm (48in) wide or 130cm (54in) wide. You must buy the same width of lining fabric as your face fabric. All seams in curtains must lie on top of one another or you will have too many seam lines showing through your curtain in daylight. The lining sateen leaves the factory folded in half, lengthways with the right side to the outside.

The quality of curtain lining material does vary considerably. Always buy good quality cotton lining sateen. Cheaper lining is sometimes a mixture of cotton and man-made fibres. They can also be poor quality cotton, over-starched, which gives a good feel to start with, but once you start working on the fabric, this will quickly wear off and the poor quality will become evident. Once the curtains are hung at the window, and without the body of the added starch, the fabric will relax and quickly sag, spoiling the hang of your curtain.

It is, in fact, better to have a good cotton lining fabric rather than an expensive face fabric. The base of a good lining will enhance the fabric whereas the cheap lining will offer little to the stability and hang of your curtain.

Once the lining is sewn into a curtain, the curtain should be dry cleaned as the face fabric may shrink or relax differently and will cause the curtain to pucker. Detachable linings can be used if you really intend to wash your curtains, perhaps in a kitchen, but will not be nearly as successful. In general, linings should be sewn into a curtain.

Thermal and Blackout Linings

There are several linings on the market today with added thermal, and blackout properties. These come in cream and white.

Thermal Linings

These linings have the same benefit as cotton lining sateen and look similar but with a slightly suede feel with the addition of extra thermal properties.

Fig 5 Thermal lining.

These are a good choice in older houses with large windows or where windows are not double-glazed and draft needs to be excluded. In the winter, they keep the heat in, and in summer, keep the heat out. They drape well.

These thermal linings fall into two types:

◆ Thermal lining, which looks very similar to the standard lining, has a thin synthetic, thermal coating. It comes in white and beige.

◆ Milium lining, which is a cotton sateen with an aluminium coating on one side and appears silvery (place this silvery side against the wrong side of the curtain face fabric).

These linings are termed under such labellings as Thermal Coated Sateen, Thermal Suede or just Thermal lining. Some are washable but most should be dry cleaned and many are FR (treated with Fire Retardant).

Fig 6 Blackout lining.

Blackout Linings

Blackout linings include all the properties of thermal linings but they do have the disadvantage of being much thicker and are more expensive. They do not hang well. But they do black out a room very well. They act as a noise buffer and muffle sound, and are a good choice for children's rooms or for light sleepers.

I think you may be disappointed if you put this blackout lining into a curtain, as they give a curtain a stiff look and they do not hang well. It is a good lining for a Roman blind, holding the folds of the blind in neat, structured folds.

These linings are termed with such labelling as Blackout Velvet Suede, Suedex Blackout lining fabric.

Interlinings

An interlined curtain is a lined curtain with the interlining sewn between the face fabric of the curtain and its lining. Interlining can enhance the look of the curtain, adding body and improving the drape giving more depth to the folds particularly in light- and medium-weight fabrics. At the same time it acts as a noise and heat insulator.

Interlining should not be used with thick fabrics such as velvet or in conjunction with thermal lining.

There are various types of interlining on the market.

- *Bump*
  122cm (45in) and 137cm (54in) wide
  This is the heaviest (it looks rather like a blanket). It is made from coarse, woven, brushed cotton and comes in various thicknesses in cream or bleached white. The bleached is slightly more expensive. It has a selvedge but once cut it frays badly. If interlining silk, bump should be used. Care should be taken that it is bleached as the unbleached will change the colour of the silk and the rough finish will show through.

- *Domette*
  122cm (45in) and 137cm (54in) wide
  This is not as thick as bump (it looks like lint or flannelette sheeting) and is made from brushed cotton. It comes in one thickness in cream and bleached white. It has a selvedge but does not fray as badly as bump. Domette improves the look of everyday medium-weight curtains. It is useful to interline a valance, where the seam lines of frills or contrasting edges showing against the light of the window can be disguised.

- *Aratex Interlining*
  This is a mixture of natural and man-made (76 per cent cotton, 21 per cent viscose, 3 per cent Polyamide), stitched and bonded producing a ribbed effect.
  It is similar in weight to bump, but not quite as soft.

- *Raised Interlining*
  A man-made stitched and bonded fabric made from 90 per cent viscose and 10 per cent nylon. It has a much harder and more ridged finish and the drape of the curtain is less satisfactory.

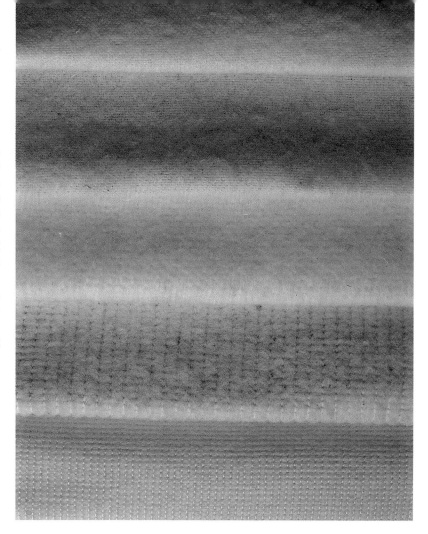

Fig 7 Interlining. From top to bottom: Domette bleached white; Domette cream; bump bleached white; Aratex; and raised.

It is similar in weight to Domette. Interlining fabric should be of the same width as the lining and face fabrics. Having curtains made professionally with interlinings increases the price considerably. It is worth learning how to do it yourself.

SELECTING A FABRIC

In large soft furnishing departments you will find the fabrics located in various sections according to their weight and composition, and labelled to indicate their composition and possible uses. There is a lot of information on the labels and it will be useful to have some understanding of what to look for and to expect, for example:

- Fabric number for identification purposes

- Colour (swatch or book) number

- Composition, e.g. 70 per cent cotton, 30 per cent acrylic

- Width of fabric

- Pattern repeat

- Washing or dry cleaning requirements

- Shrink resistance, e.g. pre-shrunk

- Fire resistance (FR)

Today, many fabrics are a mixture of natural and man-made fibres and without labelling it is difficult to tell the difference. In my college days we would do a simple experiment in the laboratory to indicate the composition of a fabric, which can be done at home provided you exercise a little caution.

The Burn Test

- Cut a small square of fabric 5cm × 5cm (2in × 2in).

- Place on an old, fireproof dish.

- Light a corner with a match. Take care to keep your fingers well away.

- When the material has burnt, look carefully at the residue.

- A natural fibre will leave a soft, light ash, whereas a man-made fibre will result in a black, tar-like substance with a slightly acrid smell. A mixed fabric will result in a combination of both.

Testing for Shrinkage: Material and Lining

To test for colour and shrinkage of fabric cut two pieces of material 12cm by 12cm (5in by 5in) and two pieces of lining the same size. All four pieces should be the same size and cut on the straight of grain of the fabric. Take a sample of material and a sample of lining. Keep the other pieces aside. Wash, dry, iron and then compare the washed fabric with the sample.

Fibres can be blended, mixed and treated to create a whole, wide variety of properties and characteristics such as:

- Washable

- Shrink-resistant (pre-shrunk)

- Fireproof

- Dry clean only, etc.

An example of recent legislation mandates the use of fireproof fabrics on furniture in property to be let. Any landlord failing to observe this ruling may find he is liable in the event of a fire.

Make up your mind what characteristics are necessary for a particular piece of work then make sure that the fabric you are buying satisfies that requirement.

This subject has become very complex and it is not within the scope of this book to go into great detail, but don't be afraid to ask if the labelling is not clear. A good store will always have an assistant with the knowledge to guide you.

Selection of Fabrics for Projects

I have, for the purpose of this book, chosen a selection of fabrics of different patterns, weaves and textures to familiarize you with fabrics and labelling, at the same time introducing techniques and learning the skills through a series of soft furnishing projects.

FABRICS FOR PROJECTS

- ◆ *Tulka Sunshine* – a 100 per cent cotton, plain weave, printed fabric.

- ◆ *Akita Gold* – a mixed, textured fabric (Jacquard weave) of 55 per cent cotton and 45 per cent modacrylic (synthetic).

- ◆ *Radley* – a 100 per cent cotton, woven pattern fabric.

- ◆ *Calico* – 100 per cent cotton, plain weave, flame retardant. For lining inner covers.

- ◆ *Doulton* – 100 per cent cotton, plain weave, printed chintz fabric.

FABRIC USED TO UPHOLSTER A CHAIR

- ◆ *Provence Blue* – a 47 per cent cotton, 48 per cent modacrylic and 5 per cent nylon fabric, flame retardant. Suitable for curtains and upholstery.

It would be impossible to choose a fabric that could be guaranteed to remain in production for an unlimited time. These fabrics, available at time of print, are only a representation.

There are, however, fabrics that have become so popular that manufacturers go on producing that same fabric for years.

- ◆ *Conway Damask* – 100 per cent cotton, a Jacquard weave suitable

Fig 8 A selection of fabrics used in the projects.

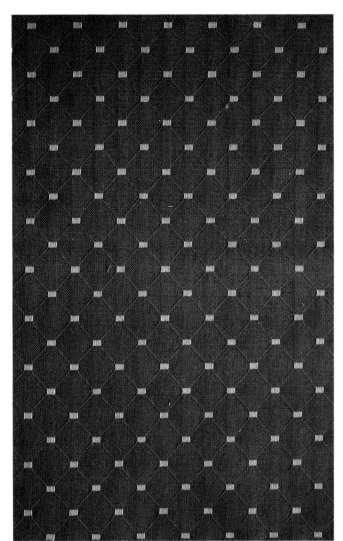 

(Left) Fig 9 Provence Blue

(Right) Fig 10 Conway Damask.

for curtains and bedcovers and general domestic upholstery if used with a flame-retardant interliner.

This Damask fabric, with the same design, has been in production for over thirty years and latterly produced in the wider width of 137cm (54in) to conform to the manufacturer's change to produce standard widths of fabric. During the last century, although enormous progress has been made in the textile industry, history still prevails, no less in the term Damask.

Originally named after a silk fabric, woven in Damascus, it was described as a patterned fabric in one colour only, woven on a complicated loom which involved small children lifting the threads from underneath the loom.

In 1834, the Frenchman, J M Jacquard, the son of a weaver, experiencing this process, invented the Jacquard loom to eliminate this necessity. This method is still used today but it is now computerized. Today, Damask is woven in cotton and mixed fibres.

2 Equipment

EQUIPMENT FOR CURTAIN AND CUSHION MAKING

◆ *Sewing machine*
A basic domestic sewing machine with a piping foot and a zigzag setting. (The sewing machine is covered in more detail in Chapter 3.)

◆ *Sewing machine needles*
9–18 fine to thick – English
  numbering
70–110 fine to thick – Continental
  numbering
Use needle size 14 for a medium-weight fabric in soft furnishing.

◆ *Iron*
A steam iron is an advantage.

◆ *Weighting bricks*
See notes on covering bricks, page 41.

◆ *Table clamps*
Two pairs of table clamps or bulldog clips (assorted sizes).

◆ *Scissors*
Cutting out scissors, 20.5–23cm (8–9in) blade.
  Small, sharp pointed, 12.5–14cm (5–5½in).

◆ *Pins*
Good stainless steel pins and glass-headed pins.

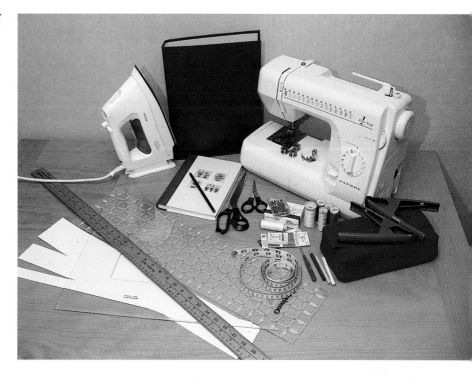

◆ *Needles*
Sharps No 7–No 9 for general work
  See 'Additional Sewing Needles' in 'Additional Equipment for Curtain Making' on page 8.

◆ *Thread*
Use a thread of the same material as the fabric to be sewn, for example, cotton thread for cotton fabric and synthetic for man-made fabrics. If the thread and fabric colours cannot be matched exactly, use a slightly darker thread. With patterned fabrics, match the thread to the dominant colour in the fabric.

Fig 11 Equipment for curtain and cushion making.

◆ *Seam ripper*
A generally useful piece of
equipment with a small curved
blade and sharp points. Replace
cover when not in use.

◆ *Measures*
– Soft tape measure (fibreglass or
linen, not plastic), the standard
150cm (60in) long.
– Metre/yardstick.
– Retractable steel tape with a
  stop mechanism.
– Small 15cm (6in) transparent,
  plastic ruler.
– Card. A sheet of card 750
microns 57cm × 81cm (23in × 32in)
obtainable from office stationery
shops for making measuring cards.
See 'Additional Equipment for
Curtain Making' below.

◆ *Large set square or modern
measuring aid*
For checking straight of grain,
checking corners are correct and
for marking out.

◆ *Pencils and chalks*
Use a soft HB pencil with a soft
point. Tailors chalk in white pencil
form. Include a pencil sharpener.

◆ *Hardback notebook (handbag size)*
For recording measurements and
plans.

◆ *Ring file plus A4 lined pad*
For recording additional notes and
making visual aids.

◆ *Brown paper*
A roll of good quality brown paper
for making paper patterns 10m ×
70cm (395in × 27½in).

◆ *Pocket calculator*

In addition to this list of equipment my
students are asked to bring a remnant of
approximately one metre or yard of
cotton furnishing fabric with a printed
pattern and a pattern repeat. This fabric
is used to visually understand fabrics
and later techniques and skills. We will
look at this more as we progress through
the book and use the fabric to make
visual aids.

ADDITIONAL EQUIPMENT
FOR CURTAIN MAKING

◆ *Work surface*
A trestle table 180cm × 70cm
(71in × 27½in) or a decorator's
table.

◆ *Ironing pad*
See note on page 20
(Watchpoints).

◆ *Additional sewing needles*
Darners or Straws (milliner's
needles, size 3–9).

◆ *Additional bulldog clips*
Selection, approximately 2.5cm
(1in).

◆ *Thread*
Bold – natural colour; strong
synthetic thread.

◆ *Staple gun*

◆ *Card*
750 microns, 57cm × 81cm (23in ×
32in). For making measuring cards.
Cut to the following widths: 2cm,
2.5cm, 5cm, 7.5cm and 10cm (¾in,
1in, 2in, 3in and 4in) for making
curtains.

WATCHPOINTS:

IRON

In achieving a really professional finish to your work the iron plays an important part. Always iron the work stage by stage. The iron should be in good working order, the lead should be sound and the plate of the iron kept clean and smooth. A cordless iron, plugged in and standing away from the work will provide a greater degree of safety.

Great care should be taken to see that the plate of an iron is clean. Always check this after ironing. Remember to use the appropriate setting for each fabric. Take special care when pressing man-made fabrics as they can easily be marked if the correct setting is not applied. Should this happen use a stick cleaner on the iron plate before using it again. Equally, you must be careful not to damage the iron plate with pins, which will destroy the surface. Ironing over pins can damage your fabric and pull threads.

ALWAYS recheck that any iron is unplugged and safely stored before leaving the room.

SCISSORS
Cutting Out Scissors
20.5cm–23cm (8in– 9in)
Buy the best quality stainless steel, standard straight blade dressmaker's scissors.

Your scissors should always be very sharp. Sharpen them when necessary either by using the sharpener that can be bought with your scissors or have them professionally sharpened. NEVER use your cutting out scissors for paper, as this will blunt the blades.

Small Scissors
12.5cm–14cm (5in–5½in)
These should be sharp with straight points. Threads cut with these sharp scissors are easier to thread and slashing material for curves and corners will be much more accurate. Make sure these scissors are sharpened often as cutting the thread blunts them.

Extra Pair of Straight Scissors
For cutting paper and making patterns.

Pinking Shears
These can be included in your workbox if you already have them, although they are not really necessary in soft furnishings. Never use pinking shears for cutting out your fabric.

PINS

Keep in a box or use pincushion. They must always be rust free – check from time to time and replace when necessary.

Do not leave pins in fabric longer than necessary and learn to use the minimum number strategically placed.

In addition, the larger sized pins can be an advantage, but are not a necessity.

NEEDLES

In soft furnishings few sewing needles are needed, but it is important to choose a needle that is appropriate for your work.

The hand-sewing needle is marked from 1–12. The smaller the number the thicker the needle.

NEVER use bent or blunt needles.

Packets of sewing needles have different names.

Sharps are those used for most general sewing. Sharps are reasonably long needles with an oval eye and are used more often in soft furnishings. No 8 is the average size, although you may want to use the range 7–9.

There may be occasions when using a fine or heavier weight fabric, when a fine needle on lightweight fabrics and a coarser needle on heavier fabrics may be necessary.

Betweens are similar to Sharps but they are shorter needles.

◆ *Darners or Straws*

– Darners These long needles have larger eyes making them easier to thread.

(continued overleaf)

WATCHPOINTS *continued*

– Straws (Milliner's needles) Very similar to Sharps but longer. Use 3–9. I find Straws easier to use than Darners.

When making curtains, long thin needles are an advantage because longer stitches are frequently used.

♦ Sewing machine needles are numbered in the opposite way to hand sewing needles. The smaller the number the finer the needle.

Use needle size 14 for a medium-weight fabric in soft furnishing.

THREADS

Mercerize (OD) Treated (cottons, fabric or thread) under tension with caustic alkali to give greater strength and imparts lustre.

♦ For general use in soft furnishings use a Mercerized cotton thread.

♦ Do not use cotton on synthetic fabrics as the cotton shrinks more than the fabric.

♦ *Tacking thread*
This is made from cotton but it is not mercerized and you should never use tacking thread for your machine or for permanent stitches.

♦ *Silk thread*
If sewing a silk fabric, use a silk thread.

♦ Keep a box for sewing threads and secure the ends.

♦ Thread should be the same content and weight on your machine bobbin and spool. A small box bought for storing spools is an inexpensive, useful addition.

WORK SURFACE

It is not a good idea to use the floor for cutting out curtains. Apart from backache there are many disadvantages. Use a trestle table, 180cm × 79cm (6ft × 2ft 3in) or a decorator's table, which is less expensive and reasonably satisfactory. If you are going to make a number of curtains the more substantial trestle table is a better buy. Both tables fold up for storage.

IRONING PAD

There are small commercial pads available, which are sold for caravans and boats. It is not difficult to make your own pad by cutting an old heavy blanket or thick piece of felt about 70cm × 60cm (28in × 24in) and making a simple cotton sheeting cover, using a strip of Velcro as a convenient closure for ease when washing the cover.

TABLE CLAMPS

These are invaluable to hold your fabric in position for cutting out and during stitching. They are expensive and a cheaper alternative is large bulldog clips plus a selection of small sizes. In addition, we will cover a brick with fabric and this will also be used for holding fabric in place.

TIP:
Pricked Fingers

If a finger is pricked and the work marked, quickly chew a piece of tacking thread and roll it into a ball and rub it onto the bloodstain in a circular movement. The thread will draw the blood away from the work. You must use tacking cotton, which is un-mercerized, as it absorbs the dampness more easily. It is sometimes necessary to repeat with a clean piece of thread. It is particularly useful on a pale lightweight fabric and it really does work!

3 The Sewing Machine

Mindful that some of my readers may be real beginners and not wishing to offend those with considerable skills, I introduce the sewing machine, which must be in good working order.

Soft furnishings for your own home can be made very well using the domestic sewing machine. If you do not already have one, I suggest a few guidelines before you purchase your machine, but above all ask for a demonstration before finally deciding. If you decide to buy a second-hand machine make sure it is in good working order and that it has a good instruction manual with it.

Pick a machine that will allow you to handle average and fairly heavy fabrics. Small portable machines should be avoided. Select a machine of a reasonable weight before you make your final choice.

You need a basic machine that has the following stitching capabilities: Straight, Zigzag and Reverse.

Fig 12 Typical sewing machine.

Straight stitch Your basic machine will come with an ordinary stitch foot (presser foot). This holds your fabric in place as you machine and will facilitate the straight stitch for straight lines of sewing.

Zigzag stitch In making this stitch the needle moves from side to side as it moves along for which you need the standard zigzag foot. It is supplied with a machine that has this stitching facility. Zigzag stitch neatens raw edges and it is also possible to use this function to gather fabric.

Note: The more modern machines may have one foot to perform both functions.

Reverse stitch Machine stitching on all seams must be securely finished off. A machine with this reverse stitch mechanism enables you to make a few stitches in reverse at the beginning and end of your work. In more modern machines a press button may operate this function.

You will also need a zip foot for stitching piping cord and zips.

Today, most machines come with a zip foot but this is not always satisfactory if used for piping. Most likely, for piping you will have to buy the piping foot separately. If this were the case I would suggest the older style, screw-on type multipurpose zip/piping foot is preferable. Most new machines today have a clip on presser foot complete with stem. You can use the older style, zip/piping foot by unscrewing the complete stem and foot and replacing it with the old-style unit.

MAINTENANCE

For those readers who already have their machine it is important to ensure that it is in good working order. When I ask students how often machine needles have been changed or if the machine has ever been serviced, there is always quite a lot of amusement.

◆ I suggest that if you are unfamiliar with or nervous of your machine, it would be greatly to your advantage to have the first service professionally done. Machines can usually be returned to the retailer or the manufacturer for servicing. Alternatively, there are many reputable sewing machine servicing organizations that will come to your home to carry out the work and you will probably learn a great deal by just watching. Those who are more familiar and experienced with their machines should follow their own instruction books.

If oiling your machine, always take great care to ensure that no oil has been left on any parts of your machine and carefully wipe all lubricated areas with a clean rag before using your machine again. It is also important to leave a piece of doubled plain cotton material under the foot for at least a day before you use your machine again to soak up any excess oil. Double check by sewing a clean scrap of double fabric.

Before beginning any piece of work it is important that you check that your machine is working properly and that the stitch is correct. Also, you should know the fibre content of your fabric because this will affect the size of the stitch you will need, the size of the machine needle and the correct type of thread to use, particularly if you are using a synthetic or mixed fabric.

Machines should be unplugged when not in use and stored at room temperature. If your machine does not have its own hard cover a soft plastic cover is perfectly adequate.

THREADING

It is important that you check with your manual that you have threaded your machine correctly. In the main, most machines thread in the same way, normally following this path:

1 The reel of thread is positioned on the pin at the top of the machine.
2 The thread is brought down through the upper tension unit which houses the tension discs (In older machines you will find the tension unit on the face of the machine and on the more modern machines it is usually concealed above the needle assembly area.)
3 Then up into the take-up lever.
4 And then down to the needle through the thread guides (refer to manual).

Check with the manual regarding the placement of your machine needle:

1 The flat side of the needle must be correctly positioned and then inserted into the clamp, making absolutely sure it is as far up as possible (failure to position the needle correctly may cause major problems).
2 Finally, make sure the clamp screw is securely tightened.

Be sure that you have filled your bobbin with sufficient thread of the same type and thickness as on the reel and that you insert the bobbin into the bobbin case correctly. Again, check this with the instruction manual.

It is important that the construction of the stitch is correct. A perfect stitch will have the threads locked between the two layers of fabric with no loops on top or bottom. It will thus look the same on both sides.

If this is not the case, check the tension (Fig 13).

Fig 13 The correct stitch.

CORRECT TENSION

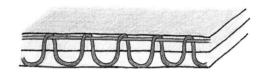

upper thread too tight
DECREASE TENSION

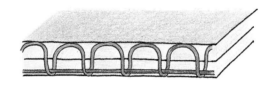

upper thread too loose
INCREASE TENSION

TENSION

The mere mention of the term tension confuses many students. Every sewing machine has two tensions:

1 The needle thread tension. The position of this tension unit will vary according to your machine. Refer to the manual.
2 The bobbin thread tension.

Tension is the amount of drag on these two threads. Both the thread and bobbin tension need to be correctly set to give you well-formed stitches.

Regarding the needle thread tension:

◆ The needle thread tension only comes into effect when the presser foot is lowered, ready to sew (i.e. the sewing position).

◆ When the presser foot is raised using the lever at the back of the machine this automatically releases the tension.

Regarding the bobbin thread tension:

◆ When the bobbin is inserted into the bobbin case correctly (check in your manual) there should be a gentle drag back on the thread. It must not be too tight or too loose.

A simple test on the thread tension:

1 Needle thread tension: Lower the presser foot to the sewing position and pull the thread through the tension unit. There must be tension at this point (i.e. a slight resistance as you pull the thread).

2 Bobbin thread tension: Thread the bobbin into the bobbin case as shown in the manual. The thread should offer some resistance when pulled. It should not pull through too easily nor offer strong resistance to pulling.

Note: The top thread tension controls the look of the stitch *under* the fabric. The bobbin thread controls the look of the stitch on the *top* of the fabric.

Basically, the tension is controllable by the upper tension knob. These controls are extremely sensitive and often, only tiny adjustments are required. Look carefully at the tension unit on the machine. Most machines are set with the tension at the midway point, 4 to 6 on the dial. The dial usually reads 0 to 9 and if necessary check with the manual.

There should be no real need to touch the bobbin tension. Here, there can be a problem if it is dirty and this is where the servicing comes in.

Note: When adjusting tension on the bobbin case, make only very slight adjustments with the tiny screwdriver that should be included with your box of attachments.

STITCH LENGTH

Once you have established that your tension is correct for your work it may be necessary to adjust the stitch length.

The stitch length control on your machine regulates the length of stitch you need – consult your manual. The higher the number, the longer the stitch. The length of stitch is the distance between the two locking points, normally numbered 0 to 4.

◆ Short stitch for fine fabrics (stitch length setting approximately 1½).

◆ Medium stitch for average fabrics (stitch length setting approximately 2 to 2½).

◆ Long stitch for heavy fabrics.

◆ When making curtain seams it is better to use a longer stitch than normal (stitch length setting approximately 3 to 3½).

◆ The gauge or thickness of the thread can also affect the quality of the stitch. Modern threads are either cotton, synthetic or a mixture and are approximately 50 gauge. This is a fine thread and will give the best stitch. Older type thread was generally 40 gauge, which is thicker. The figure 40 was normally printed on the label, so check in

WATCHPOINTS:

Before machining your fabric, ensure;

◆ You have selected the correct size of needle and thread to suit the material to be sewn.

◆ The needle is correctly threaded and that it is not bent or blunt (a new needle should be used for each new project). Blunt needles pull the threads and damage the fabric and blunt or bent needles ruin both fabric and machines and break the thread.

◆ The needle is correctly placed in the machine otherwise it will cause the thread to break and can damage your machine.

◆ The presser foot and needle clamp screws are both tight.

◆ Remember, sewing machine needles are numbered in the opposite way to hand sewing needles.

Having checked the above, now test the stitch on a doubled piece of the fabric you are about to use.

your sewing box and avoid using it for machining. Use it up for tacking.

TESTING YOUR STITCH

1 Begin by rotating the wheel by hand, move the needle to its highest position. Always turn the hand wheel towards you when hand-operating your machine.

2 Pick up your bobbin thread. Having threaded the machine needle correctly and inserted the bobbin case correctly (check in your manual) you need to raise the bobbin thread. To do this you need to have the needle raised to its highest point. With your left hand, hold the needle thread and with your right hand turn the hand wheel of your machine *towards you* so the needle goes down through the hole in the needle plate and returns to its highest point again. This will pick up the bobbin thread, which means you will have both threads coming through the needle plate on the machine.

3 Pull both threads out about 10cm (4in), leave under the foot and take to the rear of the machine.

4 Place the material under the presser foot and insert the needle into the material by hand by turning the hand-wheel towards you. Then lower the presser foot.

5 Machine about 5cm to 8cm (2in to 3in) and then look carefully at the stitch.

6 To remove the work, first turn the hand-wheel towards you until the needle is at its highest position. Then raise the presser foot and pull the material to the rear allowing the thread to take the strain against the foot of the machine. Leave about 10cm (4in) of excess thread. Most machines have a thread cutting facility – refer to the manual.

REVERSE STITCH CONTROL

It is best to begin and end seams with a few stitches taken in reverse.

1 Make sure both threads are pulled back under the presser point.

2 Lower the needle into the fabric about 1cm (½in) from the beginning of the seam.

3 Press reverse (*see* Note) mechanism for reverse stitching.

4 Stitch in reverse until the needle reaches beginning of seam (i.e. the edge of the fabric).

5 Release button for forward stitching and complete seam.

6 When you reach the other end push the reverse button and sew back over 1cm (½in).

Fig 14 Tying off ends.

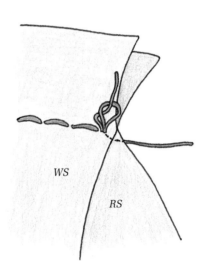

Note: Various sewing machines have different ways to engage reverse stitching. If you are not familiar with the way your machine works, consult the manual.

To tie off ends. There will be occasions when it is difficult to use this reverse mechanism, for example when joining a very narrow strip of fabric with a very short seam length.

The loose ends of thread must be securely tied off. From the wrong side of the seam or work, gently pull the end of the thread facing you. This in turn will lift the thread lying on top and you will be able to take hold of the loose loop and pull it through to allow both threads to lie to one side. Carefully tie a knot and repeat with the second close to the end of the seam line or wrong side of work. Trim off both ends leaving about 1cm or ½in of thread.

Note: To remove machine stitches, carefully clip the top machine threads approximately every 3cm (1½in) and pull out the bobbin thread from the wrong side of the work.

BASIC STITCHES FOR PROJECTS

The following are the stitches to be used in the worked projects.

◆ Backstitch

◆ Tacking stitch (sometimes called basting)

◆ Ladder stitch (sometimes called slip stitch)

◆ Slip tacking stitch (sometimes called outside tacking)

◆ Tie stitch

◆ Stab stitch

◆ Whip stitch

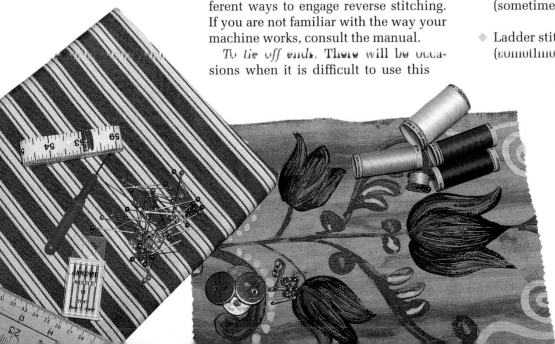

4 Preparation

Having given you a brief introduction to fabrics and their make up it is now time to understand and use your fabric. I explained that during manufacture, fibres, whether they are natural, man-made or a mixture, are spun into threads. These threads are then used to weave the fabric using different techniques to produce different weaves and effects. Long, lengthways threads run the whole length of the piece of fabric being woven and other threads are woven backwards and forwards across the width of the fabric.

Now take the small length of about one metre or yard of patterned cotton furnishing fabric and look at it carefully. (See Chapter 2 'Equipment')

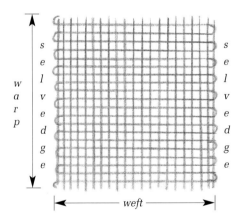

You will find as we progress with our work the term 'straight of grain' will frequently be used. This is the straight thread in your fabric. Look carefully at your fabric and you will notice that down its length, the edges are finished by a firm un-fraying edge. This is the 'selvedge'. The threads running down your fabric and parallel to the selvedge are known as the *warp* threads (or grain) and these are the strongest threads. If you hold a piece of fabric and pull it from top to bottom it will have a good firm feel. The threads running across the fabric at the fraying edge are known as the *weft* threads (or grain). If you give the fabric a tug in this direction you will feel that it is less firm than in the direction of the warp threads. These straight threads, whether they are warp or weft threads, are the threads referred to as 'straight of grain'.

It is now necessary to understand what is meant by the term *crossway*.

Oxford Dictionary: Crossway (or Bias) (Bias as in dressmaking etc.) cut obliquely across the warp.

Look at your material again, take the straight warp edge (selvedge) and fold it diagonally so that the edge lies along

(Far left) Fig 15 Weave of a fabric.

(Below) Fig 16 Crossway of weaves.

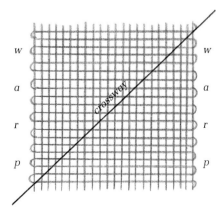

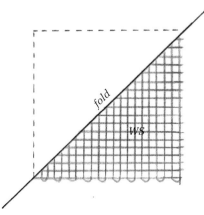

the weft thread and forms a triangle. This line of the fold running diagonally between the two threads (grains) is known as the crossway of the fabric. Give the fabric a gentle pull along this crossway fold and feel the give in it.

CROSSWAY STRIPS

There will be many occasions in our work when we need *piping*. This adds a professional finish to the work apart from its practical and decorative uses. Piping can be termed as the simplest form of border, which can be rounded, flat or frilled.

Piping for soft furnishings is made by covering piping cord with fabric, which is cut on the cross, i.e. *crossway strips*. This enables the pliable piece of fabric to mould easily round the piping cord and seam lines.

Piping is the beginning of working a fabric to advantage. It can be done in matching fabric and letting these fine lines of fabric outline and strengthen the shape in contrasting fabric, or you may use checks and stripes to give a more interesting effect. It is important that whatever fabric you choose for piping, it must be of similar weight and weave to the fabric you are using. Loosely woven fabrics are not suitable.

To be really successful, crossway strips must be cut on the *true bias*. The true bias is a line at 45 degrees to the selvedge and the weft threads and lies along the diagonal fold mentioned above. Cutting your strip at any other angle to the selvedge will not be true bias. If you cut the fabric at any other angle, it is termed a 'bias strip' – and this bias strip will not give as much as 'true bias crossway' strips and will not mould as easily around corners and curves.

PIPING CORD

The piping cord used inside crossway strips is manufactured in both cotton and synthetic material and it comes in various thicknesses and weights – fine, medium and coarse. It is numbered 0–6, the smallest number being the thinnest cord. Numbers 4, 5 and 6 are generally used in soft furnishings. Always use the cotton cord with cotton fabrics and the synthetic cord with synthetics. It is important if you are using cotton cord that it is pre-shrunk, otherwise it will shrink as you use it and pucker the covering crossway fabric.

Many cords are now sold pre-shrunk but if you are in any doubt you must shrink it yourself. Knot the two ends of the cord, place it in a pan, cover with water and bring it to the boil for about five minutes. Remove the cord from the pan and rinse it in cold water, spin it in the washing machine tied in a piece of cloth or placed in a small bag. Remove, straighten out the cord and hang it in the airing cupboard overnight.

Crossway strips should be cut to the circumference of the cord you are using plus the seam allowance.

Throughout this book number 5 piping cord will be used for the projects.

TO CALCULATE THE WIDTH OF THE CROSSWAY STRIP

Example: cut a measuring card to the 'width of the crossway strip' in the chart on page 29. (*See* Chapter 2 for making measuring card.)

Record on the card:

◈ 'crossway strips'

◈ width 4.5cm (1¾in)

◈ No 5 cord

seam allowance	+	circumference of cord	+	seam allowance	=	width of crossway strip
1.5cm (½in)	+	number 5 cord	+	1.5cm (½in)		
1.5cm (½in)	+	2cm (¾in)	+	1.5cm (½in)	=	4.5cm (1¾in)

Add this measuring card to your equipment.

STRAIGHTENING YOUR FABRIC

In preparing the fabric for any piece of work it will always be necessary to straighten it first. 'Straighten your fabric' is another term that will be in constant use.

Most of the time you are actually straightening the weft thread. When this thread has been straightened it should form a right angle with both selvedges. The easiest way to straighten your fabric in soft furnishings is to place the selvedge (warp threads) down the long straight edge of your worktable. The cut (fraying) edge will now be at right angles across your table. You can then use the 'cross' edge of the table to straighten the weft end of your fabric.

Using the 'cross' edge of your table, run your thumb along the weft to imprint a line. With the side of your chalk pencil or the blunt side of your scissors mark a line along the edge of your table through the fabric then cut along this indented line with sharp scissors and a long even cut using the whole length of the scissors blades.

On a smaller piece of fabric you can use a setsquare or one of the other useful measuring aids on the market.

In either case you could 'pull a thread'.

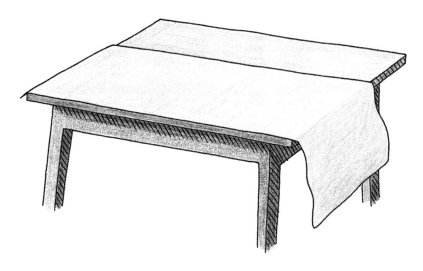

Fig 17 Straightening your fabric.

You will often meet the phrase 'pull a thread to straighten your fabric'.

On evenly woven fabrics, in particular loosely woven fabrics, this can be done without too much difficulty, but it can be time consuming. There are certain fabrics where this is not possible, for example, cotton 'sateen' lining fabric, which is tightly woven with an uneven weave for a firm finish.

Pulling a Thread

Make a short, straight cut into the selvedge near to the top, fraying edge of your fabric or where the fabric has been cut off the roll (bolt) and gently pull a single weft thread across the full width. This will leave a clear, straight line that you can then use to cut along and thereby 'straighten the fabric'.

TIP:

Material should NEVER be straightened by tearing, you should always use the methods explained above.

First Stitches

A little time and care in the preparation of each stage of your work will add up to a really professional finish.

Backstitch (Fig 18)

It is preferable to use a backstitch rather than a knot (knots unravel) to start and finish your hand stitching, whether temporary or permanent stitches.

(a)

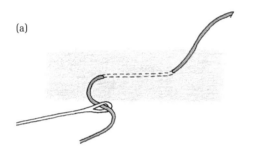

(b)

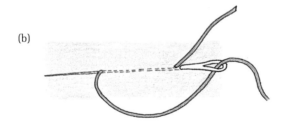

(c)

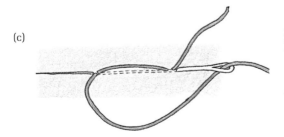

Fig 18 Backstitch.

Two backstitches should be used on top of each other.

Working from right to left (if right handed):

1 Leave a long end 5cm or 2in (*see* Fig 18a).
2 Take a stitch 6mm or ¼in then take a stitch backwards into the first stitch (*see* Fig 18b).
3 Repeat this stitch just above the first stitch (*see* Fig 18c).
4 Now begin your chosen stitch.

Tacking Stitch (Fig 19)

This is a temporary stitch to hold the fabric in place ready for machining or permanent stitching. (Use tacking cotton.)

Use a double backstitch to secure your thread with a long end. (By leaving a long end it is easier to remove these stitches after the machining is done.)

Fig 19 Tacking stitch.

Stitches are worked from right to left (if right handed). The stitch is formed with a long running stitch approximately 1.5cm (½in). Start and finish with a backstitch. Occasionally the length of the stitch may vary when holding loosely woven, fine or slippery fabrics in place. You may need a shorter stitch.

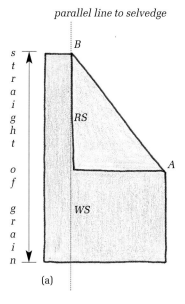

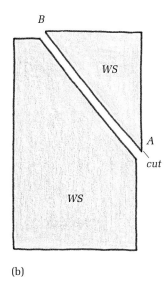

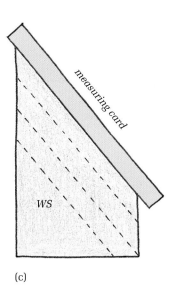

(a)   (b)   (c)

PREPARATION OF FABRIC FOR MAKING CROSSWAYS STRIPS

The Conventional Method of Cutting Crossway Strips Separately

ORDER OF WORK

◆ Iron your fabric carefully. Always iron your fabric on the wrong side and in the same direction as the selvedge (i.e. down the strong, warp threads). Any ironing after the crossway is made should be avoided because the fabric will then give and slightly stretch with the heat of the iron with the result that you would lose the proposed width of the crossway strip.

1 Straighten your fabric.
2 Fold the fabric on the crossway and very lightly, press in place (Fig 20a).

3 Cut carefully through the fold from A to B with sharp scissors (Fig 20b).
4 Align the edge of your measuring card 4.5cm (1¾in) for No 5 piping very accurately to the cut, crossway edge, and using a very sharp (HB) pencil, mark a parallel line against the other edge of the card (Fig 20c).
5 Cut exactly along the line.
6 Continue marking and cutting your strips until you have sufficient for the required length of piping.

Joining Crossway Strips

All joins made in crossway strips should be made on the straight grain of the fabric. If several joins are made, they must all face in the same direction.

Note: When using stripes, checks or certain patterns, adjust the joins to match the pattern. This may not always be possible. For example, where you want to join a crossway onto itself to create a continuous circle of strips, the final join will probably not match but try to make the join as inconspicuous as possible.

Fig 20 Preparation of fabric for making crossway strips.

Fig 21 Joining crossway strips.

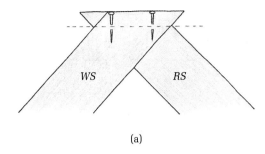

(a)

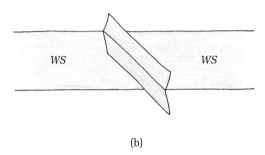

(b)

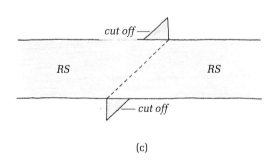

(c)

◆ Place the right sides of the crossway strips together with the short, straight edges level allowing each end to protrude to create a seam allowance of 1.5cm (½in). Pin and tack on this line which runs along the straight of grain, placing the pins in a vertical position. By placing pins in vertically it prevents the fabric moving. As you gain more experience, you will be able to omit the tacking and machine

carefully over the pins in this position (Fig 21a).

◆ You will notice that points of fabric protrude at either side. The line through the middle (i.e. parallel to the cut edges) is your stitching line. The distance between these two parallel lines should be exactly 1.5cm (½in). If this is not correct the strips will not join together accurately.

◆ As this is a short seam and the stitches must be firm, do not be tempted to do this by hand. Use a short stitch on your machine and machine accurately along this line. Carefully finish off both ends of your machining.

◆ It is important to finish off all ends of your machine stitching. This is a small line of stitching. If you find it difficult to use the reverse mechanism of your machine, tie off your ends remembering to leave long ends. Tie them close to the stitching with two firm knots.

◆ Continue joining until sufficient crossway is made.

◆ Finger press the seams open by running your thumbnail firmly against the line of stitches (Fig 21b).

◆ The seams must now be trimmed down to 6mm (¼in). Do this carefully. Finger press the seam again and cut off the protruding points of fabric (Fig 21c).

◆ Approximately 0.5m (20in) of material will give you about 9m (8¾yd) of joined crossway strips.

This amount can vary depending on the width of the measuring card. It is better to use long strips to minimize the number of joins.

CONTINUOUS CROSSWAY STRIPS

Crossway strips can be made in a *continuous strip*. It is reputed that some years ago a member of the 'Women's Institute' invented this method. How true this is I do not know. The method has both advantages and disadvantages. There are more joins and the joins may not necessarily run in the same direction, and it cannot be used effectively with striped, checked or certain patterned fabrics. However, it is a useful method if large amounts of crossway are needed.

Using this method you cannot use a piece of fabric less than 25cm (10in) wide because it is too difficult to handle and it would result in too many joins. The length of the strip must be at least twice its width. This minimum amount of fabric will produce approximately 2m (roughly 2yd) of crossway strip.

TIP FOR BEGINNERS:

I recommend you practise with the minimum amount of fabric to gain experience with this method. This sample can then be added to your file for future reference.

The following instructions are for making a continuous strip of crossway. If you feel confident, you can now follow these instructions when we begin our immediate, first project – the square, piped cushion.

MAKING THE CONTINUOUS STRIP OF CROSSWAY SAMPLE

BEGINNERS METHOD:

Prepare a piece of cotton furnishing fabric with a small pattern 25cm × 50cm (10in × 20in) on the straight of grain.

Preparation of Fabric for Making a Continuous Crossway Strip

ORDER OF WORK

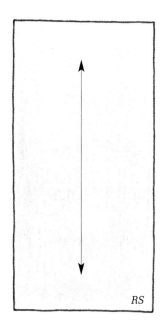

Fig 22 Continuous crossway strips, 1–5.

1   Remove any selvedge (Fig 22).
2   Iron the fabric.
3   Straighten your fabric.
4   Remember the length must be double the width or more.

5 Mark in your straight of grain with the right side of your fabric uppermost.

6 Fold over the right-hand corner allowing the edges of the fabric to be level at the left-hand side. Pin the fold in place with a single pin. Lightly press to mark the fold line (Fig 23).

7 Open out the fold and cut along the fold line (Fig 24).

8 Replace pieces, right side uppermost on your table in the original position and call them A and B.

Fig 23 Continuous crossway strips, 6.

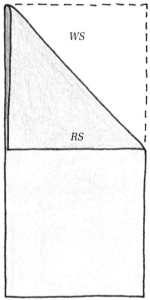

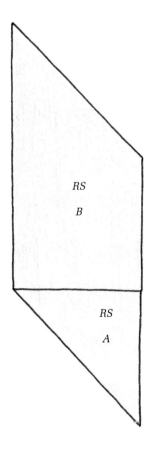

(Right) Fig 24 Continuous crossway strips, 7–8.

(Far right) Fig 25 Continuous crossway strips, 9.

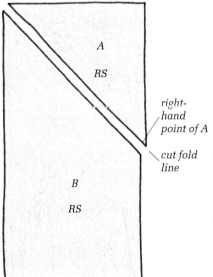

9 Take the right-hand side point of A and pull this section over and down section B to its new position underneath B (Fig 25).

10 Place section A over section B with their right sides facing and carefully match the bottom edge. It is important that both side edges are level (Fig 26).

11 Now carefully pin and tack in place

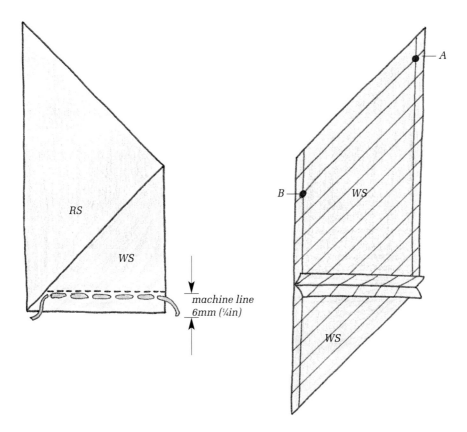

6mm (¼in) from the edge. Place your pins in vertically. This holds the fabric exactly in place.

12 Machine along 6mm (¼in) from the edge. This again must be accurate and both ends of your machining must be finished off. Use the reverse mechanism of your machine or tie off ends.

13 Remove tacking stitches and finger press seam open.

14 Turn fabric to the wrong side (Fig 27).

15 Using a sharp HB pencil held vertically, rule a line down both sides 6mm (¼in) from the edge. Make these lines very clear.

16 Draw very accurately a number of diagonal, parallel lines down the material using your 4.5cm (1¾in)

measuring card for No 5 piping cord (or appropriate size of card) to define the distance apart.

17 Mark these lines very clearly so you are able to see a distinct cross where they meet the vertical lines running down the side edges.

18 Where the first diagonal line crosses the right hand side vertical line mark a cross (X) denoting position A and where the second parallel line crosses the left hand side vertical line, mark a second cross (X) at position B. This is very important. If this is not correct the crossway strips will not cut correctly.

19 Note A and B (B is one line below A).

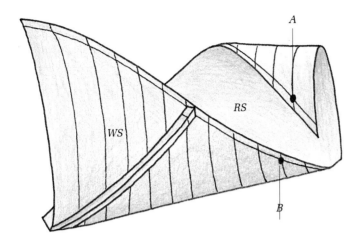

Fig 28 Continuous crossway strips, 20–21.

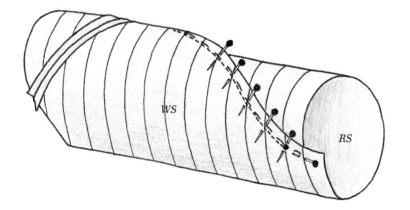

Fig 29 Continuous crossway strips, 22–27.

Fig 30 Continuous crossway strips, 28–31.

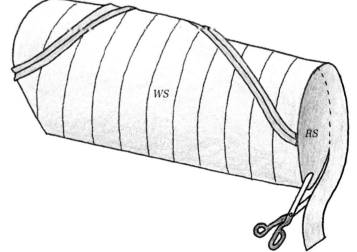

20 Form a tube with the right sides of your fabric facing and the two side lines together (Fig 28).

21 Bring point B to A and pierce your pin exactly through the centre of these two points.

22 Pin vertically bringing the point of the pin towards you (i.e. at right angles to the edge lines) (Fig 29).

23 Continue to pin the cross points along the length of the tube.

24 If this is correct you will have the edges offset at the top and the bottom. Do not worry if the last parallel line marked runs into an uneven measurement at the bottom. This will be removed when the strip is finally cut.

25 Tack exactly on the marked line, making sure the point of your needle goes through the same position as the pins you are removing. Begin with a double backstitch at the start (above B) and finish in the same way. This must be done accurately.

26 Using a small stitch, machine exactly over the line of tacking stitches. Start and finish using the reverse mechanism on your machine or tie off the ends.

27 Carefully remove tacking stitches without breaking machine stitches.

28 Open the seam out and finger press by running your nail firmly against the line of stitches or gently use the toe of your iron only on the stitching line (Fig 30).

29 Now look carefully at the tube you have created and you will note that the parallel lines you drew have become one, long continuous line around the tube.

30 Note the offset top of the tube.

31 Using sharp scissors and starting at the top (that is at the line above where points A and B meet) cut very accurately along the whole length of this line.

You have now formed a continuous strip of crossway.

THE FINAL JOIN!

When applying piping to the edges of a cushion cover, it will be necessary to make a *final join* where the ends of the crossway meet. That is, at the point where you started and finished the piping.

Over the many years I have been lecturing in soft furnishings, certain aids have become invaluable to my students. When new students join the course they are a little taken aback when I suggest making paper visual aids for some of the more difficult techniques. Encouraged by my students, I have decided to include these in my book. You may wish to make and keep them in the file we are building up as we progress through the course.

A Visual Aid for the Final Join

◆ Take a page from your A4 lined pad.

◆ Cut five 4cm (1½in) strips across the page (i.e. parallel to the lines). These will represent the crossway strips.

Now follow my instructions on making this final join on your crossway strips (completing the circle and joining it up to itself).

1 Pin the first strip at its left-hand side, about 4cm (1½in) down from the top, to a piece of A4 lined paper.

2 Mark this paper strip 'wrong side'.

3 About half-way across, fold the paper strip up so that the right-hand end is now vertically upwards (at right angles to the left-hand part of the strip) (Fig 31).

4 About 4cm (1½in) down from the first paper strip, pin two more strips of paper, one at either side, on top of each other, using the lines of your pad to keep them straight. Mark these strips 'wrong side' and A and B (Fig 32).

5 On the left strip A, repeat the fold as for the top strip and then cut off the paper along the fold line.

6 Measure back 2.5cm (1in) along the top edge of the strip, away from the 'point' of the cut and mark.

7 Bring the strip from the right-hand B side and cover the strip A.

8 Mark the top strip at the same point as strip A (i.e. 2.5cm or 1in beyond the cut point).

9 Draw a vertical line across the right-hand B strip from this mark.

10 Carefully fold the end of the strip vertically down to bring the top edge of the paper exactly onto this marked line (*see* Fig 32).

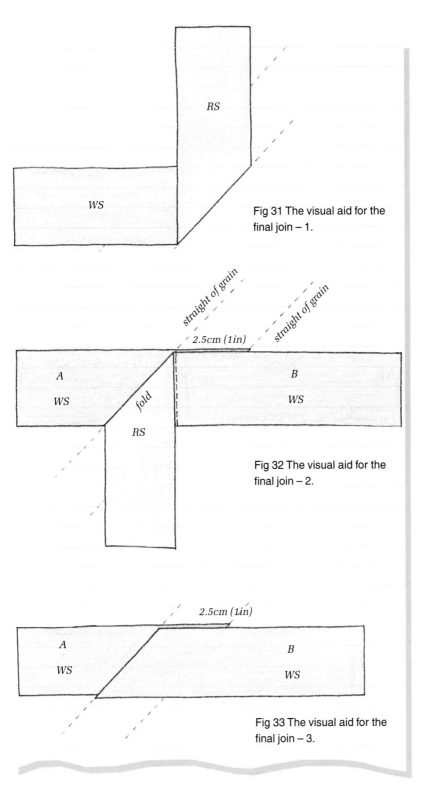

Fig 31 The visual aid for the final join – 1.

Fig 32 The visual aid for the final join – 2.

Fig 33 The visual aid for the final join – 3.

11 About another 4cm (1½in) down the paper pin another pair of paper strips in the same way repeating all the actions taken in the pair above, but this time cut the right-hand B strip along the fold line (Fig 33).

When using fabric the ends are now joined using the same method as joining crossway strips, but you are working in a smaller space. Do make sure you place the short cut edges accurately together. These ends will be on the straight of grain.

To complete the join, refer again to 'joining crossway strips' (*see* Fig 21).

12 Tack in place.

13 Check the size and position of the tacked join is accurate before machining, by allowing it to drop into place.

14 Machine finish ends carefully. Remember a smaller machine stitch for this short seam. Check your stitch first.

15 Cut back seam allowance to 6mm (¼in). Cut back the points of fabric created at the edges of the crossway strip.

16 Finger press.

You have now completed the final join.

5 Project 1 – The Basic Cushion

PRE-PLANNING

The first project, 'The Basic Cushion', will present for the beginner, and reinforce for the experienced, an understanding of fabrics.

In Chapter 1, 'Fabrics', I spoke of the need to buy all of your fabrics from one roll (bolt). Clearly when making cushions this is not necessary. In fact, very often you can pick up some very good remnants.

In understanding labels and using your fabric, there will be new words and techniques you will meet which will obviously be much more important on larger projects and certainly for curtains. So this seems a fitting time to begin.

Before calculating the amount of fabric you need, carefully look at the label and any manufacturer's notes. It is important that you know the width of your fabric and the length of any pattern repeat (marked 'PR').

Furnishing fabrics in the main are manufactured in two widths 137/140cm (54–56in) wide or 120/122cm (48in) wide. There is a trend for manufacturers to produce less of the narrower widths.

Look at your metre of fabric again.

We know the selvedges run down the length of the fabric and that the width is across the fabric, selvedge to selvedge.

Carefully look at the selvedge and the manufacturer's printed notes, if any, such as: top of fabric, allowance for shrinkage, etc. Not all manufacturers offer this information.

Before buying your fabric, you should look for flaws, usually marked in the selvedge with a coloured thread. The sales person should observe any flaws and you should not accept that fabric. If this is overlooked at the time, it is important that you check your own fabric before cutting as once you cut, the manufacturer will take no responsibility for flaws such as pulled threads, bad printing or patches of poor weave. It is important when using a fabric with a printed pattern, that the pattern is printed correctly. Some fabrics are not printed well and where the pattern is not straight this is known as the *pattern drift*. Again, the sales person should check for this.

Manufacturers allow approximately 2.5cm (1in) tolerance of pattern drift. If it is more than this, do not buy the fabric.

Obviously, once again, when making a small cushion, this will not be really necessary but it will always be necessary when calculating for larger projects, in particular curtains. So this is a sound routine to follow.

Make sure your fabric is cut straight in the shop. In the main, good shops will do this for you.

Before beginning each piece of work or checking for pattern drift, your fabric must be straightened.

To Check the Pattern is Printed Straight (Pattern Drift) (Fig 34)

Use your metre of fabric.

1 Straighten fabric (if necessary, refer back to 'Straightening Your Fabrics', page 29).
2 Cut off the straightened edge. With a patterned fabric, it will immediately show up if the pattern is accurately printed on the straight grain.
3 Lay the fabric, wrong side uppermost on the table and bring the left-hand selvedge over to the right-hand selvedge, *turn under the selvedge allowance* on the left-hand side of your fabric just inside where the printing on the fabric begins, next to the selvedge. Run you fingers or back of your scissors down the fold to crease in a sharp fold.
4 Place this fold over and on top of the flat selvedge of the right-hand side of your fabric and bring it to the next complete pattern (or motive). The pattern should match (Fig 34a).
5 If the drift from the top of the two selvedges is more than 2.5cm (1in) you should return the fabric to the shop or manufacturer (Fig 34b).

Fig 34 Checking for pattern drift.

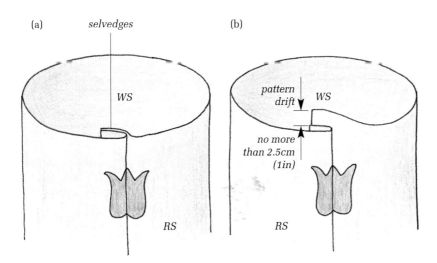

Length of Pattern Repeat (PR)

This is the distance from the top of one pattern to the top of the next identical pattern. Likewise you can check this by bringing selvedges to selvedge, across the straightened end of the fabric. If correct the pattern will match and you can check the length of your pattern repeat.

There may be occasions when the pattern will not appear to match. This is not a pattern drift but what is known as a half drop pattern repeat usually denoted on the label as HDPR or 'Repeat'. On the whole, manufacturers are producing less of these fabrics but you must be aware of it. What it basically means is that the pattern is printed on the diagonal. This becomes much more important when making larger soft furnishing projects and very important when making curtains. This will be discussed more fully in the section on Curtains.

The Brick

During the first meeting of a new course, we run through the equipment list as in the Chapter 2 of this book 'Equipment'. There are always questions about *The Brick*. And when I ask my students to look for a household brick, wash it, dry it and then cover it with fabric, there is always a lot of amusement and wondering what this soft furnishing course is all about! In fact, this brick will prove invaluable throughout all the work. Although, once again, we are only dealing with a small piece of fabric for the cushion, it is not long before it is agreed *the brick is a must*.

To Cover the Brick

Wash and dry the brick. Place in an airing cupboard for a few days. If possible,

find a brick with a centre indent. This area can then be filled with a piece of fabric and can be used as a convenient pin cushion when pinning out patterns and working on your fabric.

◆ Cut a piece of medium-weight furnishing fabric or calico approximately 43cm × 46cm (17in × 18in) cut to the straight of grain.

◆ Fold over to the wrong side 2.5cm (1in) along the 43cm (17in) edge and iron into place.

◆ Place the fabric on the table with the wrong side uppermost and the ironed-in fold running along the top edge.

Place the brick in the centre of the fabric. *Note:* If you have a brick with a centre hole filled with fabric, just run a bit of Sellotape over the top to hold the fabric in place. Place this onto the wrong side of the fabric, as this will be the top side of the brick when in use. It is a good idea to roughly cover the brick with a piece of fabric as a lining before making the top cover (Fig 35).

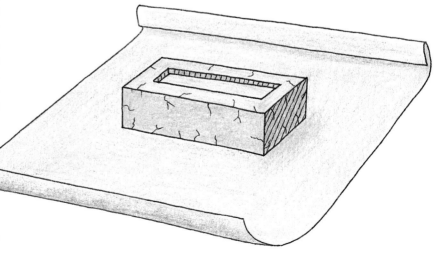

Fig 35 Making a parcel of the brick.

Fold the fabric over the brick making a parcel, bringing the folded edge over the fabric with the raw edge.

◆ Fold the ends in like a parcel and bring the ends up and over onto the face of the brick. Roughly stitch in place (Fig 36).

Fig 36 Folding and stitching the parcel.

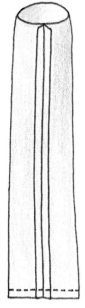

◆ Turn the brick over with all the joins underneath.

Set aside.

Fig 37 Making a handle for the brick.

Prepare a Handle for the Brick

1 Cut a strip of fabric 12cm (5in) wide and 70cm (27in) long on the straight of grain.

2 Bring the long edges together to form a tube with the right sides of the fabric together.
3 Pin, tack and machine using a 1.5cm (½in) seam allowance.
4 Press the seam to open.
5 Allow the opened seam to lie down the centre of the tube and run a line of machine stitching across the bottom of one end through all thicknesses (Fig 37a). This will enable you to push the blunt end of a pencil against the stitching line in order to turn the handle right side out.
6 Once turned to the right side, press the handle and strengthen by running a line of machine stitches from top to bottom along both long sides.
7 Form the handle into a circle (Fig 37b). Overlap the already neatened short end over the raw edge end by 1.5cm (½in) and machine in place through all thicknesses along this neatened edge. Repeat with another parallel line of stitches towards the raw edge end. This will join and strengthen the handle ready to be place around the brick.
8 Place the handle, now a circle, around the brick lengthways with the join underneath and covering the ends of the folded parcel ends.

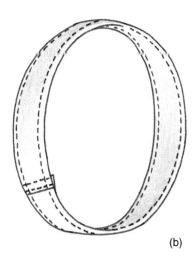

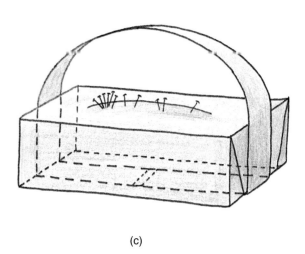

(a)   (b)   (c)

9 Roughly sew in place along both edges of the handle, along the bottom of the brick and up the two sides (Fig 37c).

Note: If you prefer to buy a piece of heavy tape in place of making the handle, buy 70cm (¾yd) of strong, webbed carpet tape 5cm (2in) wide and attach in the same way. However, this is a useful exercise as it forms a practical run for making ties for certain cushions and curtains, for example, today's fashionable tab headings for curtains.

THE BASIC CUSHION

Our first piece of work will be a simple, square, piped cushion using a printed patterned cotton furnishing fabric which is easy to handle. Not only will you be handling and beginning to understand your fabric but you will be involved with several techniques and skills needed as you progress into more advanced work.

NEW TECHNIQUES AND SKILLS
• Measuring the cushion
• Pre-planning and estimating fabric
• Making a paper pattern
• Cutting out
• Making and using piping
• First pattern layout
• Cutting out your fabric
• Tacking piping into a seam and negotiating a corner
• Using the piping foot
• Machining piping into a seam
• Pivoting a fabric on the sewing machine needle
• Making the final join in a crossway strip using the visual aid
• Joining the piping cord
• Using zigzag stitch for neatening seams
• Closing an opening by hand stitches
STITCHES
• Ladder stitch

MATERIALS FOR THE WORK PROJECT
• A square feather cushion pad (if allergic to feathers, use man-made filling – terylene/dacron), 40cm × 40cm (16in × 16in)
• 70cm (¾yd) of printed, patterned, cotton furnishing fabric
• No 5 piping cord (cotton) the length of four sides of the pad plus 10cm (4in)
• Matching cotton thread
• Brown paper for making pattern
• Zip/piping foot
• Measuring card 4.5cm (1¾in) for making crossway strips, using No 5 piping cord

PREVIOUSLY LEARNED TECHNIQUES AND SKILLS
• Checking your sewing machine and stitch
• Finishing the threads on lines of machining
• Cutting crossway strips
• The conventional method
• The continuous strip method
• Making a paper visual aid
STITCHES
• Back stitch
• Tacking stitch

Fig 38 The basic piped cushion.

For the example project I am using a square feather cushion pad 40cm × 40cm (16in × 16in). The example fabric is a printed, patterned, cotton furnishing fabric.

The first fabric chosen is Tulka Sunshine, a cotton furnishing fabric of medium weight with a plain weave and a printed pattern. It is a stable fabric, easy to work with. You will see from the photograph, it has a large pattern. By using this fabric to full advantage will demonstrate a clear placement of the pattern bringing out a strong colour and motif.

Cushions are not expensive and on the whole I think it is unnecessary to make your own cushion pads. It is essential that you buy a good, well-filled cushion pad, as this will form a sound foundation for your cushion. Using old cushions is not always successful as very often, with constant use, the feathers will have broken down and the pad becomes flat and shapeless. Choose a pad of good feathers (down, and down and feather are available but much more expensive). Or for those of you that are allergic to feathers, you can use a man-made terylene/ dacron-filled pad, although this will not be quite as successful as a feather filling. Do not be tempted to buy the foam chip fillings as these give a very uneven finish to your cushion. If you should wish to

Fig 39 Tulka Sunshine.

make your own feather pad then feather-proof ticking fabric must be used for the base.

For any soft furnishing project, there are certain pre-planning steps that must be undertaken:

1 Decide on your project (in this example the Basic Cushion)
2 Choose your fabric
3 Understand fabric characteristics (by going to the shop and reading the label)
4 Create a cutting plan
5 Estimate the amount of fabric
6 Record all the above.

My students have found it extremely useful to keep a simple but permanent and easily portable small, hard-backed notebook. I think you would also find this a most useful item. In this notebook we record pre-planning as follows:

Pre-planning:

◆ Select size of cushion

◆ Select fabric

◆ Width of fabric

◆ Pattern repeat

◆ Natural, man-made or mixed

◆ Any special properties

As we discussed earlier in fabrics, it is necessary to understand the labelling when selecting your fabric. You need to know the width of the fabric and any pattern repeat before you are able to estimate the amount of fabric needed for your project.

You will also find it useful to record other information about each of your projects to take along with any extra notes you may want to carry forward. From time to time I will suggest:

 RECORD IN YOUR NOTEBOOK

Measuring a Soft Cushion Pad

Fig 40 Measuring a soft cushion pad.

◆ Plump up your cushion pad and using a soft tape measure take a

loose measurement from seam to seam. Do not indent the cushion (Fig 40).

This will be the cutting size of your cushion cover. A seam allowance of 1.5cm (½in) is now used so in fact making the cushion cover smaller than the cushion pad. The reason you do not add a seam allowance to the measurement of a feather or other soft cushion filling such as terylene/dacron is because, by making the cover smaller, you will tighten up the cover and have a nice firm cushion rather than a loose one.

Order of Work for Cushion Project (Fig 41)

Make a cutting plan as in the diagram below. This does not need to be to scale, simply a visual aid and a record for future reference and for calculating the amount of material you will need to buy and as a cutting plan for your fabric. From the cutting plan (below) it is easy to visualize where you should be able to find the fabric for your piping. It also

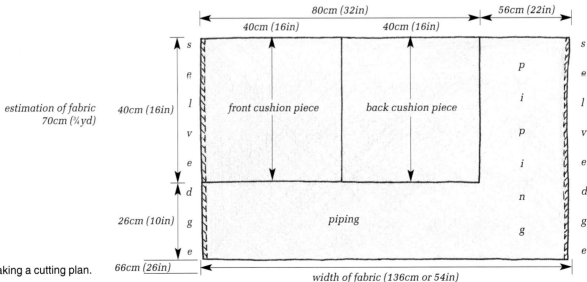

Fig 41 Making a cutting plan.

gives sufficient space to move your paper pattern to centralize any pattern on the fabric. Of course this depends on the fabric you pick, plain or patterned. You will learn by experience to adjust accordingly.

The following will give you an outline of the way your notebook should look for the first project:

 RECORD IN YOUR NOTEBOOK

WORKED PROJECT

Project 1: Basic Cushion Cover
Size of cushion

Pre-planning
Selection of fabric
Fabric content
Width of fabric
Pattern repeat

Cutting plan
copy the plan into your notebook
Amount of fabric
– amount needed
– size of piping cord
– amount of piping cord

Useful information

Project 1: Basic Cushion Cover
Size of cushion
– 40cm × 40cm (16in × 16in)
My selected fabric
Tulka
100 per cent cotton
Width 137cm (54in)
Pattern repeat 64cm (25in)
– Plain weave

Cutting plan (*see* Fig 41)

Amount of fabric
– 70cm (¾yd)
– No 5 piping cord
– 1.7m (1¾yd)

Useful information

best possible condition. For this small cushion it is sufficient to remember the basic understanding of your fabric (i.e. the width of your fabric, the selvedge and the straight of grain). If the fabric is creased, iron it and make sure the cut edge of your fabric is straightened (to the straight of weft grain) and is cut at right angles to the selvedge.

Basic Understanding of Your Fabric

Whatever piece of work you embark on you must make sure the fabric is in the

Making a Paper Pattern from Your Cutting Plan

◆ Make a brown paper pattern to the measurements of your cushion.

◆ Fold the paper into four to make sure it is correctly cut.

◆ Open out pattern.

◆ Mark in your straight of grain by drawing a line down the centre of your paper pattern.

◆ Mark the top centre of your pattern by folding the pattern in half, down the straight of grain and clipping a small 'V' out of the paper to indicate the centre and top of your fabric.

◆ Look after this pattern carefully for future use and record onto it the amount of material required, size of piping cord, width of crossway, length of piping cord and any special comments that might prove useful in future work (for example, when using a soft feather/dacron cushion pad, no seam allowance is added to the measured size of your cushion).

Fig 42 Using the pattern on the fabric to advantage.

TIP FOR BEGINNERS:

You may find it easier to cut two identical pattern pieces, one for the front and the other for the back.

Preparing to Cut Out for the First Time

Preparation of fabric:

◆ Iron your fabric if necessary.

◆ Straighten your fabric.

Now look carefully at your material. If using a patterned fabric it is quite usual to have the front and back of your cushion identical, and in making our first cushion we will do just that. A piece of patterned fabric can very often be used to bring up different motifs and colours, for example, a centre rose or a bird or perhaps a detailed stripe. By folding your paper pattern into four again, it is possible to move it around on the fabric to find a balance centre of a pattern motif or colour (Fig 42 left) and then to visualize such effects by opening out the paper and pinning a rough shape (Fig 42 right).

As an alternative, a different effect can be achieved by backing your cushion

with a plain or contrasting fabric or perhaps using contrasting piping. You must remember if you do use two fabrics they must be of equal weight.

First Pattern Layout

Note: Do not use the selvedge.

- Centralize the pattern using your cutting plan as a guide.

- Now pin your paper pattern onto the material.

Use as few pins as possible and get into the habit of placing these pins in the most necessary areas of the fabric. Remember, you do not use the selvedge. The first two pins must be placed on the straight of grain. Only one pin is necessary at each corner, but should be kept away from the corner. This enables you to cut evenly and quickly and without catching the pins with your scissors and blunting them (Fig 43).

Cutting Out for the First Time

- Cut out. Use the whole blade of your scissors and make long, even cuts holding the fabric flat with your other hand. This may sound very unnecessary, but in time you will find it saves time and minimizes damage to your fabric.

- Remove your paper pattern.

- Mark the centre top of your fabric, on both the back and front pieces, by folding your fabric in half, down the straight of grain.

- Clip the edge of the fold at the top of the fabric to create a small 'V'.

- Record the following useful information on the paper pattern for future use, and store paper pattern.

Fig 43 Pinning pattern in place.

Information to Record on your Paper Pattern for the Worked Project

- Size of pattern (40cm × 40cm or 16in × 16in)

- Amount of piping cord and size (1.70m or 1¾yd)

- Amount of fabric needed (70cm or ¾yd)

Estimated from your cutting plan and depending on the size of your fabric pattern you would need to buy approximately 70cm (¾yd) of face fabric.

Note: If using a contrasting fabric for your piping you would need to buy 25cm (¼yd) for continuous strip crossway or 50cm (½yd) for the conventional method. If using a striped fabric, use the conventional method.

ORDER OF WORK TO MAKE THE FIRST CUSHION

Piping

Prepare sufficient crossway strips to go round the four sides of your cushion plus an extra 10cm (4in).

Follow the instructions for making crossway strips. You may use the conventional method (i.e. cutting strips separately), or you may wish to use the continuous strip method as a useful exercise. At this stage of the course, I would suggest you use your patterned fabric or a plain matching fabric for your piping. Do not use stripes or checks at this stage unless you are experienced.

Front Cushion Piece

APPLYING PIPING CORD TO CUSHION

The bias strip with the cord inside is *tacked* directly onto the front cushion piece. This should be done accurately and using the thread matching your fabric rather than your tacking thread.

There are two reasons for tacking your piping into place with matching thread.

1 It is not necessary to machine the piping to the front cushion piece.
2 This line of tacking then acts as a guideline for the line of machine stitching that attaches the front and back cushion pieces together. It also eliminates the need for a double line of machine stitching. If the machining is accurate, it will not be necessary to remove these tacking stitches.

It is important that you begin your tacking with a *backstitch* and that you position and insert the piping cord into the crossway strip accurately.

Note: There are a variety of ways for joining piping cord from layering the ends of the cord and recreating the twisted ends, or by binding the ends with tape. All are correct. As beginners and beyond, we have found the following method most successful: Begin by binding the end of your cord (Fig 44).

(a)

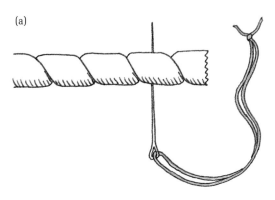

(b)

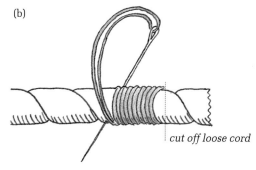

cut off loose cord

1 Straighten out the piping cord.
2 Use a matching thread and double it and tie a knot to keep the ends together.
3 Pierce the needle into the cord approximately 1.5cm (½in) from the end (Fig 44a) and bind the cord over and over with thread. This must be firm but not too tight or you will lose the shape and width of your cord. Keep the threads close and even for about 5mm (¼in).
4 Finish off with a backstitch through the binding and clip off the threads (Fig 44b).

(Far right) Fig 44 Binding the end of your cord.

5 With very sharp scissors, cut off the loose cord where you began binding. Care must be taken not to catch the stitches.

6 The cord should then be encased in the prepared crossway strip.

7 Check that the cut end of the crossway strip is at the correct angle.

8 Place the cord onto the wrong side of the strip along the centre. Allow the bound end of the cord to protrude approximately 1.5cm (½in) beyond the end of the strip.

9 Bring the two raw edges of the strip together making sure that it is folded so that the longest side of the cut end of the crossway extends behind the cord and both edges are even.

10 Hold together with three pins.

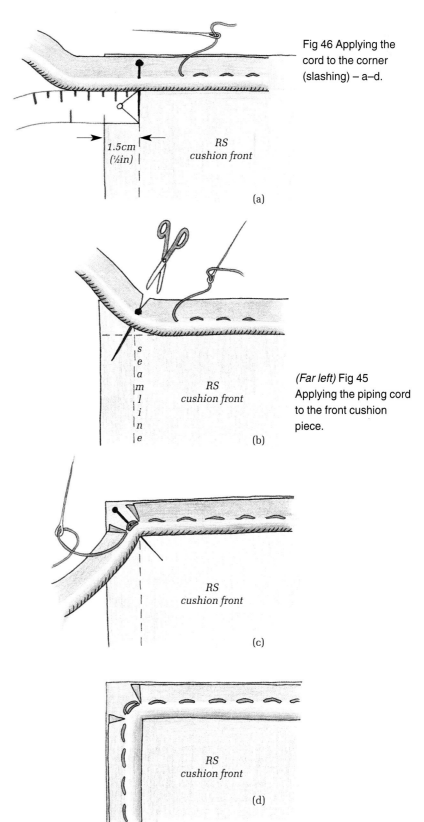

Fig 46 Applying the cord to the corner (slashing) – a–d.

1.5cm (½in)

RS cushion front

(a)

RS cushion front

(b)

(Far left) Fig 45 Applying the piping cord to the front cushion piece.

RS cushion front

(c)

RS cushion front

(d)

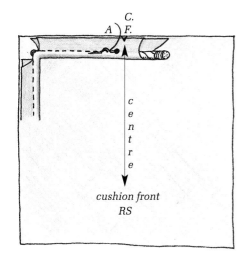

1 With the right side of your front cushion piece uppermost, find the marked centre (**V**) of the cushion. Allow 2.5cm (1in) of pinned piping to extend to the right of the centre mark

2 With the raw edges of the piping matching the raw edges of the front cushion piece place the first pin in place through all layers 2.5cm (1in) to the left of the centre at point A and begin tacking using a double backstitch (Fig 45).

Follow the diagram (Fig 46) and using only the minimum number of three pins:

1 Pin and close-tack the cord to within 2.5cm (1in) of the corner.
2 Now using a tape measure or a small ruler, measure 1.5cm (½in) from the side edge of the corner and place a steel pin (not fibreglass ended) vertically through the piping (*see* Fig 46a).
3 Using your very sharp, small scissors slash through the crossway strip, with a straight cut to the top of the pinhead (*see* Fig 46b).
4 Now gently mould the piping around the corner and continue your tacking, and at the very point of the slash do two small backstitches on this weak point. This must be accurate to avoid the corners of your cushion becoming 'ear shaped' (*see* Fig 46c).
5 Turn the work and continue tacking along this side making sure the raw edges of the piping accurately match the raw edges of the side being piped and that your tacking stitches remain even and tight up to the cord using only the minimum number of pins. Too many pins pull and distort the crossway. Work on three pins, removing and replacing as you work (*see* Fig 46d).
6 Repeat at corners 2, 3 and 4.
7 Continue tacking along the top edge of the cushion until you reach a point 5cm (2in) from the end of the crossway where you began.

Once again this may seem unnecessary, but it will make the final join much easier as it leaves a space in the unstitched piping to complete the join without having to unpick any stitches to complete the final join technique.

The question is often asked 'What happens if you meet a join in your crossway strip at the corner?'. If the crossway has been machined and finished accurately there will not be a problem.

(Far right) Fig 47 Joining the crossway – the final join.

Joining the Crossway – The Final Join

Join the two ends of your crossway with the help of your *visual paper aid – the final join* (Fig 47).

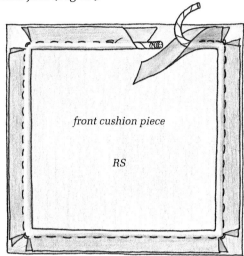

front cushion piece

RS

Joining the Cord

The circle of piping cord must now be completed by butting up the two ends of the cord. Repeat the process of binding the cord (Fig 48).

1 Let the second end of the cord fall evenly into place over the top of the first bound end of cord (*see* Fig 48a). Pierce your needle through the cord adjacent to the first bound end of the cord. The position of the needle marks the point where this end of the piping cord will butt up against the first bound end.
2 Starting from this point, bind the second piece of cord firmly, 5mm (¼in) away from the fraying end. Then over bind half way back towards the end again and backstitch off. But this time leave the thread attached.
3 Cut off the loose end of fraying cord at the edge of the binding, butt up the

(a)

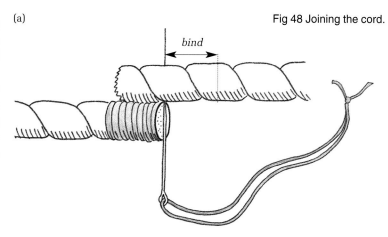

Fig 48 Joining the cord.

two ends of cord and secure in place with two or three stitches bringing the two cords together. Finish off thread (*see* Fig 48b).

4 Let the joined cords drop into place into the already joined crossway strip and encase the cord again, matching the edges of your crossway. Pin in place along the edge of the cushion and complete the tacking.

(b)

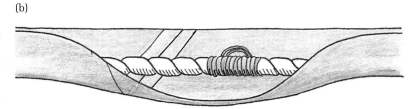

Using your Piping Foot for the First Time

For the beginner, using the piping foot for the first time, I am going to go into a little extra detail at this point. For the more advanced – bear with me!

Check your machine stitch on a double piece of matching fabric. The stitch should be a medium stitch length approximately 2 to 2½ (Fig 49).

This first line of machining is used to attach the piping to the front cushion piece along the bottom edge seam line where the opening will be closed by hand. In order to strengthen the opening it is necessary to machine along and slightly beyond the two bottom corners by extending the machining by 2.5cm (1in) into each side edge. At the same time this serves as a practice run using your piping foot and negotiating a neat corner by the technique of pivoting your fabric on the machine needle.

Attach the piping foot to your machine. The single foot shape allows the machine needle to stitch close to the encased piping cord.

Follow Fig 49 accurately.

Lower the machine needle into point A close up to the piping cord and just inside the line of tacking. Secure the thread with the reverse mechanism. The bulk of the fabric will be lying to the left and the outside. Machine almost to the corner. Leave

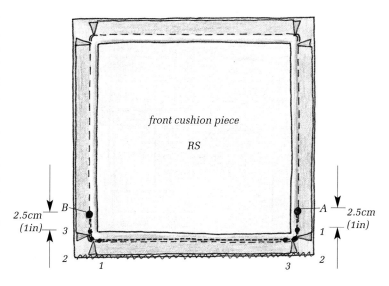

your needle in the fabric, lift the presser foot and slightly turn the fabric (i.e. pivoting the fabric on your needle). Lower the presser foot again and carefully take another machine stitch. Repeat exactly on the corner and once more, as you turn

Fig 49 Using the piping foot for the first time and pivoting the fabric on the machine needle.

your fabric, to run along the bottom edge. Continue machining along the bottom edge keeping the piping foot and needle close to the piping cord. And just inside your tacking line.

Repeat the pivoting (1, 2 and 3) at the second corner and machine up to point B. Finish off the ends and remove the fabric from machine.

(Right) Fig 50 Machining a guideline for the opening.

Using the Zigzag Foot for the First Time

For the beginners this may be the first time using the zigzag stitch.

TEST THE ZIGZAG STITCH

If you are unsure read again the zigzag facility in Chapter 3 ('The Sewing Machine').

Use a piece of matching single fabric and set the sewing machine stitch length to 4 and set the stitch width to approximately 3–4. Zigzag stitch along the raw edge so that the needle pieces the fabric just short of the outside edge.

Check the stitch is correct.

Once the stitch looks correct machine the length of the bottom edge of the front cushion piece to correspond with the line of machine stitching attaching the piping. Do not zigzag up into the side edges as above (*see* Fig 50a).

Set aside front cushion piece.

Back Cushion Piece (Fig 50)

Place the back cushion piece on the table with the wrong side uppermost. Fold up the bottom edge for a seam allowance of 1.5cm (½in) and iron-in the fold to the wrong side (*see* Fig 50a).

(a)

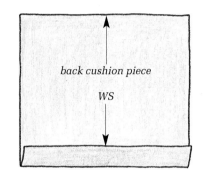

(b)

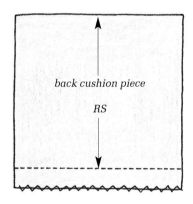

◆ Open out the fold (*see* Fig 50b) and machine a straight line of stitching on the flat, marked fold line 1.5cm (½in) from the bottom of the raw edge. This line of stitching is used as a guideline when closing the opening of your cushion and adds strength.

◆ Finish off the bottom raw edge with your machine zigzag stitch to correspond with the line of machine stitching.

Joining Front and Back Cushion Pieces (Fig 51)

◆ Place the back and the front sections of the cushion together with their right sides facing, pinning each corner carefully into place. Add another pin at the centre of the seam line of each side. Note placing of pins. You may need two pins for a large cushion along the seam lines.

◆ Tack front to back *all* round making sure all edges are together and that the corners are correct. This ensures accuracy for machining front and back pieces together.

The front and back cushion pieces are now machined together and the prepared, marked opening left un-machined. The opening is now strengthened at the two bottom corners (Fig 52).

Using your piping foot, lower the needle into the line of machine stitching along the bottom edge at point C (i.e. 2.5cm or 1in from left-hand corner). Use reverse stitch to begin and machine over the line of machine stitching up to the corner. Pivot your needle in the same way as used to attach the piping to the front cushion piece.

◆ Continue machining along all three sides until you reach the bottom edge of the other side, remembering to pivot your needle at the corners.

◆ Extend machining another 2.5cm (1in) along the bottom edge to point D covering the line of machining marking the opening. Use reverse stitch to finish.

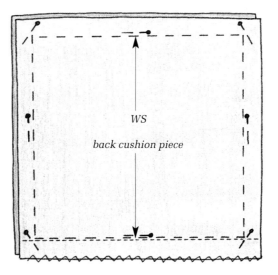

Fig 51 Joining front and back cushion pieces.

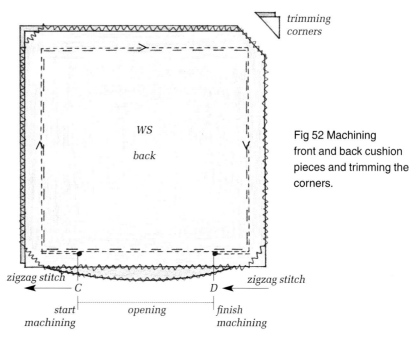

Fig 52 Machining front and back cushion pieces and trimming the corners.

◆ Trim off each corner as in above diagram to remove bulk.

When trimming a corner it is important that you do not cut too close to the machine stitching at the corner.

◆ Finish the raw edges with the zigzag stitch through all layers

to correspond with the line of machine stitching C to D joining back to front cushion pieces.

◆ Turn the cushion to the right side.

◆ Iron.

◆ Insert pad. Do make sure that the corners of the cushion pad are placed evenly into each of the cushion cover corners by putting your hand inside the cover and easing them into place.

The First Opening

Closing an opening by hand is the basic, simple opening for cushions. The seam is closed with a ladder stitch (Fig 53).

Fig 53 Ladder stitch.

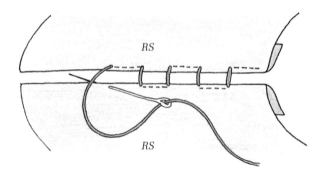

To join folded edges invisibly together from the right side of the fabric, working from right to left (if right handed), slip the needle along the fold line along one side for about 6mm (¼in).

Bring the needle out of the fold and into the fold line on the opposite side 6mm.

Draw up the stitches firmly but not over-tight otherwise the stitching line will show.

Closing the Opening of the Cushion with Ladder Stitch

Close the seam opening of the cushion along the bottom edge.

The front and back pieces should fall into place along the seam line, marked by the line of machining attaching the piping on the front cushion piece and the line of machining marking the opening line on the back cushion piece.

Pin together at the centre of the opening and add two or three pins either side to hold the opening in place.

Work from right to left (if right handed).

Using a double matching thread, knot the ends together and fasten on your thread by inserting the needle into the machined line of stitching about 1.5cm (½in) from the starting point of the opening. Leave a long end of thread. The end will be snipped off later. Run the needle to the starting point and secure the thread with a small backstitch.

Now begin your ladder stitch. Slip the needle along the opening's piped edge of the front cushion piece immediately above the line of machining attaching the piping through the piping seam allowance 6mm (¼in). Bring the needle out and into the opposite matching marked fold line of the back cushion piece.

Continue ladder stitching up to the end of the opening. Finish off with a small backstitch and run the thread into the machined line of stitching 1.5cm (½in) in the same way as fastening your thread.

Cut off both long ends of thread.

6 Zips in Cushions

When we made the first basic cushion we closed the opening in the seam by hand stitching using the ladder stitch. Although an extremely neat and adequate closing it does have the disadvantage of requiring these stitches to be removed for laundering or cleaning. Therefore, as an alternative you may prefer to use a zip, which will produce a strong, neat closure. This is much more difficult to insert and you will need to be both patient and very accurate to achieve a really professional finish.

Zips are available with metal and nylon teeth in a large range of colours, weights and sizes. Zipping in continuous lengths can also be bought, but I would not advise these at this stage as they come with loose locks and are difficult to apply. They are stronger however, and may be used in large cushions and in much more advanced soft furnishings.

Good dressmaking zips are the best and easiest to use in most soft furnishing. Here are a few pointers in selecting zips:

◆ Ensure that the opening will be large enough for the cushion pad to be slipped through easily, because too small an opening will strain the zip at the base and weaken the teeth at the end stop.

◆ Measure the size of the intended opening.

◆ Buy the nearest available size of zip. A slightly larger zip is better than a smaller size. Adjust the opening size accordingly.

◆ Select a colour that is the nearest match with the fabric (Fig 54).

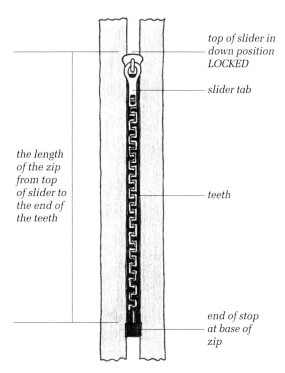

the length of the zip from top of slider to the end of the teeth

top of slider in down position LOCKED

slider tab

teeth

end of stop at base of zip

Fig 54 The zip – 1.

57

Fig 55 The zip – 2.

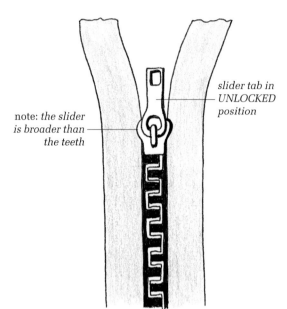

note: *the slider is broader than the teeth*

slider tab in UNLOCKED *position*

◆ When the slider tab is in the down position the zip is locked.

◆ When the slider is in the up position the zip is open.

◆ The length of the zip is measured with the zip closed from the top of the slider to the end stop at the base of the teeth.

◆ Take care not to iron over zip teeth, especially in the case of nylon zips, as this can damage both teeth and iron.

TIP FOR BEGINNERS:

I would suggest for those inserting a zip for the first time that you make a sample of *inserting a zip into a flat seam*. This sample can be added to your file for future reference.

Those who have already used zips or feel confident with their sewing skills may wish to put a zip straight into a back opening for the next project, 'The Basic Round Cushion'. The following instructions are applicable in both cases.

SAMPLE – INSERTING A ZIP INTO A FLAT SEAM

Materials Needed for Making a Sample

◆ A brown paper pattern 30cm (12in) wide × 25cm (10in) deep. This can then be kept to record information.

◆ 20cm (8in) zip.

◆ Coloured sewing thread to tack the stitching line.

◆ Zip foot for the sewing machine.

When inserting a zip a seam allowance of 2cm (¾in) is used for the opening.

1 Cut two identical pieces of fabric using the brown paper pattern, remembering your straight of grain.
2 Zigzag stitch over the two, straight long cut raw edges for the zip opening.
3 Place the two right sides of the fabric together with the zigzagged edges level and pin in place.
4 Start with a backstitch and tack along the seam allowance using a small tacking stitch. Finish with a backstitch. It is important that these stitches remain firm when setting in the zip and that this tacking line is accurate. If you don't feel confident, rule a line with a

sharp, chalk or HB pencil along the seam line and follow that line.

5 The correct length of the opening must be marked before you begin machining.

INSERTING A ZIP INTO A FLAT SEAM AND CENTRAL OPENING (Fig 56)

Machine stitch the seam up to the marked zip opening 4cm (1½in) from both sides.

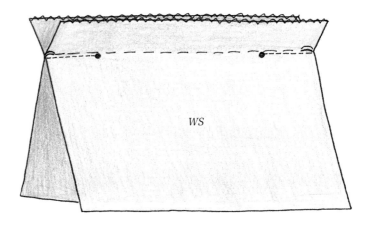

(Above) Fig 56 Preparing the opening, tacking and machining.

> **TIPS FOR THE EXPERIENCED:**
>
> Extend the machining by 3mm (⅛in) at this point. This makes it possible to slip the top of the slide and stop at the base of the zip just underneath the machining.

Reverse to secure the stitching and strengthen this point.

Note: The amount of seam allowance you need to machine both sides of the opening is approximately 4cm (1½in). Obviously, if you cannot buy exactly the correct length of zip, remember to go up to the next (longer) size. Any excess length of zip will slightly reduce the amount of machining necessary beyond the opening length.

1 Iron the seam open along the machine stitched and un-stitched tacked section using the toe of the iron to press the turning firmly into place. This will sharpen the crease line along the zip opening. If this is done correctly it should not be necessary to press this section again.

2 Re-mark the position of the ends of the opening with a vertical pin.

zip slide in UNLOCKED position

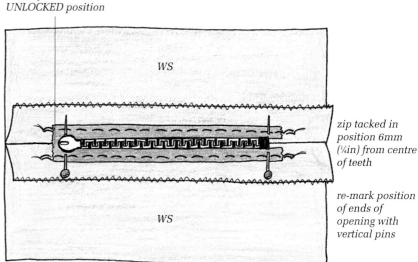

zip tacked in position 6mm (¼in) from centre of teeth

re-mark position of ends of opening with vertical pins

Fig 57 Tacking the zip onto the opening.

3 Lay the right side of the zip over the tacked seam allowance on the wrong side of the opening with the teeth of the zip centred exactly over the centre of the seam (Fig 57).

4 Place the top of the zip slide in the unlocked position to the marked position of the opening and place the end stop of the base of the zip to the marked position at the other end of the tacked opening.

Pin the zip in place through the tape and all layers and carefully tack one side at a time with a line of straight tacking stitches through all layers 6mm (¼in) from the centre of the teeth of the zip. Keep this very accurate, as it is your guideline for machining. It is a good idea to tack this line for the machining in a contrasting colour. Use your small ruler to check.

Turn the work to the right side with the zip tacked in position ready to top stitch into place.

1 Attach the zip foot to the machine.
2 Check your machine stitch on a small piece of your face fabric. The stitch should be strong and firm but you will have to test your own machine, probably a No 2 to 3 stitch length will be adequate.
3 Lower the needle into the right-hand side into the prepared tacking line 5cm (2in) from the top of the zip (Fig 58). The tab remains in the unlocked position. Do not use the reverse stitch but leave long ends of thread to be tied off on the wrong side after the zip has been machined into place. Machine accurately to the first corner where your vertical pin marks the end of the stop at the base of your zip. Leaving the needle in your work lift the presser foot and pivot the work at right angles. Lower the foot and machine a straight line of stitches close to the end stop to the point of the next line of tacking stitches, i.e. a parallel line.
4 Leaving the needle in the work, lift the presser foot and pivot your work again. Lower the foot and continue machining along the tacking line. Stop machining 6cm (2½in) from the end of this line and leave the needle in your work and lift the presser foot. The following procedure will prevent the stitches widening as the machining passes by the slider.
5 Look carefully at Fig 59. This is what is happening underneath your work. You cannot turn it over as the machine needle is holding it on the right side.
6 Carefully put your hand underneath the work and push the slider down the zip teeth about 8cm (3in) and past the point where the needle is in the work and past the foot. Now lower the presser foot and continue machining to the corner where the top of the slider would normally be. Leave the needle in the work, lift foot, pivot at right angles and complete the stitching to the opposite corner. Repeat the

process. Now your work is in the same position on the line of tacking where you began.

7   Continue machining up to the starting point and precisely cover the first three stitches (Fig 60).

8   Remove the work from the machine leaving long ends. Pull the threads to the wrong side of the work. Carefully tie off all the ends on the wrong side of the work. This must be correct or the join will look untidy.

9   Remove all tacking.

10 It should not be necessary to iron the zip opening if you ironed it correctly

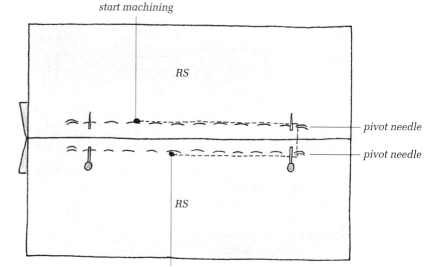

start machining

RS

pivot needle

pivot needle

RS

*leave needle in work
lift presser foot and manoeuvre zip
slide down zip teeth from
underneath your work*

(*Above*) Fig 58 Machining the zip into the opening.

(*Left*) Fig 59 Manipulating the slider of the zip to facilitate easy machining.

(*Below*) Fig 60 Completing the machining of the zip.

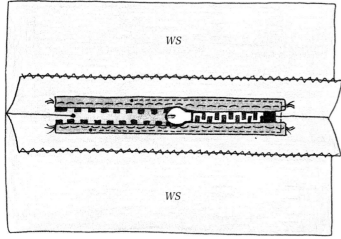

WS

WS

a view of what is happening underneath your work

when you closed the opening with your tacking before inserting the zip.

Note: If making the cushion, before placing back cushion piece to front to complete, open the zip to its full extent.

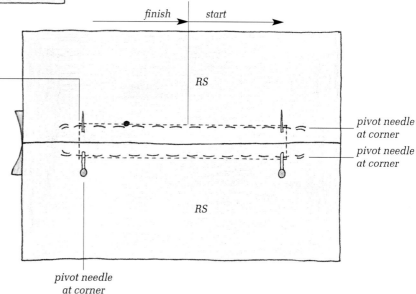

start machining on the marked tacking line

finish   *start*

*finish machining
cover the first three
stitches accurately*

RS

*pivot needle
at corner*

*pivot needle
at corner*

RS

*pivot needle
at corner*

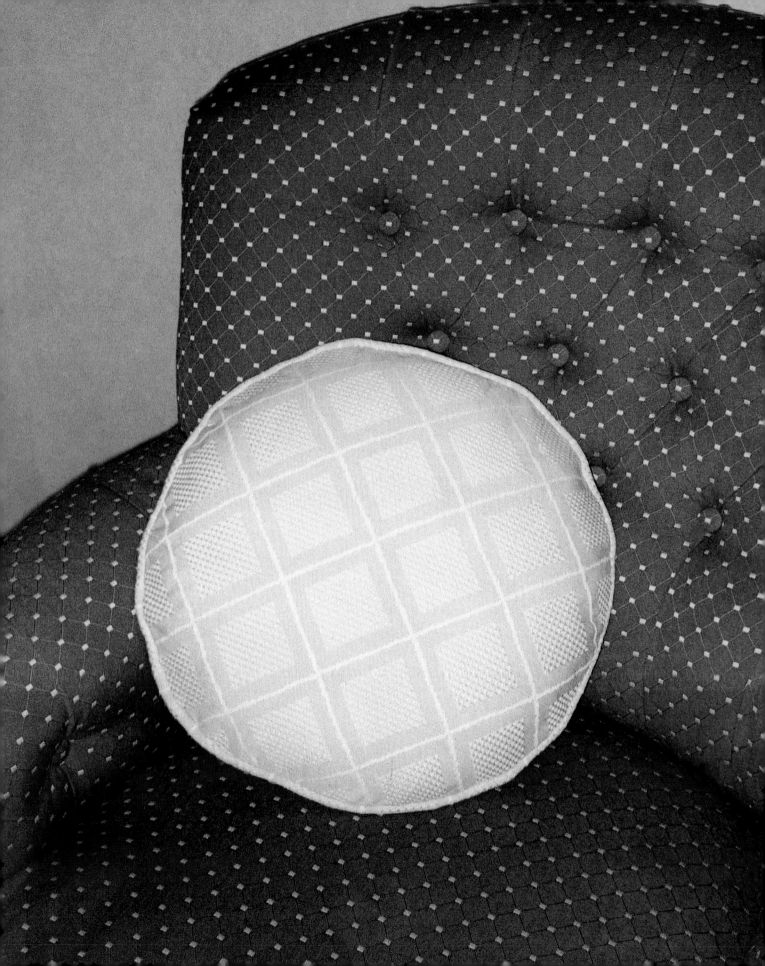

7 Project 2 – The Basic Round Cushion

The next project will be a flat, round cushion, inserting a zip into a flat seam for a back opening.

For the example project I am using a round, feather cushion pad, 40cm (16in) in diameter. I would suggest you choose

NEW TECHNIQUES AND SKILLS

- Inserting a zip in a flat seam
- A fabric pattern match
- Making a round paper pattern
- Planning a layout with a pattern match
- Inserting piping into a round cushion
- Clipping notches

STITCHES
- Slip tacking

MATERIALS FOR THE WORK PROJECT

A round-shaped, feather cushion pad, 40cm (16in) in diameter

- 70cm (¾yd) of cotton furnishing fabric
- No 5 piping cord (cotton) the length of the circumference plus 5cm (2in)
- Matching cotton thread
- Brown paper for making pattern plus 1m (1yd) string plus drawing pin
- Zip
- Zip/piping foot
- Card for cutting crossway strips

PREVIOUSLY LEARNED TECHNIQUES AND SKILLS

- Planning a layout
- Estimating fabric
- Making and inserting piping in a seam line
- Pivoting a fabric on the sewing machine needle

STITCHES
- Back stitch
- Tacking stitch
- Ladder stitch

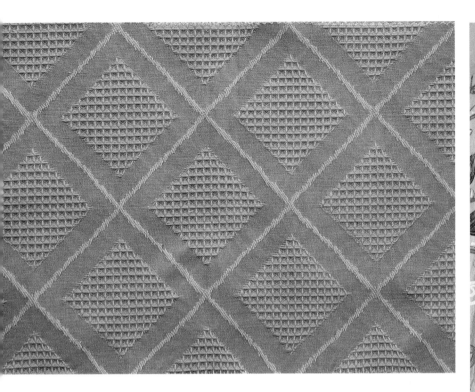

(Above) Fig 61 Akita Gold.

(Far right) Fig 62 The basic round cushion.

a pad of the same size to enable you to follow my measurements.

The example fabric is a textured cotton and man-made furnishing fabric, with a pattern repeat that will necessitate a pattern match along the seam line of the zip.

PROJECT 2
THE ROUND CUSHION

This is another stable, medium-weight furnishing fabric, easy to work with. The fabric is woven with a Jacquard weave and a self-coloured pattern and an arrangement of threads producing a raised textured surface.

It has a pattern repeat of 9.5cm (approximately 4in), which will introduce the first pattern match. The label tells me – mixed fibres of 55 per cent cotton, 45 per cent Modacrylic. It is flame retardant and must be dry-cleaned.

TIP FOR BEGINNERS:

Beginners who are a little nervous can pick a plain, cotton fabric or one with an overall design that does not need pattern matching.

For the more advanced, choose a textured, patterned fabric with a pattern repeat.

Acrylic fibres are man-made entirely from mineral sources.

Modacrylics are a modified form of acrylic fibres, which have been developed to produce flame-retardant fabrics. The label tells me dry clean only, and on larger projects this is good advice, as this fabric does not tolerate heat. For this small cushion, with care, it can be washed using warm water, rinsed well, with an added fabric conditioner. Do not wring or twist. Use only a very light cool spin and then allow to dry naturally. Use only a cool iron.

INSERTING A ZIP INTO A FLAT SEAM

Zips can be inserted into the back of a round, square or rectangular cushion.

The zip should be placed across the middle of the cushion or a third of the way down into a flat seam.

The neatest position for the zip in a round cushion is one third of the way down so that it does not run across the full diameter, and is less conspicuous. The opening placed in this position is perfectly adequate to allow you to insert your pad without straining the ends of the zip. Of course there is a disadvantage in placing a zip across the back of your cushion in that you cannot reverse the cushion.

PATTERN MATCHING

In this project, the first fabric pattern match is introduced.

I suggested at the beginning of this project that beginners should use a fabric which does not necessitate pattern matching.

In order to keep the continuity and build up skills and techniques throughout this course, I might suggest for those students who are not pattern matching their zip closure, a small practice sample might be added to their files.

Those who have already pattern matched or feel confident enough may immediately pattern match the zip opening. The following instructions are applicable in both cases.

The easiest way for the beginner is to take about *20cm (8in) off their metre or yard of their sample fabric length*. You have already straightened this fabric earlier, when understanding the pattern drift and pattern repeat.

The excess can be cut off and kept, leaving you with a sample of about 20cm × 30cm (8in × 12in) to put into your file.

First Pattern Match

The professional can do this without tacking but for the beginner, and beyond, and to ensure accurate pattern matching, it is much better to tack your fabric into place using slip tacking, sometimes referred to as 'outside tacking'. This is a tacking stitch that is worked on the right side of the material. After slip tacking, the fabric can be folded with the right sides together and machined on the tacking line (Figs 63 and 64).

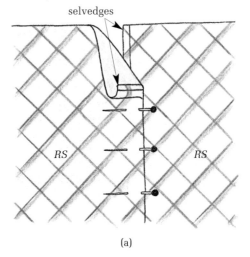

(a)

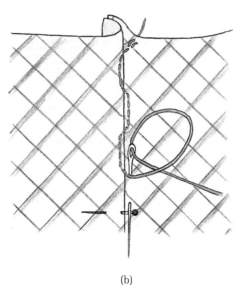

(b)

Fig 63 Slip tacking – 1.

(a)

(b)

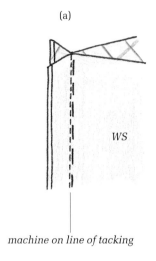

WS

machine on line of tacking

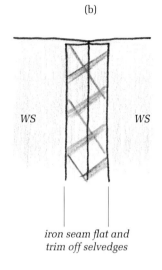

WS   *WS*

iron seam flat and trim off selvedges

(Above) Fig 64 Slip tacking – 2.

(a)

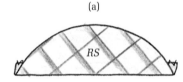

RS

RS

Fig 65 Pattern matching the opening for a round cushion.

(c)

(b)

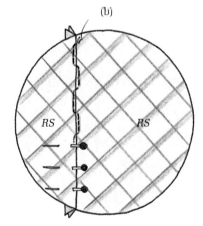

RS   *RS*

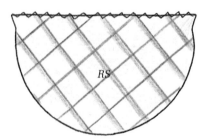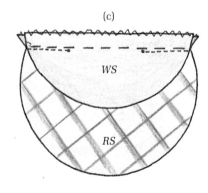

WS

RS

Slip Tacking Stitch (Outside Tacking)

This stitch is used for matching the pattern on fabrics that must be held accurately in place before machining. It is worked on the right side of the material.

1 Lay the lower back cushion piece on the table right side uppermost. Open out and flatten the ironed-in seam line.
2 With right side uppermost, lay the upper back cushion piece with the seam line ironed-in onto the flattened out seam line of the lower back cushion piece.
3 Pin in place with pins in horizontal position, carefully matching the pattern.
4 Use only 2 or 3 pins.
5 Slip the needle along the folded left-hand edge 1.5cm (½in). Then take another 6mm (¼in) stitch through the flat piece of fabric next to the fold (Fig 65). Repeat to the end.
6 Turn the fabric to the wrong side – it will appear to be tacked as a normal seam (*see* Fig 64).

Now follow the instructions for the sample – inserting a zip into a flat seam (page 59).

ORDER OF WORK FOR THE SECOND PROJECT

Inserting a Zip into the Back Opening of a Round Cushion

MAKING A CIRCULAR PATTERN

Measuring a Circular Cushion (Fig 66)

Although this is another feather/Dacron-filled soft cushion and we added no seam allowance to the measurement of the basic square, feather/Dacron cushion, then taking the seam allowance of 1.5cm (½in) to firm up the cushion.

In the case of a round cushion a little extra ease is necessary to accommodate the curved seam allowance which is more bulky than the straight seam. So in this case we *add* 6mm (¼in) all around to the measured size of the cushion and make the paper pattern to this size. A 1.5cm (½in) seam allowance is then used when making up the cushion.

Plump up the cushion pad and using your soft tape measure, measure loosely across the centre (diameter) of the pad.

Record the exact measurement = 40cm (16in).

Add ease of 6mm (¼in) all around:

6mm + 40cm + 6mm = 41.2cm
(¼in + 16in   + ¼in = 16½in)

PREPARE TO MAKE A PAPER PATTERN

To make a paper pattern the same size as the pad:

1 Cut a square of brown paper to this measurement, 41.2cm (16½in), and carefully fold into four (quarters). It is important that this is accurate. Place a pin in the centre to make sure it stays in place (Fig 67).
2 With string, a sharp pencil and a large drawing pin, make a string compass.
3 Tie the pencil to one end of the string. Hold the pencil, point down, on one corner of the square. Stretch the string along one edge to the next corner (this will be the radius of the pattern, i.e. 20.6cm or 8¼in).
4 Place a piece of card under the folded corner and pierce the string, the corner of the paper and the card with a drawing pin. Carefully draw an arc across the paper between the opposite corners, keeping the pencil vertical.

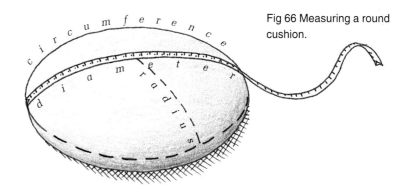

Fig 66 Measuring a round cushion.

Fig 67 Making a string compass and paper pattern.

(a)

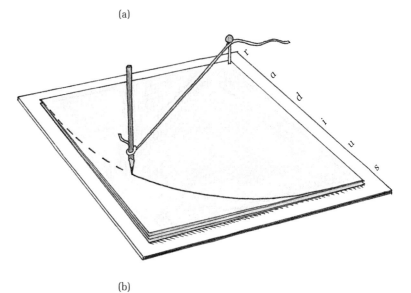

(b)

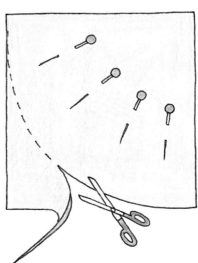

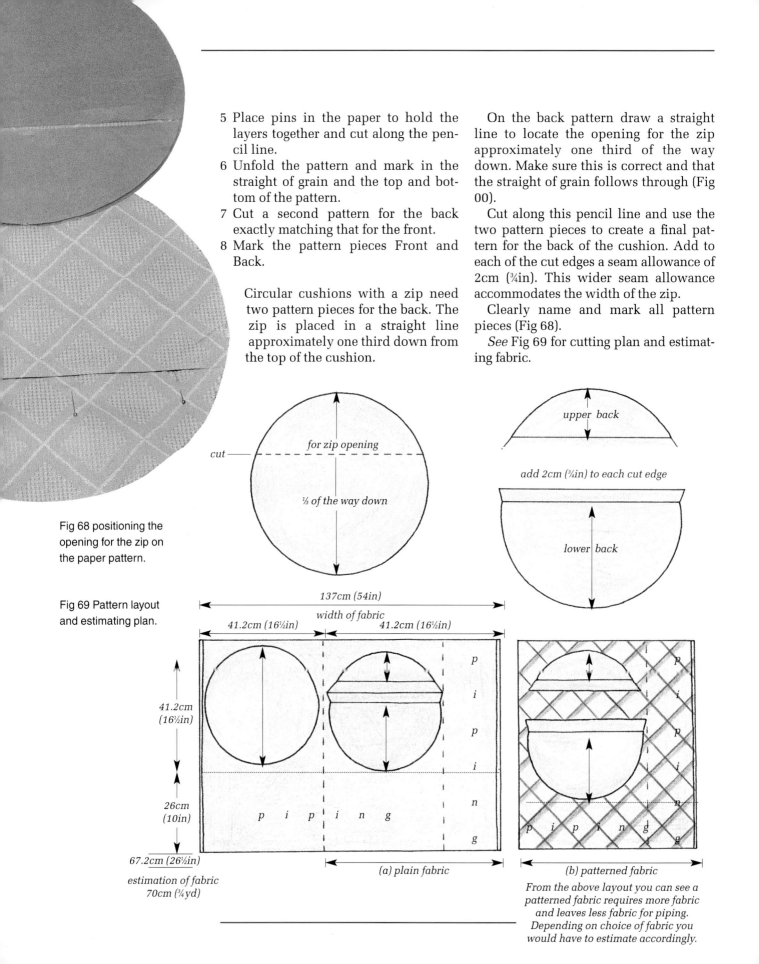

5 Place pins in the paper to hold the layers together and cut along the pencil line.

6 Unfold the pattern and mark in the straight of grain and the top and bottom of the pattern.

7 Cut a second pattern for the back exactly matching that for the front.

8 Mark the pattern pieces Front and Back.

Circular cushions with a zip need two pattern pieces for the back. The zip is placed in a straight line approximately one third down from the top of the cushion.

On the back pattern draw a straight line to locate the opening for the zip approximately one third of the way down. Make sure this is correct and that the straight of grain follows through (Fig 00).

Cut along this pencil line and use the two pattern pieces to create a final pattern for the back of the cushion. Add to each of the cut edges a seam allowance of 2cm (¾in). This wider seam allowance accommodates the width of the zip.

Clearly name and mark all pattern pieces (Fig 68).

See Fig 69 for cutting plan and estimating fabric.

cut — for zip opening

⅓ of the way down

upper back

add 2cm (¾in) to each cut edge

lower back

Fig 68 positioning the opening for the zip on the paper pattern.

Fig 69 Pattern layout and estimating plan.

137cm (54in)
width of fabric
41.2cm (16½in)   41.2cm (16½in)

41.2cm
(16½in)

26cm
(10in)

p i p i n g

67.2cm (26½in)

estimation of fabric
70cm (¾yd)

(a) plain fabric

(b) patterned fabric

From the above layout you can see a patterned fabric requires more fabric and leaves less fabric for piping. Depending on choice of fabric you would have to estimate accordingly.

CUTTING OUT

Look carefully at your fabric and if, for example, there is a bird or a particular flower or a definite textured pattern or colour you want to centralize, then position your pattern as we did in our basic square cushion.

It is not necessary that the back of the cushion matches the front, as you would probably leave the cushion *in situ* with the zipped side behind. What is most important when using any patterned or textured fabric with a definite woven pattern, is that *the pattern remains complete when the zip is closed*. So a certain amount of planning and looking at your fabric is essential before placing the pattern pieces on the fabric.

Look carefully at the pattern layout (Fig 70).

1 Place the front pattern in place on your fabric.
2 Place the upper half of the back pattern piece in place with the 2cm (¾in) seam allowance added.
3 Fold over the seam allowance on the lower half of the back pattern.
4 Look down your fabric for the pattern match of the upper and lower back pattern pieces.

Note: At the moment the seam allowance of the upper back piece is flat, so you would have to note the seam line.

Project 2: Basic Round Cushion
Size of cushion

Pre-planning
Selection of fabric

Fabric content

Width of fabric
Pattern repeat

Cutting plan –
copy the plan into your notebook
Amount of fabric
– amount needed
– size of piping cord
– amount of piping cord

Useful information

Project 2: Basic Round Cushion
Size of cushion
– 40cm (16in) diameter
My selected fabric:
Akita Gold
– a plain colour, textured weave
Content: 55 per cent cotton,
45 per cent modacrylic
Width 1.37m (54in)
Pattern repeat 9.5cm (4in)

Cutting plan (Fig 69)

Amount of fabric
– 1.10m (43in)
– No 5
– 1.2m (47in)
– 32cm (12in) zip

Useful information
– Flame retardant
   Suitable for curtains and bed covers, also for general domestic upholstery and loose covers
– Dry clean only

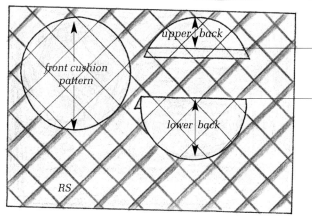

Fig 70 Pattern layout for a patterned fabric for the round cushion.

5 Roughly pin in place making sure that the straight of grain follows through on both the upper and lower sections of the back pattern.

CUSHION FRONT

Cut the *front* pattern piece.

Set aside.

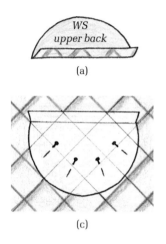

(a)

(c)

Fig 71 Planning and cutting the back cushion sections.

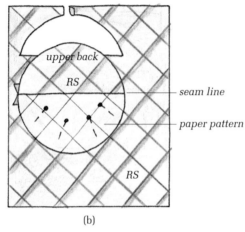

— seam line

— paper pattern

(b)

CUSHION BACK (Fig 71)

1 Cut out the upper part of the back remembering the 2cm (¾in) seam allowance that has been added to the pattern for the zip opening and angle the seam allowance out at each side. The pattern for the lower section of the cushion back remains roughly pinned in place on the material.
2 Remove the paper pattern from the upper section and fold over the seam allowance of the fabric 2cm (¾in) to the wrong side and press into place.
3 With the right side of the fabric facing you and the seam allowance folded under, align this folded edge of the upper back section fabric to the straight edge of the lower back brown paper pattern piece, still pinned roughly in place on the material. Check the seam

allowance is folded back on the paper pattern of the lower section. Now make sure the pattern on the fabric matches and the straight of grain runs through. If necessary, reposition the lower back paper pattern on the fabric before cutting. After checking that the pattern is correct, remove the *upper* section of fabric (*see* Fig 71b).

Set aside.

4 Cut the lower section of the back cushion piece remembering the seam allowance that has been added to the pattern. Angle the seam allowance out at each side (*see* Fig 71c).
5 Remove the paper pattern.
6 Neaten the edges of the two back sections of the zip opening by zigzagging along both straight cut edges.

*If the material you are using is patterned you must now pattern match (*see* page 66 – Pattern Matching for the Round Cushion).*

In order to insert the zip, refer to page 59 for all sample instructions and diagrams, 'Inserting a Zip in a Flat Seam'.

Piping

Make up sufficient crossway for the piping round the edge of the front cushion piece plus 10cm (4in).

ATTACHING PIPING TO THE ROUND EDGE OF THE FRONT SECTION OF THE CUSHION

When applying crossway and sewing a curved seam, as in a round cushion, it is important that the piping moulds well and sits evenly in the seam allowance.

To do this, V-shaped notches should be cut into the seam allowance of the crossway at regular intervals around the edge as shown right (Fig 72).

Encase the bound end of the cord into the crossway strip. Check the correct angle of the cut end of the crossway strip and place the first two pins into position using the same method as the basic, square cushion. Using matching thread, start with a backstitch, then begin tacking for about 4cm (1½in) as shown here.

Place the third pin into the crossway and through the piping at the first point to be slashed, approximately 5cm (2in) from the beginning of the tacking. The method we will use will be exactly the same as making a straight cut to the top of the pinhead on the square corners of the first cushion. Continue tacking close to the cord and double backstitch at the point of each slash. Continue in this method pinning and slashing only the crossway strip at regular intervals until you come to your *final join*.

The final join is done in exactly the same way as your first cushion. Once again, you can use your visual paper aid if you are unsure.

Open the zip before placing the back cushion piece to the front cushion piece.

Joining the Back and Front Cushion Pieces (Fig 73)

With the right sides facing, place the back cushion piece to the front cushion piece and match the centre top and bottom V. Secure in place with pins and, keeping the raw edges together, carefully tack on the seam lines through all layers. Keep the tacking stitches close to the piping cord.

Machine just inside the tacking line, keeping your piping foot close to the piping cord.

1 Turn the cushion cover with the wrong side front uppermost.

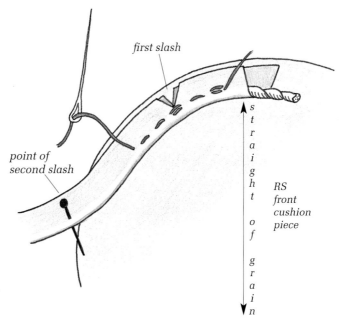

Fig 72 Slashing V-shaped notches.

2 Complete the notch by trimming out a V through all layers in exactly the same position as you slashed and double backstitched the piping. Do take care that you do not clip the backstitch.
3 Using your zigzag stitch, finish off your raw edge, sewing through all thicknesses.
4 Turn cushion cover to the right side.
5 Press.
6 Place cushion pad into the cover, easing it into shape.
7 Close the zip and plump up into shape.

Fig 73 Joining the back to the front cushion pieces and completing the notches.

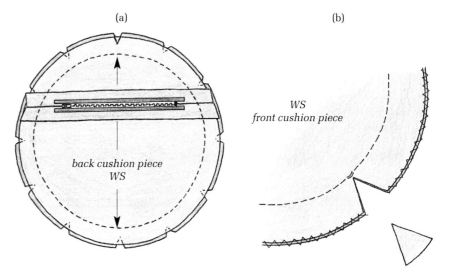

8 Project 3 – Boxed Cushions

These cushions are sometimes referred to as welted cushions. Deeper and firmer cushions need a welt. This is a piece of material inserted between the top and bottom sections of the cushion that forms the side of the boxed (or welted) cushion. The depth of the welt is the depth of the cushion. These cushions can be square, rectangular or round, or cut to the exact shape of the seat.

The next project will be a square, boxed cushion using a block of foam as the base. Calico will be used for the cover. For the cushion cover an even, striped cotton furnishing fabric will be used.

In this project it will be necessary to make two separate covers:

RADLEY GREEN REGATTA STRIPE

A medium-weight cotton furnishing fabric, easy to work with. The fabric has a woven pattern, easily identifiable with the colours showing on both sides of the fabric, checks and stripes being the simplest woven pattern using a plain weave. Using this striped fabric will demonstrate the techniques to give you the skills in working with striped fabric.

CALICO

A plain woven cotton fabric. It is used for lining fabrics for upholstery. The label tells me – Flame Retardant.

Fig 74 Radley Green Regatta Stripe.

Fig 75 Checked fabric.

This project is made up of two parts:

Part 1 The Calico Lining Cover for Foam with a Ladder-Stitched Closure.

Part 2 The Cushion Cover with Piping and a Zip in the Centre of the Back Welt.

It would be a useful exercise to treat both as separate projects. First, to plan, make and complete the lining cover for the foam before tackling the more advanced work on the cushion cover itself. The former will usefully serve as a practical run in some of the new techniques we will use. We will approach them as follows:

(The Radley Green check matches the Radley Green stripe, and as can be seen from the photograph on page 72 it can be used to complement the striped fabric and add interest by using it for scatter cushions using the basic soft square cushion. In this case I have used the checked fabric for the piping, but interest could have been added by using the striped fabric for the piping.)

PROJECT 3 – PART 1
THE CALICO LINING COVER FOR FOAM WITH A LADDER-STITCHED CLOSURE

For the example project I am using a block of foam, the dimensions are: 43cm × 43cm square × 5cm depth of welt (17in × 17in × 2in). THIS WILL BE USED AS A

NEW TECHNIQUES AND SKILLS	MATERIALS FOR WORK PROJECT	PREVIOUSLY LEARNED TECHNIQUES AND SKILLS
◆ Use of calico	◆ Block of foam for base	◆ Planning a layout
◆ Planning a layout for the calico base	◆ Calico	◆ Estimating fabric
◆ Planning a layout using a weft straight of grain	◆ Matching thread	*STITCHES*
◆ Making and inserting a welt	◆ Brown paper for making pattern	◆ Back stitch
		◆ Tacking stitch
		◆ Ladder stitch

GARDEN SEAT. The example fabric is calico lining fabric.

I would suggest you pick a similar, small, square seat cushion. Use a piece of foam cut to the exact size of your seat and the required depth of your welt. Foam can be bought in various weights and thicknesses. Although cutting the foam oneself with a sharp knife is widely practised, I would suggest that for a little extra cost you may buy the foam cut to shape from a good upholstery shop or department store. Bear in mind that it is now mandatory that the foam is fireproof.

Foam is firm, but with constant wear it can break away at the edges. To avoid this the foam is first covered with calico, which will also act as a firm base for your cushion cover. You can ask for it to be netted by the supplier, which means the foam is encased in a fine netting cover, which will be quite satisfactory for fairly light foam, but you will still get a firmer foundation using calico,

You will need to make a pattern for the purpose of buying the foam pad:

◆ Measure the length and width of the cushion.

◆ Cut a pattern to this size from your brown paper and place it on the seat to check it is correct.

◆ Write on the paper pattern the size of the cushion and the depth of the welt and the purpose for which the cushion is to be used – this will ensure that the correct density of foam is ordered and that it is cut to the exact size.

◆ Make two identical patterns – one for yourself and one for the shop. Ask the shop to return its copy with the cut foam.

Fig 76 The garden seat project.

THE EXAMPLE BOXED CUSHION

The dimensions are: 43cm × 43cm square × 5cm depth of welt (17in × 17in × 2in). The *foam* is cut to these measurements.

Paper Pattern for the Calico

Make a pattern piece for each section of the cover. This will make it easier for you to lay the pattern pieces on to the fabric accurately.

When using foam, which is a more rigid filling, it is necessary to *add* a seam allowance of 1.5cm (½in) to all sides of the brown paper pattern (Fig 77 overleaf).

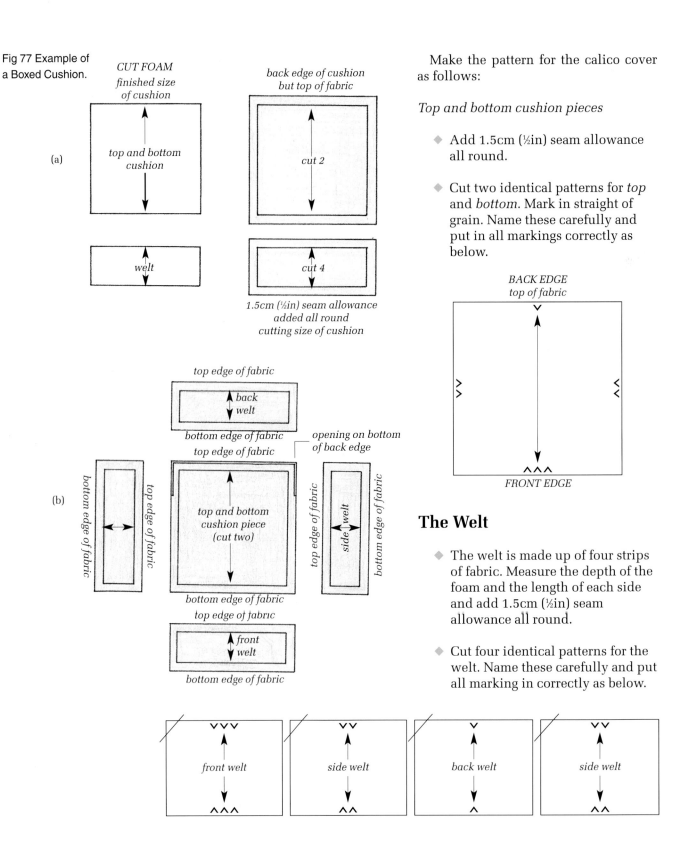

Fig 77 Example of a Boxed Cushion.

CUT FOAM
finished size of cushion

(a)

top and bottom cushion

welt

back edge of cushion but top of fabric

cut 2

cut 4

1.5cm (½in) seam allowance added all round cutting size of cushion

(b)

top edge of fabric

back welt

bottom edge of fabric
top edge of fabric

opening on bottom of back edge

bottom edge of fabric
top edge of fabric

top and bottom cushion piece (cut two)

top edge of fabric

bottom edge of fabric

side welt

bottom edge of fabric

bottom edge of fabric

bottom edge of fabric
top edge of fabric

front welt

bottom edge of fabric

front welt

side welt

back welt

side welt

Make the pattern for the calico cover as follows:

Top and bottom cushion pieces

◆ Add 1.5cm (½in) seam allowance all round.

◆ Cut two identical patterns for *top* and *bottom*. Mark in straight of grain. Name these carefully and put in all markings correctly as below.

BACK EDGE
top of fabric

FRONT EDGE

The Welt

◆ The welt is made up of four strips of fabric. Measure the depth of the foam and the length of each side and add 1.5cm (½in) seam allowance all round.

◆ Cut four identical patterns for the welt. Name these carefully and put all marking in correctly as below.

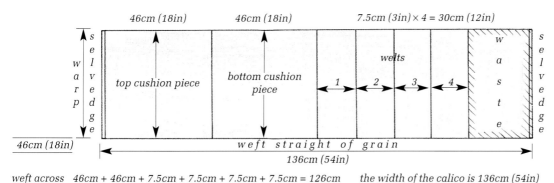

Fig 78 The cutting plan.

weft across   46cm + 46cm + 7.5cm + 7.5cm + 7.5cm + 7.5cm = 126cm
           (18in   18   3   3   3   3   48in)
warp down   46cm

the width of the calico is 136cm (54in) from this cutting plan the minimum amount of fabric would be 50cm (½yd)

PLANNING AND ESTIMATING THE FABRIC

The cutting plan is described in Fig 78.

This is an important and useful exercise in planning the layout for the calico lining cover. The width of the calico is 136cm (54in) and you will see from the cutting plan that the minimum length of calico you would buy would be 50cm (½yd). Because this is only the lining and so as not to be extravagant with the material you may cut the four pieces of welt in the direction of the weft straight of grain. However, when you are using the face fabric where there is a pattern or a texture you must make sure the warp straight of grain follows through otherwise the pattern will not match.

✎ RECORD IN YOUR NOTEBOOK

DEMONSTRATION PROJECT

Project 3(1): Boxed Cushion
Calico lining cover for foam block
Dimension of foam, cushion block

Pre-planning
Selection of fabric
Fabric content
Width of fabric
Pattern repeat (not applicable)

Draw a cutting plan
Amount of fabric
– amount needed

Useful information

Project 3(1): Boxed Cushion
Calico lining cover for foam block
43cm × 43cm square × 5cm
depth of welt (17in × 17in × 2in)
My selected fabric:
Calico natural
100 per cent cotton
Width 136cm (54in)

Cutting plan (Fig 78)
Amount of fabric
– minimum: 50cm (½yd)
– width: 136cm (54in)

Useful information on the label
– Flame retardant
– Dry clean only

CUTTING OUT

1 Place the paper pattern on the fabric, first pinning the straight of grain into place and remembering to use as few pins as possible but correctly placed as previously described.
2 Cut out.
3 Remove the pattern making sure each section of fabric is carefully marked.
4 Record notes on paper pattern.

ORDER OF WORK

Making up the Welt

1 Place the four sections of the welts on the table, right sides uppermost. Check that they are in the correct order and the pattern markings are correct. *FRONT SIDE BACK SIDE*
2 Join the four short end sections of welt together to form a circle. Placing the right sides fabric together, pin and tack along the seam using a 1.5cm (½in) seam allowance (Fig 79a).
3 Machine accurately in place along the seam line and leave 1.5cm (½in) unstitched at top and bottom. Use the reverse stitch on the machine or tie off the ends securely, as these are weak points. Use a marker pin inserted vertically into the fabric at each point before machining.
4 Press all seams evenly open from top to bottom. There is no need to neaten the seams on this calico lining (Fig 79b).

Fig 79 Pinning, tacking and machining welt seams.

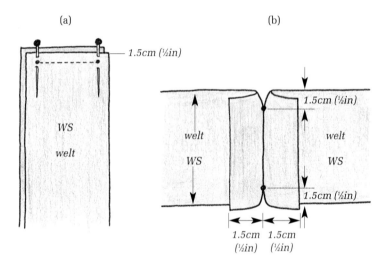

Fig 80 Pressing up the seam allowance and marking the opening on the bottom back edge of the welt.

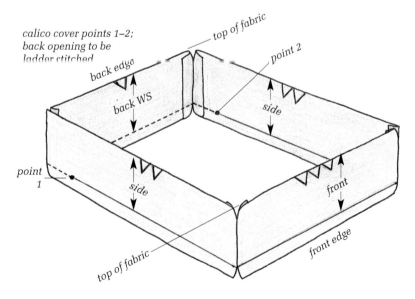

Prepare the Welt for the Opening

In order to accommodate the rigid foam pad, the opening along the bottom back edge of the calico cover must be extended into the sides. For this size of foam it is sufficient to allow 4cm (1½in) extension and the line marking the opening to be ladder stitched must be strengthened.

◆ Press up the seam allowance to the wrong side of the bottom edge of the welt along the front, back and two side edges (Fig 80).

◆ Flatten out the ironed-in fold line along the bottom edges of the welt along the back edge and side edges. Machine a line of stitching along the flattened indented fold line from point 1 of the side welt seam 4cm (1½in) up to the top corner. Pivot your needle exactly at the point where seam lines meet on the corner and continue your line of machining along the fold line to the next corner. Pivot your needle accurately on the corner again and continue machining down to point 2, which is 4cm (1½in) into the second side.

Joining the Welt to the Top and Bottom Sections of the Cushion

TOP SECTION

It is important that the following instructions are correctly followed:

Note: the *top cut edge* of the fabric has now become the *back edge* of the cushion. Use your markings very accurately. This may be confusing at first, but unless it is correct, continuity of any pattern from back edge to front edge and down into the front welt will not be achieved.

Although the calico is an unpatterned fabric and there is no need to pattern match, if using a striped or patterned fabric this order of work is essential. By following these instructions it will serve as a practice run (Fig 81).

1   Place the top cushion piece right side uppermost on the table. With the right sides of the fabric facing, place the top edge of the back welt piece to the top edge of the cushion top matching the centre markings keeping edges level (**V**).

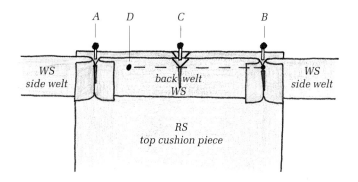

2   Make sure that the short seams of the welt at either side are pressed open and flat.

3   Place pins A and B in a vertical position exactly on the points where the machining of the welt seam finishes, i.e. 1.5cm (½in) from the ends.

4   If the seam allowance of the welt is correct, the turned back 1.5cm (½in) will be level with the side of the cushion cover. This is most important and it must be 'spot on'.

5   Place the third pin in the vertical position at C, the centre.

6   Mark at point D along the seam line 2.5cm (1in) from point A.

7   Tack into place through A, D, C and B very accurately along the seam line.

8   Take the work to the machine and lower the machine needle into the work at the point D. Leave long ends on the machine thread and do not use the reverse stitch.

9   Machine to point B. Machine accurately along the 1.5cm (½in) seam allowance.

10   Leave the needle in the work at point B exactly on this point. Lift the machine foot and pivot the work for the next section of the welt. With the foot still up, push the fabric to the left and align the next section of the welt to the side edge of the cushion (**VV**).

11   Lower the machine foot (Fig 82).

Fig 81 Joining the top of the welt to the top cushion piece.

Fig 82 Machining the top
of the welt to the top cushion
piece.

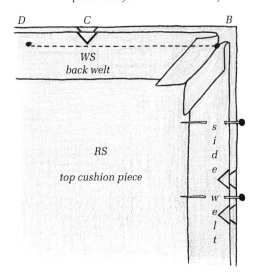

*leave needle in work EXACTLY at this
point B, then lift machine foot and
pivot work for the next section of welt*

WS
back welt

RS

top cushion piece

*s
i
d
e*

*w
e
l
t*

the bottom back edge and sides. This marks the position for the back opening. Machine a line of stitches along the back edge of the bottom section of the cushion, and the extended position of the opening of the edge starting on the side edge 4cm (1½in) (**VV**) below the corner and finishing the same distance below the adjacent corner (**VV**). Points 1 and 2 (*see* Fig 83).

2 This line of machining strengthens the opening and gives a guideline for the ladder stitching to be used for closing the opening to correspond with the line already prepared on the welt.

3 There is no need to finish the raw edges of the calico lining.

4 The bottom section of the cushion is now stitched to the welt using the same technique as for the top cushion piece. But in order to incorporate the opening a different order of work is necessary.

5 With the right sides facing, making sure all edges are level and the short seams of the welts are pressed open and flat, begin by pinning and tacking

12 From this point it is not possible to tack accurately, but using the pins vertically to hold the work in place, proceed in exactly the same order of work as Stage 1, i.e. pin A, B and C.

13 Between A and C and C and B you will need two or three more pins, again in the vertical position.

14 Very carefully continue machining exactly on the seam line of 1.5cm (½in). If you are careful it is possible to machine with these vertical pins in place and over them.

15 At the next corner repeat the process then again at corners 3 and 4.

16 Finally, you will reach point D again. Machine over the first two or three stitches leaving long ends, tying them off on the reverse side.

17 The welt is now ready to be attached to the bottom section of the cover.

BOTTOM SECTION (Fig 83)

1 With the wrong side of the bottom cushion piece uppermost, iron-in the 1.5cm (½in) seam allowance along

(Far left) Fig 83 Marking the
position for the back opening.

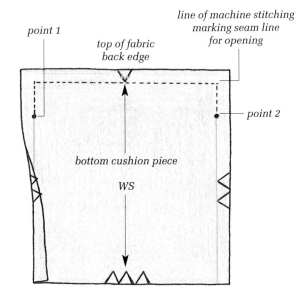

point 1

*top of fabric
back edge*

*line of machine stitching
marking seam line
for opening*

point 2

bottom cushion piece

WS

the right-hand side section of the bottom cushion piece to the side welt (**VV**). Tack along the whole length of the side.

6 Start machining at point 2 using the reverse stitch to strengthen this weak point. Machine down to the corner.

7 Turn the corner pivoting the needle as before and, using your pins in the vertical position, pin and machine the bottom edge of the welt to the bottom edge of the cushion cover (**VVV**). This is now the front edge of the cushion.

8 Turn the next corner, pin and machine the second side (**VV**), machining over the vertical pins as in the top cushion.

9 Finish the machining at point 1 with reverse stitches.

10 Clip across each corner

11 Press the seam allowances towards the welt.

12 Turn the cover to the right side and press.

13 Insert the foam pad into the opening.

14 Close the opening, making sure the extended opening is correctly placed at the corners, and strengthen this point using three closer stitches.

15 Ladder stitch into place as for the basic cushion (*see* Fig 84).

16 Follow instructions as for ladder stitch.

PROJECT 3 – PART 2
THE BOXED CUSHION COVER, PIPED, WITH A ZIP SET IN THE CENTRE OF THE BACK WELT

There are important considerations to be made before we embark on the boxed cushion cover, which is to be piped with a zip set in the centre of the back welt.

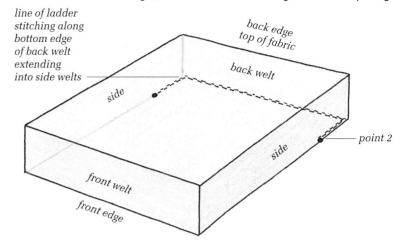

Fig 84 Position of ladder stitching for the back opening.

line of ladder stitching along bottom edge of back welt extending into side welts

back edge top of fabric

back welt

side

side

point 2

front welt

front edge

(Below) Fig 85 Zip in the welt of the boxed cushion.

NEW TECHNIQUES AND SKILLS	MATERIALS FOR WORK PROJECT	PREVIOUSLY LEARNED TECHNIQUES AND SKILLS
◆ Cutting crossway strips using striped fabric ◆ Planning a layout with stripes ◆ Pattern matching stripes ◆ Tie stitch for holding stripes in place ◆ Inserting a welt into a piped seam	◆ Calico covered block of foam ◆ Face fabric ◆ No 5 piping cord the length of four sides × 2 plus 15cm (6in) ◆ Matching thread ◆ Brown paper for making pattern ◆ Zip ◆ Zip (piping) foot ◆ Card for cutting crossway strips	◆ Cutting, making and the final join in crossway strips ◆ Planning a layout ◆ Setting in a zip ◆ Pattern matching ◆ Making and inserting a welt
STITCHES		*STITCHES*
◆ Tie stitch (for stripes)		◆ Back stitch ◆ Tacking stitch ◆ Ladder stitch ◆ Slip tacking

◆ When using a patterned, textured, striped or checked fabric, there must be a continuity of pattern from the top of your cover into the front welt and the pattern must be centrally placed.

◆ The four pieces of welt must run in the same direction, down the warp grain and welt pieces must be cut identical. This means along the front edge and back edge the pattern will follow through, but it is not possible at the sides, but it is still necessary to have the fabric running in the same direction.

◆ The zip is set in the centre of the back welt. This section is made up of two strips of fabric extending into the side welts to allow the zip to turn at each corner and running into the side welt by 5cm to 10cm (2in to 4in) depending on the size of the cushion.

◆ It will become apparent when making the paper pattern that the back welt extends into the side welts to accommodate the zip. The side pattern pieces are shortened. In addition, the back welt pattern depth becomes deeper with the addition of the two 2cm (¾in) seam allowances for the zip to be inserted.

◆ The zip opening must be constructed so there is a continuity of pattern and must be pattern matched.

To demonstrate all these important considerations the fabric I have chosen for the cushion cover is a simple, woven, even-stripe cotton furnishing fabric (Fig 86).

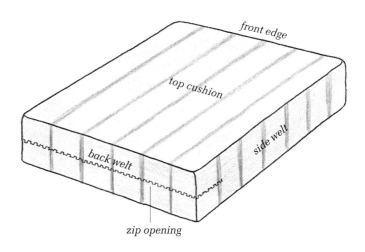

WATCHPOINTS:

◆ Not all striped and checked fabrics are even. Some are printed, so you must be aware of any pattern drift. Others are multi-coloured and you may wish to centralize a wider stripe or a particular colour.

◆ If making a cushion where the width of your fabric is shorter than the length of the front welt, the centre panel of your fabric must be centralized. Any extra width of fabric must be added in equal proportions at either side. In the same way, the top and bottom cushion pieces must match and the matched seam line must run through from the top of the cushion into the front and back welts.

Making a Visual Aid for Fabric Layout and Positioning the Zip in the Welt

I think, like my students, you will find making a paper visual aid will again considerably help you to plan your fabric layout and help position your zip accurately in the welt.

Please note: When making this visual aid use either metric or imperial measurements as they stand

i.e. 1.5cm (½in)
8cm (3in)
18cm (7in), etc.

In order to illustrate the method of constructing the pattern, and to enable the use of the A4 paper for this visual aid, I have assumed:

The depth of foam to be: 5cm (2in)
The block to be: 18cm × 18cm
            (7in × 7in)
            square.

Note: For the worked project, the dimensions of the paper pattern must be adapted to your own boxed cushion.

Fig 86 Example of the positioning of stripes and zip.

ORDER OF WORK

1 Take two pages from your A4 lined pad and cut *three* 8cm (3in) wide strips *across* the pad; these will become the two side and the front welts.
2 Cut another strip *down* the pad 12cm (4½in) wide; this will become the back welt.

Fig 87 Making a visual aid for inserting a zip into a welt.

3 Name each piece, and mark RS and WS.

4 Mark a seam allowance of 1.5cm (½in) along both long edges of all *four* strips.

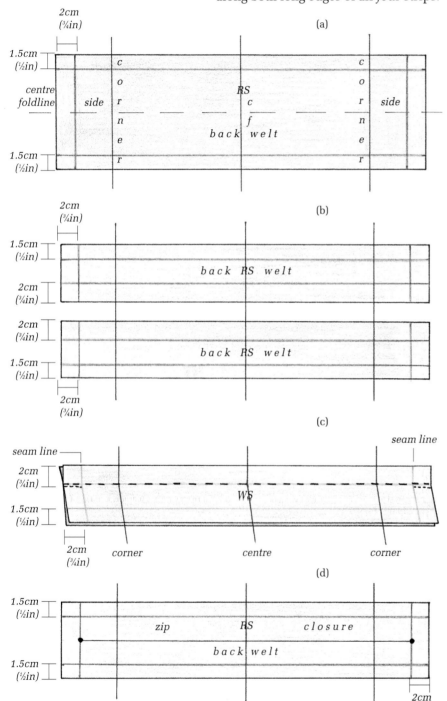

Back Welt

See Fig 87: making a visual aid for inserting a zip into a welt (a).

1 Mark a horizontal line along the centre of the back welt strip.

2 Mark a vertical line down the centre of the back welt strip.

3 Mark two additional vertical lines down the back welt strip. The distance of each line from the centre line must be half the width of the foam block, this will mark the corner of your cushion. In this visual aid: 9cm + 9cm = 18cm (3½in + 3½in = 7in).

4 Mark two further vertical lines down the strip a distance of 4cm (1½in) outside the corner marks. These two marks will define the end of the zip opening running into the side welt.

   Note: This measurement depends on the cushion's size 5–10cm (2–4in).

5 Two further lines must be added for the 2cm (¾in) seam allowance, one at each end. (This extra seam allowance is necessary to accommodate the end of the zip.)

See Fig 87: making a visual aid for inserting a zip into a welt (b).

6 Take the back strip and fold it in half along the marked horizontal centre line. Cut into two equal widths along this line. This cut marks the seam line where the zip will be inserted.

7 Mark each cut edge of the paper with a 2cm (¾in) seam allowance. This extra seam allowance accommodates the width of the zip.

See Fig 87: making a visual aid for inserting a zip into a welt (c).

8 Place the two right sides of the paper together and pin or staple along this seam line.

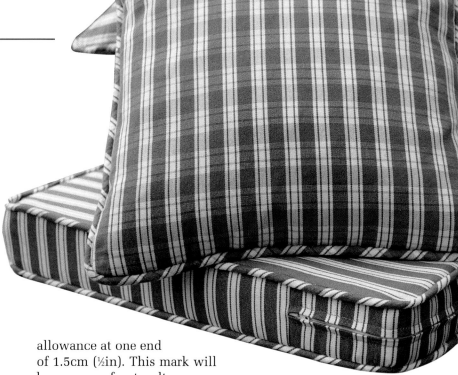

9 *In fabric, this would be tacked and the zip would be inserted as 'Inserting a Zip in a Flat Seam' (page 65).*

10 *In fabric, machine at each end up to the position marked for the zip.*

11 *Open out and press seam allowance. In fabric, the raw seam edges would then be neatened by the zigzag stitch.*
   Note: When using fabric with a printed pattern, stripes or a textured pattern, the seam line of the zip must be pattern matched.

The side welts will now be completed in paper (*see* Fig 87d).

12 Take the back welt strip and fold in the two, short end seam allowances 2cm (¾in).

13 Take one side welt strip and mark a seam allowance of 2cm (¾in) at one short end. This seam allowance is necessary to accommodate the end of the zip. Place the seam allowance, right side to right side, against the seam allowance of the back welt strip, i.e. 2cm (¾in) seam allowance.

14 *At this point if working with fabric, pin, tack and machine the seam (on the paper aid, clip together).*

15 From the marked corner of the back welt strip, measure the length of the block side (in this case 18cm or 7in) and mark a vertical line across the side welt piece to mark one front corner and a further line 1.5cm (½in) to mark the seam allowance.
   Note: This is not necessary when working in fabric as the adjustments are made on the paper pattern.

16 Now repeat for the other side, thereby creating three of the four welts.

17 Cut off the waste.

18 Take the final strip (marked 'front welt') and mark across to give a seam allowance at one end of 1.5cm (½in). This mark will become one front welt corner.

19 Make a second mark across the strip a distance of the width of the block (again, 18cm or 7in in this case). This will be the other front welt corner and a 1.5cm (½in) seam allowance.

20 Complete the square by joining the front welt strip at the two front welt corners with the previously joined back welts and side welts.

21 In the case of a paper aid, clip in place *or if working with fabric, machine stitch, and leaving a 1.5cm (½in) unstitched at either end of the line of machining, remembering to finish off the ends.*

22 Store visual aid in your file.

Paper Pattern for Cushion Cover

Note: The two identical pattern pieces for the top and bottom and the front welt pattern of the calico lining cover can be used again. Mark this information on your paper pattern.

The sides and back pieces cannot be used again. You will have to cut the back

Fig 88 Pattern for cushion
cover.

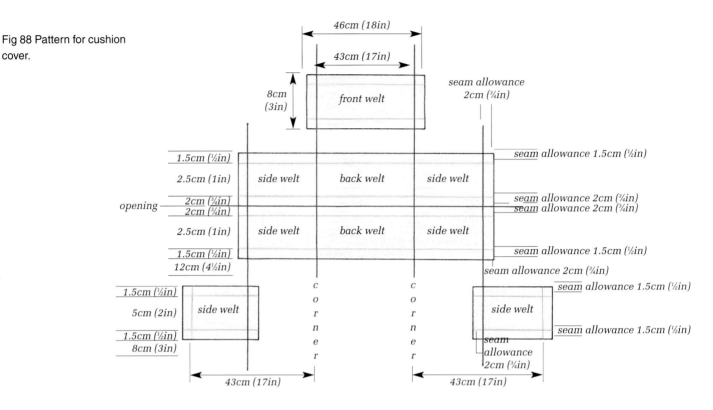

Fig 89 Pattern pieces
for the cushion cover.

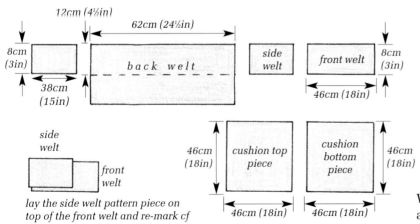

and two side pieces of pattern to accommodate the zip (Fig 88).

Make the pattern for the cushion cover (Fig 89).

Using the diagram above and using the same dimensions as the foam base 43cm × 43cm × 5cm (17in × 17in × 2in) adding a 1.5cm (½in) seam allowance all round.

Note: You must make adjustments to these measurements for the size of your own block of foam.

THE WORKED PROJECT

Cut the following pattern pieces:

◆ 2 pattern pieces for top
   and bottom sections:
   46cm × 46cm (18in × 18in)

◆ 1 front welt pattern:
   8cm × 46cm (3in × 18in)

◆ 2 side welt patterns:
   8cm × 38cm (3in × 15in)

◆ 1 back welt pattern piece:
   11cm × 62cm (4½in × 24½in)

When using stripes, leave the back welt as one piece. The lengthwise cut will be made later. Leaving it as one piece will make it easier to keep the vertical stripes in position when cutting out.

Note: Making the back welt pattern. Look at the Layout Plan carefully, the seam allowance on each half of the back opening for the zip has a 2cm (¾in) added to each edge and the seam allowance joining back welt to side welt is 2cm (¾in).

RECORD IN
✎ *YOUR NOTEBOOK*

Planning and Estimating Fabric

The cutting plan is illustrated below.

Fig 90 Layout plan of worked project.

Project 3(2): Boxed Cushion
Cushion cover for calico-covered foam block
for garden seat cushion
Dimension of calico covered block

Pre-planning
Selection of fabric

Fabric content
Width of fabric
Pattern repeat (not applicable)
Draw a cutting plan
Amount of fabric
– amount needed

Useful information

DEMONSTRATION PROJECT

Project 3(2): Boxed Cushion
Cushion cover for calico-covered foam block

43cm × 43cm square × 5cm
(17in × 17in × 2in)
My selected fabric:
Radley Green
(woven striped fabric)
100 per cent cotton
Width 136cm (54in)
No pattern repeat
Cutting plan (Fig 90)
Amount of fabric
– width: 70cm (28in)
– 62cm (24in) zip

Useful information on the label
– Suitable for curtains and bed covers, also light domestic upholstery if used with a flame retardant interior
– Dry clean only

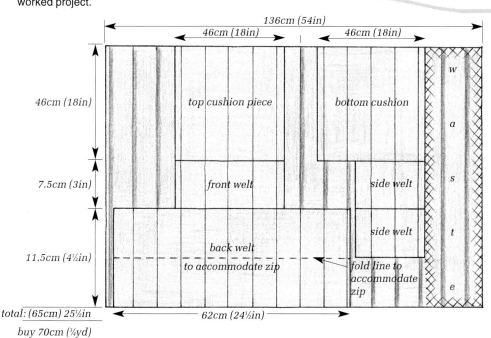

	136cm (54in)	
	46cm (18in)	46cm (18in)

46cm (18in)   top cushion piece   bottom cushion   w a s

7.5cm (3in)   front welt   side welt   s

11.5cm (4½in)   side welt   t

back welt
to accommodate zip   fold line to accommodate zip   e

total: (65cm) 25½in
buy 70cm (¾yd)

62cm (24½in)

ORDER OF WORK

Cutting out

1 Place the pattern pieces onto the fabric, taking care to centralize the stripes on the front and back sections, the front welt and the extended back welt.
2 Place the side welts to centralize the same stripes on the centre front (CF) markings. These are already marked on your pattern.
3 Pin in the straight of grain, i.e. down each matching stripe, and follow the usual pinning routine.
4 Cut out.
5 Remove paper pattern and record all relevant information on each carefully named pattern piece.
6 Mark all relevant fabric pieces.

Set Aside.

Piping

1 Cut sufficient piping for cushion top and bottom pieces.
2 Prepare sufficient crossway strip to go around four sides plus a little extra for matching stripes in the joins × 2 plus 10cm (4in) (i.e. for top and bottom cushion pieces).
3 Crossway strips in striped fabric cannot be cut using the continuous strip method. Cut stripes separately until you have sufficient to make up the required length. Prepare in the usual way.

Care must be taken when joining stripes. Match stripes as accurately as possible.

Piping the Top and Bottom Pieces

Place the top and bottom cushion piece RS uppermost on the table.

Pipe round cushion bottom and top pieces as for the basic flat, square cushion.

◆ The final join (use paper aid). You may find it difficult to match the stripes exactly at this point. Arrange the final join in the most inconspicuous way possible.

Making up the Welt

1 Place the four sections of the welt on the table, right side uppermost.
     Side Back Side Front
2 Check they are in the correct position and the pattern markings are correct.
     Now set aside the back welt, which will be made up separately.
     Join Side–Front–Side welt in this order.
3 With right sides facing, join the side welt to the front welt at either side, along the short ends. Remember to machine very accurately on the seam line, leaving the last 1.5cm (½in) at both ends of the seam and finishing machine threads securely, as this is a weak point.
4 Press open the short seams and finish the short seam raw edges of the seams with zigzag stitch.

Set aside.

THE BACK WELT

In fact, it is not at all difficult, because you have already had a practice run of *inserting a zip in a flat seam* when inserting the zip into the back of the round cushion.

If you made a sample for your file of 'Inserting a Zip in a Flat Seam', use it or follow all the instructions applicable to it (*see* page 65).

Note: When cutting out in striped fabric, the back welt was left as one piece as this makes it easier to keep the stripes following through when cutting out; let it remain so until you reach the stage of cutting it in half to make the opening for inserting the zip.

In the case of a patterned fabric it would be necessary to cut the paper pattern in half, along the opening line to accommodate a pattern match.

Inserting the Zip into the Centre, Back of the Welt

STRIPED FABRIC

1 Fold the welt in half along the lengthwise, marked centre line. Iron into place and cut very accurately along this ironed mark. This will accommodate the zip.
2 Zigzag both these cut edges.
3 Place the two right sides of the opening together with the zigzagged edges level. Pin in place on the 2cm (¾in) seam allowance we allowed when making the paper pattern.

I am now going to introduce you to a stitch that you will find extremely useful when matching stripes or holding your fabric in a particular position, which must be very accurate, the *Tie Stitch* (Fig 92).

1 Use a double length of thread and knot the ends. Use a different coloured thread as these threads are later removed and it is important that you do not cut the permanent machine stitches.

2 From the wrong side of your seam, pierce the needle into the centre of the stripe at the marked centre point of the opening, exactly on the seam line, i.e. 2cm (¾in) from the edge. Follow the needle through the right side of the matched seam line into the centre of the stripe.

Fig 91 Selection of cushions for garden seats.

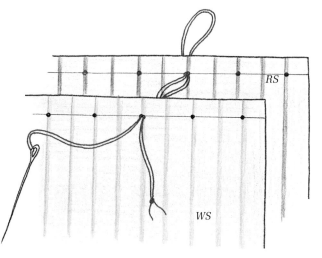

Fig 92 Tie stitch.

3 Pull the thread through leaving a 5cm (2in) loose end of knotted thread.

4 Return the needle, catching one thread of the fabric, through the same position, back to the centre point of the wrong side of the seam allowance now facing you.

5 Pull the threads tight so that the gap in the fabric closes and the stripes lie exactly on top of one another.

6 Tie the ends tightly with two secure knots, clip off the second end leaving a 5cm (2in) loose end of threads.

7 Repeat at both ends and then add extra ties in between – probably two or three but always exactly in the middle of the stripe.

8 Now follow all instructions for 'Inserting a Zip into a Flat Seam' (*see* page 65).

Fig 93 Marking the corners.

1 Lay the finished back welt with the zip opening complete, wrong side uppermost, on the table and mark the corners (Fig 93).

2 Mark in the corner lines point A and the seam allowance 2cm (¾in) at the two side ends and zigzag raw edges.

Mark in a 5cm (2in) line, through the centre of the marked corner line A exactly on the seam line 1.5cm (½in) from both long edges at either side.

3 Machine a line of stitching along all four, marked lines. This strengthens the point where the corners of the welt are attached to the back of the cushion, a natural weak point.

1 Place in correct order on the table (Fig 94).

2 Place the two short ends of the side welts and back welts, with right sides facing. Pin and tack in place on the 2cm (¾in) seam allowance line.

   Note: The whole length of this short seam is machined. Finish seams with reverse stitch.

3 Place the front welt short ends, with right sides facing to the side welts. Pin and tack in place on the 1.5cm (½in) seam allowance.

4 Machine the front and side welt seams leaving 1.5cm (½in) open at either end of the seam. Finish seams carefully, this is a weak point.

5 Finish the raw edges of these short seams with the zigzag stitch.

6 Press seams open.

Fig 94 Joining the completed zip section to the front/side/back/side sections.

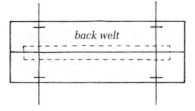

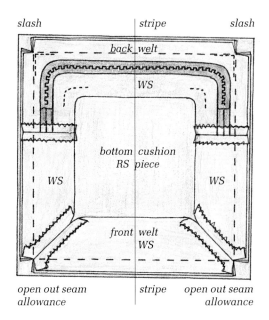

slash | *stripe* | *slash*

back welt

WS

bottom cushion
RS piece

WS | *WS*

front welt
WS

open out seam | *stripe* | *open out seam*
allowance | | *allowance*

JOINING THE WELT TO THE TOP AND BOTTOM SECTIONS OF THE CUSHION

Inserting the welt in between the top and bottom cushion pieces, which are piped, is less complicated than the technique used to place the welt into the unpiped top and bottom pieces of the calico base (Fig 95).

1 Lay the piped cushion bottom piece on the table with the right sides uppermost.

2 Place the bottom edges of the welt with their right sides facing onto the cushion bottom of the *two front welt corners*.

3 Carefully open out the 1.5cm (½in) unstitched welt seam allowance and place it on top of the corner of the cushion piece, exactly on the split where you have slashed and re-inforced the piping with the double backstitch.

4 At the *two back welt corners*, carefully slash the seam allowance on the welt to the line of strengthening

stitches exactly on the point of the marked corner. You can treat this in the same way as if you were laying the unstitched welt seam over the piped corner by opening out the slash. This is a weak point, so do be careful that you do not clip too close to the machine line.

5 Place the centres of the front and back welts to the cushion bottom. It is important now that the stripe follows through. Use the tie-stitch to centralize the stripe and again at intervals between the centre and the corners.

6 Place the centres of each of the welt sides to the cushion bottom making sure that the edges are even and pin in place. You will not have a continuation of the stripe here.

7 Once you have checked that the stripes follow through from the back welt and over the cushion into the front welt, and all the corners are correctly placed and all edges are even, tack all the way round, through all thicknesses close to your piping tacking stitch line.

8 Using your piping foot, machine accurately all round, keeping your stitches close to your piping, taking care at the corners and using the method of pivoting your needle as in the basic cushion.

9 Clip the corners.

10 Finish raw edges all round with the zigzag stitch.

Note: Open the zip.

JOINING THE WELT TO THE CUSHION TOP

1 Repeat the whole process as for joining the welt to the cushion bottom piece.

2 Turn cushion cover to right side and press.

3 Place the calico covered base into the cushion cover and close the zip.

(Far left) Fig 95 Joining the welt to the cushion bottom piece.

9 Project 4 – Invisibly Inserting a Zip in a Piped Cushion

In this worked cushion sample, I am using the same fabric as for the Basic Cushion but with a different placement of the pattern on the fabric to demonstrate use of fabric to create a different cushion (*see* photo opposite).

Pre-plan and select your own cotton furnishing fabric.

ORDER OF WORK

◆ Cut out your cushion using the same paper pattern and cutting plan as for the Basic Cushion. Adjust size of paper pattern if necessary.

◆ Make up sufficient crossway for piping the cushion.

NEW TECHNIQUES AND SKILLS
◆ Invisibly inserting a zip into a piped seam
STITCHES
◆ Whip stitch
◆ Stab stitch

MATERIALS FOR WORK PROJECT
PRE-PLAN
◆ Select your own fabric
◆ Choose a cushion
◆ Cutting plan
◆ Estimate fabric
◆ Cut out
◆ Make up sufficient crossway for piping the cushion

PREVIOUSLY LEARNED TECHNIQUES AND SKILLS
◆ Refer back to previous project where necessary

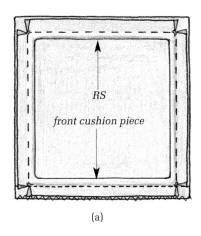 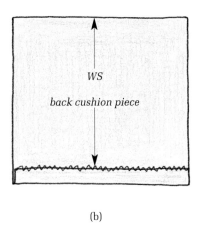

(a)

(b)

Fig 96 Preparation of front and back cushion pieces.

3 Zigzag the length of the bottom edge to correspond with the line of machining.

The Back Section of the Cushion (Fig 96b)

4 Place the back cushion piece on the table, wrong side uppermost and iron up the seam allowance of 1.5cm (½in) to the wrong side. Open out the fold and zigzag the length of the bottom edge.

The Front Section of the Cushion (Fig 96a)

1 Tack the piping cord encased in the crossway strip to the right side of the front section of the cushion following the usual procedure for piping and taking care at the corners and the final join of the crossway.
2 Machine a line of stitching against the piping right across the bottom edge. It is important that this line of machining is as close as possible to the piping.

Prepare the Opening for the Zip (Fig 97)

1 Place the front cushion piece on the table, right side uppermost, and the back cushion piece, wrong side uppermost.
2 Flatten the fold on the back section of the cushion, making sure the fold line remains clearly indented.
3 Place the right sides of the back and front cushion already piped pieces together along the bottom edge with the zigzagged edges level.
4 Pin and tack along the seam line using a 1.5cm (½in) seam allowance. It is important that this is accurate. Use a smaller tacking stitch with a long end to start and finish.
5 Machine the seam up to the zip opening on both sides 4cm (1½in) and extend the machining by 3mm (⅛in) at this point. This makes it possible to slip the top of the slide and the stop at the base of the zip just underneath the machining. Use your reverse stitch to secure the stitching and strengthen this point.
6 Iron.
7 Remove *all* tacking stitches and open out the seam.

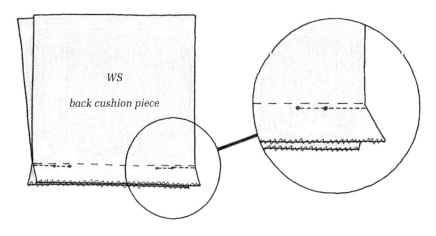

Fig 97 Preparing the opening for the zip and machining.

To Insert Zip (Fig 98)

1 Open the zip to the full extent and with the work remaining wrong side uppermost.
2 With the tab in the unlocked position, place the zip face down onto the

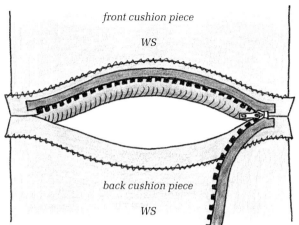

pressed, piped back seam allowance of the front cushion piece.

3 Push the teeth of the opened right half of the zip right up to the piping and tack in place. It is important that the teeth lie as close as possible to the piping. Therefore use a slightly smaller tacking stitch to ensure stability.

Note: Tack only through the zip and seam allowance, NOT through to the front of the cushion cover.

Make sure that the tab is in the unlocked position and that the end stops at both ends of the zip lie 3mm (⅛in) over the machine seams at both ends.

4 Machine as close as possible to the teeth, approximately 3mm (⅛in), making absolutely sure that you only sew through the seam allowance, and your stitches do not show on the right side of your cushion. Use the technique of pushing the zip up and down to avoid losing your straight line of machine stitching. The machining should start and finish just beyond the end of the zip at both ends. Finish off the ends.
5 Close the zip and keep the tab in the *unlocked* position.

(Above) Fig 98 Positioning the teeth of the zip against the piping.

(Top left) Fig 99 Positioning the pattern to find the centre for the cushion.

(Bottom left) Fig 100 Laying the pattern on the fabric to create a different cushion.

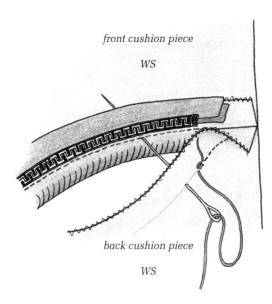

front cushion piece

WS

back cushion piece

WS

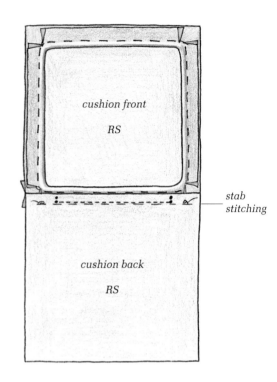

cushion front

RS

cushion back

RS

stab stitching

(Right) Fig 101 Bringing the unpiped edge of the back cushion piece over the piping and positioning the back seam line along the edge of the zip teeth.

(Far right) Fig 102 Position of front and back cushion pieces now joined along the zip opening and stab stitch.

6   Fold the front cushion seam allowance back and flat onto the wrong side of the front cushion piece, to bring the piping to the edge of the opening and butting against the pressed down seam allowance of the back cushion piece (Fig 101).

7   With the wrong side of your work still uppermost, push the unstitched side of the zip out of your way.

Bring the unpiped edge of the back cushion piece over the piping. The already ironed-in seam line of the back cushion piece must lie *exactly* on top of the line of piping machine stitching. Then tack firmly into place on this line as follows. Secure your tacking thread and pierce your needle into the wrong side of the ironed-in crease line and immediately opposite into the piped machine seam line of the front cushion piece, down between the piping and the edge of the machining of the zip teeth. Once again, take care to tack only through the seam allowance of the top cushion piece and not on to the top of the cushion.

8   *Turn the work to the right side.*
Your line of tacking should have

neatly closed the cushion opening (Fig 102).

With the right sides uppermost, open out and flatten on the table the front and back cushion pieces, now joined along the zip opening.

9   Run a straight line of tacking stitches on the back cushion piece, through all thicknesses just under the edge of the zip teeth, which you can feel with your fingers. Leave sufficient room to manoeuvre the zip up and down approximately 6mm (approximately ¼in) from the tacked, closed seam line, using your small ruler.

10   Machine through all thicknesses on the line of tacking, beginning and finishing at the top and bottom stops of the zip, leaving long ends on both ends of the machining. This thread can then be used to return these stitches at the top and bottom of the zip up to the piping with small *stab*

stitches, which is difficult to do by machine. They can then be carefully tied off or you may prefer to machine the whole length of tacking line along the bottom edge of the cushion opening. Strengthen the ends of the zip with a whip stitch – *see* Whip Stitch.

STAB STITCH

This is a small stitch used to secure several layers of fabric that should appear as a small stab stitch on the top surface of your fabric. There will be several occasions when making soft furnishings when you will find this a most useful stitch.

The stab stitch is worked in a similar way to the backstitch but, by taking the stitch backwards and inserting the needle only one or two threads behind the thread you have just pulled through, the top stitches appear much smaller. Take the next stitch by sliding the needle underneath the fabric 6mm (¼in) in front of this point. Continue for as many stitches as required (*see* Fig 102). *Note:* Smaller stitches for the ends of the zip.

WHIP STITCH

This stitch is used to join two edges by hand, so is useful to secure the zip tapes together above the top of the slider. The stitch is worked from left to right – if right handed. Use three or four firm, neat overstitches to hold edges together.

Remove all tacking.

Note: Open the zip and complete the cushion.

Joining the Back to the Front (Fig 103)

1 Bring the right side of the back cushion to face the right side of the front cushion with the wrong side of the front

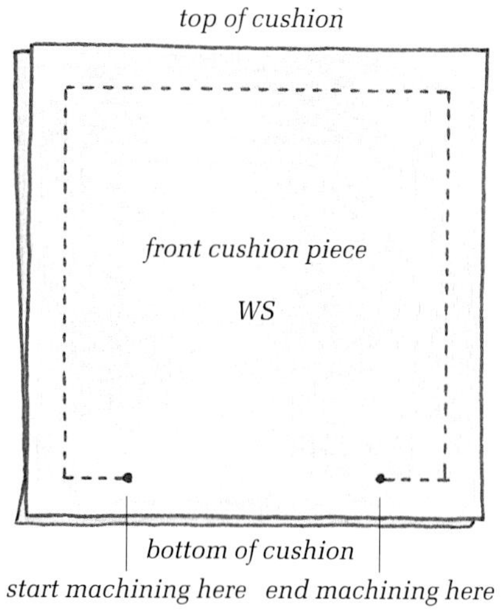

Fig 103 Joining the back and front cushion pieces.

section facing. This will enable you to use your line of piping tacking stitch as a guide line to machine the three remaining sides of the cushion cover.

2 Pin all corners in place.
3 Tack the remaining three sides into place making sure that all the edges are even. Machine into place (*see* Fig 103).

   Note: To enable you to machine accurately round the piped corners, begin your machining along the bottom seam line approximately 2.5cm (1in) from the bottom left-hand corner. Then, exactly covering the machine stitches along the bottom edge, complete the corner and continue machining close up to the piping *just* inside the line of tacking on the other three sides. Complete the final corner and machine exactly over the bottom line of machine stitching by 2.5cm (1in). Finish off ends.
4 Trim off corners.
5 Using your zigzag stitch, finish off the raw edges on the remaining three sides, stitching through all layers.
6 Turn the cushion cover to the right side and press.
7 Put the cushion into the cover, remembering to even out the corners of the pad and close the zip.

10 Project 5 – The Footstool

sing the combination of techniques and skills from the first section of this book, the footstool will embrace all we have covered so far. Those who wish may test their knowledge by making the footstool.

The final project in this section of the book is the footstool. In each of the four cushion projects you have handled and used a selection of different fabrics: a plain woven fabric with a printed pattern, a woven textured fabric with a pattern

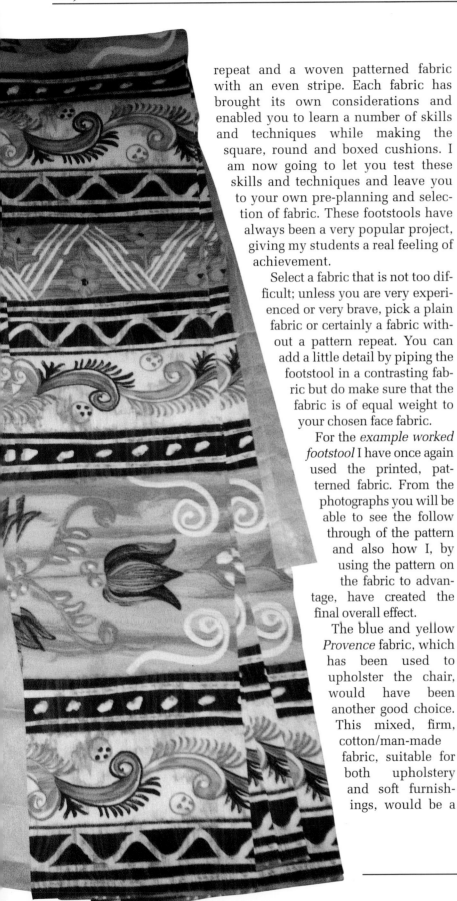

repeat and a woven patterned fabric with an even stripe. Each fabric has brought its own considerations and enabled you to learn a number of skills and techniques while making the square, round and boxed cushions. I am now going to let you test these skills and techniques and leave you to your own pre-planning and selection of fabric. These footstools have always been a very popular project, giving my students a real feeling of achievement.

Select a fabric that is not too difficult; unless you are very experienced or very brave, pick a plain fabric or certainly a fabric without a pattern repeat. You can add a little detail by piping the footstool in a contrasting fabric but do make sure that the fabric is of equal weight to your chosen face fabric.

For the *example worked footstool* I have once again used the printed, patterned fabric. From the photographs you will be able to see the follow through of the pattern and also how I, by using the pattern on the fabric to advantage, have created the final overall effect.

The blue and yellow *Provence* fabric, which has been used to upholster the chair, would have been another good choice. This mixed, firm, cotton/man-made fabric, suitable for both upholstery and soft furnishings, would be a good compromise between a completely plain fabric and a patterned fabric. It would be necessary to have continuity of the line of spots, but with the use of the tie stitch this would not prove too difficult.

USEFUL GUIDE IN PREPARATION FOR FIRST PROJECT

Pre-planning, Selecting and Estimating Fabrics

- ◆ Decide on size of footstool.

- ◆ Make a brown paper pattern and order block of foam.

- ◆ Order boxed, feather cushion or soft foam block for cushion.

- ◆ Make a cutting plan, follow the diagrams and adjust if necessary.

- ◆ Pre-plan and select fabric.

- ◆ Estimate fabric.

- ◆ Record all relevant information in your notebook.

- ◆ Make a paper pattern. Use cutting plans 1 and 2 and adapt if necessary.

- ◆ Preparation of fabric. Check for flaws in fabric, iron if necessary, and straighten fabric.

- ◆ Lay paper pattern on fabric checking straight of grain.

- ◆ Follow the usual procedure of pinning and cutting fabric.

- ◆ Remove all pattern pieces, store carefully for future use, recording all relevant information.

- ◆ Mark all fabric pieces.

This example worked footstool is made up with a heavy block of foam mounted on a piece of MDF (medium density fibre board), 1.5cm (½in) deep to form the base with a welted (boxed) feather cushion for the cushion top.

Note: The addition of the base board has evolved over the years. It is not a necessity, but it has become increasingly popular. It is perfectly adequate to make the footstool without the base board, in fact it makes it lighter to move around. The addition of the board gives more stability, in particular, on wooden floors. Some of my students also add wheels to the board for easy mobility. Slight adjustments to the base block and valance patterns would be necessary for the footstool without the board or with wheels.

The following dimensions for a footstool have proved most successful and are used for the worked project, and all paper pattern plans are to these dimensions. You may make a footstool slightly smaller or larger and you will have to adapt these pattern plans to your own requirements.

A block of foam
46cm × 46cm × 25.5cm
(18in × 18in × 10in) deep

A base board
46cm × 46cm × 1.5cm
(18in × 18in × ½in) thick

A boxed feather cushion
51cm × 51cm × 10cm
(20in × 20in × 4in) deep

THE WORKED FOOTSTOOL PROJECT

The Footstool Base

The block of foam for the base must be made of heavy-density foam. We used 6LB-REC. A good upholstery shop or large department store can order this for you. You must state this requirement on your pattern when ordering your foam.

The Boxed (Welted) Feather Cushion

In order that the feather cushion may sit evenly on the foam block base it is necessary to buy a cushion 5cm (2in) larger than the top of the block.

Fig 104 The footstool and materials.

The dimensions of the boxed feather cushion with a 10cm (4in) welt to sit on the base block of 46cm × 46cm (18in × 18in) would now be 51cm × 51cm × 10cm (20in × 20in × 4in).

There are two reasons for this larger sized cushion:

◆ As for the basic feather cushion, the patterns for the top and bottom pieces are cut to the size of the cushion, in this case 51cm × 51cm (20in × 20in).
Note: As with the basic cushion, the seam allowance is not added to this measurement but remains the same at 1.5cm (½in). In other words, you are making a cover 48cm × 48cm (19in × 19in) when finished.

◆ The other extra 2.5cm (1in) is added to the finished size of the cushion because once it is in place on the foam base, the feathers inside the cushion will take up the width, otherwise the cushion would appear to be too small for the base.

When ordering a boxed feather cushion state that it is for a seat and ask for it to be channelled. This means the feathers are held in a series of parallel channels. This allows for a more even distribution of the feathers and eliminates some of the problems of feather or down cushions having permanently to be puffed up, as no doubt those of you who already have chairs or settees with these cushions know to their cost.
Note: As some people are allergic to feathers, in this case ask for the cushion

to be filled with the Dacron filling or, alternatively, you may replace the soft filled boxed cushion with a block of soft foam. If this is the case, you must make a paper pattern to match the size of the base block and state on the pattern that it is for a cushion, as you would need a lighter and softer density of foam. The foam would have to be cut 46cm × 46cm × 10cm deep (18in × 18in × 4in).

The base block must be covered with a calico lining cover. Do not use netting to cover this foam, as this heavy block needs a firm base where the footstool sits directly onto the floor or carpet.

The calico block is then itself covered with a removable face fabric loose cover made up of a piped, welted top extending into a lined valance at the base of the welt with a deep inverted pleat at each corner, often called an American pleat.

THE EXAMPLE WORKED FOOTSTOOL

◆ A block of foam 46cm × 46cm × 25.5cm (18in × 18in × 10in) deep plus a base board 46cm × 46cm × 1.5cm (18in × 18in × ½in) deep

◆ A boxed feather cushion 51cm × 51cm × 10cm (20in × 20in × 4in)

Prepare the Block by Adding the Board

Use adhesive PVA woodwork glue. Spread the glue generously and evenly over the board and place the block of foam onto the glued surface of the board and press well down into place. Leave in this position overnight to make sure it is dry and firm.

Pattern Layouts for the Example Worked Footstool

The following patterns and layouts can be used – *all 1.5cm (½in) seam allowances are added.*

Footstool Base Calico Cover

The following pattern plan is for a calico cover for the base block of the foam and board.

Cut   48cm × 48cm × 29cm deep
           (19in × 19in × 11½in)

Finished 46cm × 46cm × 27cm deep
              (18in × 18in × 10½in)

Base Block

LAYOUT (a) (Fig 105a)

Cut two pieces 48cm × 48cm (19in × 19in) for the base block top and botttom.

Cut four pieces 48cm × 29cm (19in × 11½in) for the base block welt.

LAYOUT (b) (Fig 105b)

Note: If using a *soft foam block* for the cushion, you would have to make a pattern for a calico fabric cover for this cushion. Remember, you *add* a seam allowance for foam.

Calico cover for a soft foam cushion.

Cut   48cm × 48cm × 13cm deep
           (19in × 19in × 5in)

Finished 46cm × 46cm × 10cm deep
              (18in × 18in × 4in)

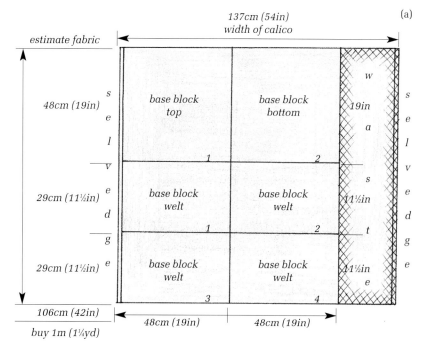

◆ Make a brown paper pattern from the plan.

◆ Mark and name each pattern piece.

Fig 105 Calico cover cutting plan (a). Calico cover cutting plan if using a soft foam block for the cushion (b).

LAYOUT (b) IF USING A FOAM BLOCK FOR THE CUSHION

Cut two pieces 48cm × 48cm (19in × 19in) for the base block top and bottom.

Cut four pieces 48cm × 13cm (19in × 5in) for the base block welt.

Face Fabric Cutting Plan (Fig 106)

The following face fabric pattern plan is for the boxed, feather/Dacron top cushion cover and the removable base block loose cover incorporating the valance to cover the calico covered base block of foam.

Boxed Cushion

Cut	51cm × 51cm × 13cm deep (20in × 20in × 5in)
Finished	48cm × 48cm × 10cm deep (19in × 19in × 4in)

Base Block Overall Finished Loose Cover
46cm × 46cm × 27cm (18in × 18in × 10½in) deep

Note: This cutting plan can only be used for a plain fabric or a fabric with no pattern repeat.

Adjustment to the layout would have to be made for patterned, striped or textured patterned fabrics and the calculations of fabric adjusted accordingly. If even or uneven stripes were used, you would have to align the cushion and welt top and block welts and continuity into the valance. If a patterned fabric is used you would have to ensure that the pattern was placed to follow through any pattern and pattern matching.

Note: The question is often asked of how to achieve a pattern match.

Look carefully at the photograph of the footstool on page 98. To exactly match the pattern where each line of piping cuts across would be extremely difficult and visually the placement of the design on you fabric may not look good at this particular point. But you must have a visual continuity of the line of pattern from the top cushion piece down into the front welt.

Look carefully at your material and select an area of pattern suitable for each of the cushion welts, the block welts and the valance pieces. Once you have selected the design for each of these sections they must appear to have an overall pleasing appearance (Fig 107).

Remember each of the four cushion welts, block welts, valance pieces must be identical so that from the side view each of the four sides of the footstool

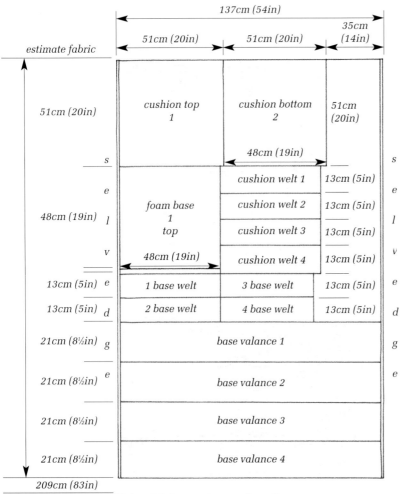

Fig 106 Face fabric layout and cutting plan for a plain fabric. Adapt for patterned or striped fabrics.

209cm (83in)

2.10m (2½yd) + sufficient fabric to make 9.5m (10 yd) crossway look exactly the same when these sections are put together.

The more you work with fabric the easier you will be able to visualize the placement of the design.

◆ Make a brown paper pattern from the plan. Cut a separate pattern for each piece.

◆ Mark in the straight of grain and the top of the fabric.

Cut the cushion top and bottom pieces and the block top piece with the placement of the pattern identical if using a patterned fabric.

All 1.5cm (½in) seam allowances are added.

Cut 1 piece for each
 Cushion top 51cm × 51cm
       (20in × 20in)
 Cushion bottom 51cm × 51cm
Cut 1 piece
 Foam base top 48cm × 48cm
       (19in × 19in)
Cut 4 pieces
 Cushion welt 51cm × 13cm
       (20in × 5in)
Cut 4 pieces
 Foam base welt 48cm × 13cm
       (19in × 5in)
Cut 4 pieces
 Foam base   21cm × width
 valance   of fabric (137cm)
       (8½in × 54in)

Note: If omitting the board or adding wheels adjust the length of the valance accordingly.

If using a soft foam block for the cushion the size of the patterns for the cushion top and bottom would have to be reduced to the size of the foam plus the seam allowance. Before cutting out fabric, read 'Preparation to Make a Valance' and make the visual aid on pages 112–13.

Cut 1 piece for each
 Cushion top 48cm × 48cm
       (19in × 19in)
 Cushion bottom 48cm × 48cm
       (19in × 19in)
Cut 4 pieces
 Cushion welt 48cm × 12.5cm
       (19in × 5in)

Set aside.

Fig 107 Suitable choice of pattern for each of the cushion welts, block welts and the valance pieces as seen in the footstool on page 98.

ORDER OF WORK FOR CUTTING OUT FABRIC

Calico Cover

◆ Lay the paper pattern onto the straightened and ironed calico

◆ Pin in place following the usual procedure

◆ Cut out, remove all paper patterns and mark each fabric piece

Set aside.

Face Fabric Cushion Cover and Removable Loose Cover for Base Block

◆ Lay the pattern onto the prepared fabric and pin in place
Note: If using striped or patterned fabrics ensure continuity of stripes or pattern down your fabric

◆ Cut out, remove pattern, name and mark each fabric piece

Set aside.

Store all pattern pieces with recorded names and sizes for future use.

ORDER OF WORK FOR FOOTSTOOL

Piping

You will see from the photograph on page 98 of the completed footstool that there are four lines of piping, two on the feather cushion and two on the base block welt.

Make sufficient crossway strips for piping the cushion top four times.

Use the conventional method or continuous strip method, according to fabric and personal choice.

In the worked project it was necessary to use the conventional method.

Set aside.

The Calico Base Cover

The base block calico cover is put together using the same order of work and techniques as for the basic calico covered block of foam with two exceptions.

That is to say: the size of the opening must be extended into the side seams to within 5cm (2in) of the whole length of the side seams. This is to facilitate placing the block into the cover. The heavy density of the foam makes it very rigid and particularly with the base board of wood in place (Fig 108).

◆ The top section of the cover is used to accommodate the opening along the top welt seam line. The reason for this procedure is that the bottom of the block will take more wear than the top which is covered with the face fabric loose cover with the boxed cushion sitting on top.

It is most important that the lines of machine stitching marking the opening for the ladder stitch are accurate and clearly marked on both the calico top block piece and the corresponding line along the top edge of the calico welt.

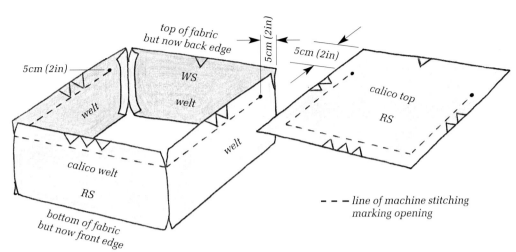

top of fabric but now back edge

5cm (2in)

WS

welt

welt

5cm (2in)

5cm (2in)

calico top

RS

weit

welt

calico welt

RS

bottom of fabric but now front edge

– – – *line of machine stitching marking opening*

Fig 108 Marking the position of opening for the calico cover.

ORDER OF WORK

Welt

Place in the correct order the four pieces of welt with the right sides uppermost, on the table. Check all markings are correct.

1 Make up the welt in the usual way placing right sides together and forming them into a circle, leaving the 1.5cm (½in) seam line open at either end of the short seams. Particular care must be taken to finish off the ends, as these are weak points particularly with this heavy block of foam and board against the corners.
2 Press seams open. There is no need to neaten the seams for the calico cover.
3 The *bottom* piece of the calico base must now be worked onto the bottom edge of the calico welt. Follow the same order of work as the basic calico covered foam (*see* Fig 81). Remember that pinning accuracy and tacking are most important along the back edge. Begin your machining at point D then carefully pin and machine the remaining three sides, returning to point D.
4 Work the *top* piece of the base block calico, attaching it to the top of the welt following the same order of work as for the construction of a ladder-stitched opening. Using the machine line, of the already marked opening, begin and end at a point in the side seam 5cm (2in) from the corner of the back edge (*see* Fig 108). Do remember to tack the whole length of the right-hand side seams into place to stabilize before machining and ensure the corners are correct. Then carefully pin the front edge and second side using vertical pins and carefully machine over these pins. Finish your machining 5cm (2in) from the top of the left-hand side.
5 Iron unneatened seams into the welt at the top and bottom.
6 Place the block into the cover and close the opening with the ladder stitch using a double thread or a heavier thread called *Bold* (*see* Chapter 2 'Equipment' page 18). You may find it easier to use a 5cm (2in) curved needle.
7 Do remember to take care that the corners are accurate and the seam lines on the welts are set exactly on each corner point of top and bottom cover pieces.

Set aside.

BOXED FEATHER CUSHION COVER

A zip should not be placed in the centre of the welt, as it is too conspicuous. It is perfectly adequate to use a ladder-stitched opening at the bottom of the welt along the back edge.

The opening must be extended into the side welts by 10cm (4in) to facilitate inserting the bulky feather cushion. Equally so the line of machine stitching marking the opening must be clear and strong.

ORDER OF WORK

1 Place the top and bottom sections of the cushion right side uppermost on the table.
2 Pipe each section as for the basic square cushion. Care should be taken at each of the corners and the final join in the crossway strip.

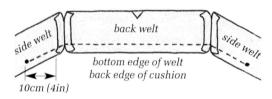

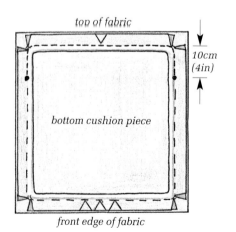

front edge of fabric

Fig 109 The position of the opening.

Bottom Cushion Piece (Fig 109)

3 Machine a line of stitching close to the piping along the top edge, extending into the sides by 10cm (4in). The top edge of fabric has now become the *back edge* and where the opening is placed.
4 Neaten the edges with the zigzag stitch to correspond with this line of stitching.

Set aside.

Welt

Place the four sections of welt, right sides uppermost, on the table. Check the top edge of fabric and markings.

1 Make up the welt as for the basic welted cushion forming a circle and leaving the 1.5cm (½in) of the seams unstitched at both ends and securely finished.
2 Iron open all seams at these short ends and finish these raw edges by using the zigzag stitch.
3 Iron in the seam line 1.5cm (½in) along the bottom edge of the back welt and two side welts.
4 Open out and use the ironed-in marked line to machine a line of stitching along the seam line along the bottom edge of the back welt extending into the side welts by 10cm (4in) to mark and strengthen the opening for the ladder stitching.
5 Neaten the edges by zigzag stitch to correspond with this line of stitching.

Joining the Top and Bottom Cushion Pieces to the Welt

1 Place the piped top cushion and the completed welt on the table. Check

once again that all the markings are correct.

This is particularly important if using a patterned fabric to ensure the continuity of pattern over the top of the cushion and down into the front welt. *Note:* The back welt is identical to the front welt piece but it will run in the opposite direction to the top cushion piece. This is correct. If using a striped fabric this would follow through. In both cases the side welts would not.

For all of the reasons stated above, the cushion cannot be reversed on the stool base.

2 Pin and tack the top cushion piece to the top of the welt using the same method as the basic piped, welted, cushion cover. Take care to set the corners accurately by opening out the prepared welt seams at each corner.

3 Machine into place, close to the piping, remembering to pivot your needle when negotiating the corners.

4 Finish all raw edges with zigzag stitch to correspond with the line of machining.

Attach the Bottom Cushion Piece to the Bottom Welt

Use the same method as the top section when positioning corners. *Tack all round to stabilize.*

1 Machine, starting the stitching at the point of the completion of the line of stitching for the opening 10cm (4in) from the top of the left-hand, top corner. Use reverse stitch when commencing machining as this is a weak point.

2 Continue machining round the cushion and up into the second side, stopping short of the last 10cm (4in) (i.e.

the point of the strengthening line for the opening). Secure the ends of the stitching.

3 Zigzag stitch the raw edges of the seams to correspond with the line of stitching and remember to trim off corners.

4 Remove all tacking and turn the cushion cover to the right side and press.

5 Place the cushion into the cushion cover making sure it is well evened out.

6 Ladder stitch to close the opening using a double, matching thread and taking care to set the corners accurately in place. This is a weak point. Shorten the distance between each stitch at this point making sure you catch the seam line of the welt to marry up exactly on the corner of the cushion bottom piece.

Set aside.

ORDER OF WORK FOR THE REMOVABLE FACE FABRIC LOOSE COVER FOR THE BASE BLOCK

Block Top

Place the block top piece, right side uppermost on the table and pipe all round using the same method as the already piped top and bottom cushion pieces.

Set aside.

Block Welt

Place the four welt sections with the right sides uppermost on the table and check all markings are correct.

(Far right) Fig 110 Attaching the piping to the bottom edge of the base cover welt.

◆ Pin and tack into place, right sides facing at short ends, to form a circle. *Note:* In the case of the welt seams leave the 1.5cm (½in) unstitched only at the top of the seam. Take the line of machine stitching right to the bottom of this short seam and reverse stitch to finish off ends of machining.

◆ Press all four short seams open and neaten the raw edges of these short seams with the zigzag stitch.
The bottom edge of the welt is now piped using exactly the same method of commencing and finishing a piping around a circle and completing with the final join.
Pin and tack the piping along the bottom edge of the welt on the right side of the fabric (Fig 110).

Fig 111 Block top in position.

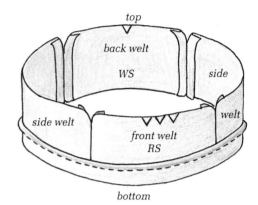

◆ Machine into place all round through all layers close to the piping.

Joining the Block Top Piece to the Welt

1 Place the piped block top piece right side uppermost on the table.
2 The prepared welt is now attached.
Note: If using patterned fabric it is important that the pattern follows through. Check that you are placing the top of the front welt piece to the bottom edge of the top block piece.
3 Pin and tack the welts into place checking accuracy at corners and centre markings. In the case of patterned or striped fabric it will be necessary to use the tie stitch to ensure a continuity of pattern; for example, if I had used the fabric *Provence* with the spot the line of the spots would have to follow through.
4 Machine into place close to the piping.
5 Finish off all raw edges to correspond with the machining, taking care to clip each corner accurately.
6 Press if necessary.

Place the completed top and welt face fabric section of the base block loose

cover onto the completed calico covered foam and pull it well down into place.

It is a good idea to use long, glass headed pins to pierce through the line of piping machine stitching and into the foam at intervals along each side. This ensures it is well in place (Fig 111).

Preparation to Make the Valance

Cut one extra strip of brown paper the full width of the face fabric and the depth of the valance paper pattern, in this case 137cm × 21cm (54in × 8½in).

Cut a card 20cm (8in) wide and the cutting depth of your valance, 20cm × 21cm (8in × 8½in). This is a *pleat measuring card*. Mark the centre with a **V** and draw a clear pencil line down the centre of the card (Fig 112).

Mark on the card:

Seam line allowance	1.5cm (½in)
Finished depth of the valance	16cm (6½in)
Hem allowance	2.5cm (1in)
Seam allowance	1.5cm (½in)
Depth of card	21.5cm (8½in)

Cut a second card – *Measuring card for checking hemline the finished depth of the valance* as for the worked project 16cm (6½in), 20cm (8in) wide and mark in the line down the centre (Fig 112).

Use this measuring card for checking the hemline. This now enables you to check the measurements for the finished valance. With the top section of the block loose cover now in place check this length of the valance.

It is sometimes necessary to adjust the hemline of the valance. If, for example you have a thick carpet the hemline should just clear this, otherwise the valance will not hang well should it

touch the surface. Whatever surface the footstool sits on there should be a clearance of about 3mm (⅛in) below the edge of the valance.

Note: The pattern for the valance has an allowance of 2.5cm (1in) for the hem plus 1.5cm (½in) seam allowance top and bottom.

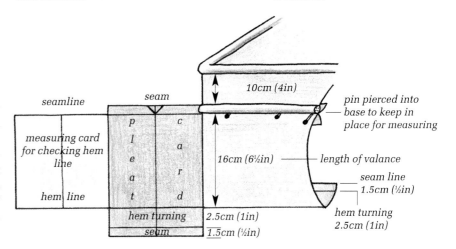

Fig 112 Checking length of valance.

MAKING A PATTERN FOR THE VALANCE AND PLEATS

Note: Patterned fabrics. It is necessary to have the whole width of fabric if using a patterned fabric or uneven stripe fabric. Use the following prepared paper pattern on your fabric to enable you to centralize any pattern on the fabric at the centre front of your block. You may now have to adjust the *finished depth* of the valance on your pleat marking card.

Using your pleating card and the prepared strip of brown paper:

◆ Mark the strip of paper 'RS' (right side) and 'WS' (wrong side).

◆ Follow the diagrams – Pattern for valance pleating (1 to 5), Figs 113–17.

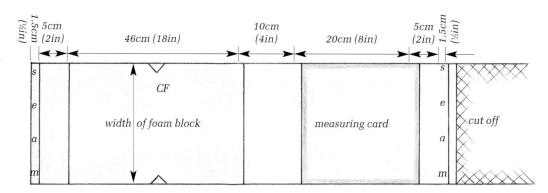

Fig 113 Pattern for valance pleating (1).

With the RS of the paper uppermost mark across the whole width of the paper in the following order (Fig 113):

Note: The 5cm (2in) at either side of the strip may appear confusing. The reason is that in order to have the join of the fabric hidden behind the pleats, these *two half pleats* become the underside of the pleat at each corner.

1 From the left hand side of the paper, mark off 1.5cm (½in). Draw a vertical line. This is the 1.5cm (½in) seam allowance.
2 Mark off another 5cm (2in) and draw another vertical line. This is the *half pleat.*
3 Mark off the width of the block 46cm (18in) and draw another vertical line. Mark in the centre of the block **V** top and bottom.
4 Mark off 10cm (4in). Draw another vertical line.
5 Mark off 20cm (8in). Now check the width of your pleating card (i.e. 20cm or 8in wide is correct). Draw another vertical line.
6 Mark off 5cm (2in). This is the *other half of the pleat.* Draw another vertical line.
7 Mark off 1.5cm (½in). This is your seam allowance. Draw another vertical line.
8 Check all measurements are correct and cut off excess paper.

Once this pattern is complete and checked, replace the marked pattern on the table right side uppermost and work from the left-hand side.

Note: In the following instructions, for convenience I have highlighted *fabric* in italics. This will be used when making up the pleats.

The following order of work must *first* be used to make the pleat in the paper pattern for two reasons: to enable a final check on the already made fabric top cover, and as a practice run for pleating the fabric valance.

ORDER OF WORK

1 Fold the seam allowance of 1.5cm (½in) and the 5cm (2in) to the wrong side onto itself along the crease line. *If working in fabric – iron.*
2 Follow Fig 114.
3 Turn the paper to the wrong side and place the *pleat marking card* up against the fold. The fold should now

Fig 114 Pattern for valance pleating (2).

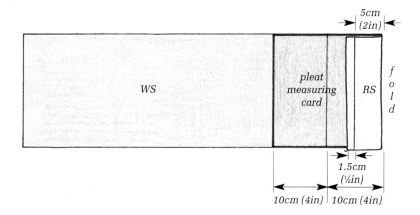

lie over the card *If working with fabric, iron in place.*

4 Turn the paper/*fabric* to the right side and check that the finished width of the block is correct to the next vertical line (in this case 46cm or 18in). *If working with fabric, tailor tack top and bottom to mark this line* (Fig 115).

5 Turn the paper/*fabric* with the wrong side uppermost (Fig 116).

6 Place the measuring card against the fold. *If working with fabric, place against the tailor tack top and bottom.*

7 Fold the paper/*fabric* over onto the card from the left hand side and pull evenly into place, and bring the paper/*fabric* up to the line marked in the centre of the card, i.e. 10cm (4in). Carefully fold it back onto itself and crease. *If using fabric, iron in the fold.* This must be correct, as it is the centre of the pleat.

8 Turn the paper/*fabric* with the right sides uppermost and removing the card from behind and now placing it in the same position and pushed up against the last fold made. *If using fabric, iron in fold* (Fig 117).

9 Bring the paper/*fabric* back onto itself and onto the card and crease against the right hand side of the card. *If using fabric, iron in fold.* You will notice that once again you have only half the pleat plus the seam allowance.

When the paper pattern is complete, check against the finished bottom edge of the finished block top cover.

MAKING THE VALANCE

Now work in fabric.

Tailor Tack (A Marking Stitch)

Traditionally you would regard a tailor tack (Fig 118) as belonging to dress-

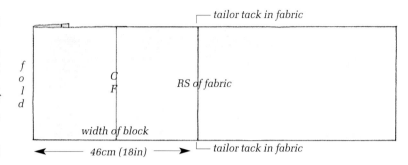

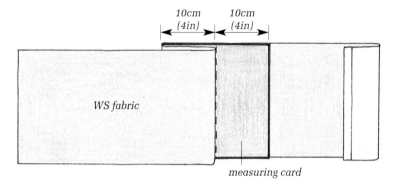

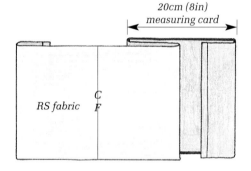

(Top) Fig 115 Pattern for valance pleating (3).

(Above) Fig 116 Pattern for valance pleating (4).

(Left) Fig 117 Pattern for valance pleating (5).

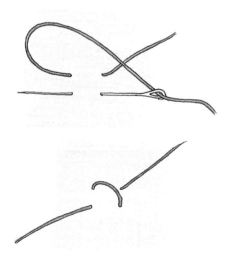

Fig 118 Tailor tack.

making where a double thread and a small loose loop stitch is made to transfer markings on a paper pattern onto fabric pieces. However, there are occasions when we have found this a most useful marking stitch in soft furnishing rather than using pins, which tend to wriggle out or pencils which either rub out or blur the marks. Adapt the tailor tack by using only a single thread and tightening up the loop.

ORDER OF WORK – MAKING THE PLEATS

1 Place the four pieces of Valance right sides uppermost on the table with the top edges of the fabric in place.
2 Using your *pleat marking card* follow the same order of work as the paper pattern. It is most important that this is accurate, take your time.

   Note: If using a patterned fabric use the *width of the block* marked on your paper pattern to centralize your pattern or stripe.

   This will mean placing your pattern on your fabric at this point. You will then be left with excess fabric at the left-hand side.
3 Repeat on each of the four sections of the valance.
4 Set each section aside as the pleating is completed.

Making Up Your Valance

1 Place the four *pleated* sections of the valance on the table, right sides uppermost.

   You are now going to form the four sections of the valance into a completed circle.
2 With right sides facing, pin and tack the seam allowance along the short (depth)

edges together. *Note:* It is important that the seam allowance of 1.5cm (½in) is very accurate or you will destroy the accuracy of your planned pleating.
3 Machine along the seam line using your reverse mechanism at the beginning and ends of all the seams.
4 Press all seams open. Take care you do not over press the lines already ironed in for your pleats. There is no need to finish the seam edges as these seams are encased by the lining.

Set aside.

Lining

It is easier to leave the cutting of the lining fabric until we reach this stage in the order of work.

This is the first time lining fabric has been used. Read again 'Lining Fabrics' in the chapter on fabrics.

It is important that a good quality cotton sateen lining fabric is used.

It is difficult to denote the right and wrong sides of lining fabric. The right side is the shinier side. If you place the lining fabric over the back of your hand and hold it up the light you will see the shinier side more easily. Lining fabric is sold doubled with the two selvedges together and with the right side (shiny) on the outside. The fabric can be cut in the doubled position.

It is important that you straighten your fabric along the weft grain before you cut your first depth of lining. Each subsequent piece of fabric can then be measured off to this straightened line.

It is not necessary to cut off the selvedges on lining fabric.

1 Carefully measure the circle of joined up valance. With the measurements we are using it ought to be approximately 345cm (136in). Fabric always takes up

a fraction of the measurements once it is machined and pleated.

2 The depth of lining is now cut 5cm (2in) shorter than the depth of the fabric valance pattern.

3 The pattern has to be checked for allowances for board and any adjustments made to the depth of the valance allowing for floor clearance.

4 The length of the lining should match up with the joined up circle of valance sections.

5 *It is not* necessary that the seam lines should fall onto and match those of the face fabric short seam lines.

6 *It is* necessary that you make allowance for joining your widths of lining with 1.5cm (½in) seam allowances when estimating your width of lining fabric.

7 Make a paper pattern or measure and cut the valance lining fabric. Use a measuring stick or steel measure, not a fabric tape measure, as this will stretch.

You can make your own layout cutting plan from the above instructions. Check that all is correct before cutting your lining fabric.

8 Join the widths of lining fabric along the short ends using 1.5cm (½in) seams to the same measurements as the circle of valance face fabric.

9 Press all seams open. It is not necessary to finish seams.

Joining the Lining to the Valance (Fig 119)

JOINING THE CIRCLE OF FACE FABRIC AND LINING FABRIC TOGETHER

To join the circle of face fabric and lining together with right sides facing place the raw bottom edge of the valance face fabric (now in a circle) against the raw bottom edge of the lining fabric (now in a circle); this must be accurate.

1 Pin and tack in place and machine all round this bottom edge using the 1.5cm (½in) seam allowance. This must be accurate (*see* Fig 119a).

2 Press both seam allowances together and down towards the face fabric and towards the hemline. You now have a complete circle of fabric with the lining and face fabric joined together.

Fold the face fabric and lining together with the wrong sides facing each other and bring the two raw edges of the two fabrics together along the top edge of the valance. This must be accurate (*see* Fig 119b).

This will create the hem allowance of 2.5cm (1in) of face fabric below the line of machining attaching the face fabric to the lining, and create the hemline along the bottom edge.

3 Iron this hemline into place.

4 Pin and tack these long, raw edges together (*see* Fig 119c).

5 Use a long stitch length (approximately No 4) on your machine and, on firmer fabrics, a No 16 (Continental 110) sewing machine needle.

6 Machine a line of stitching just inside the 1.5cm (½in) seam allowance around the whole length of the circle.

Note: This holds the two fabrics as one while the pleats are re-pleated on

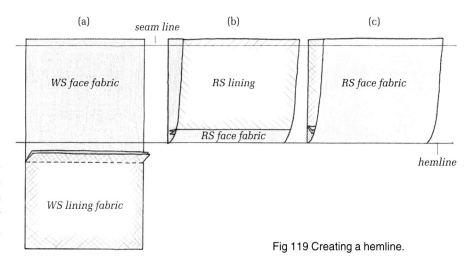

Fig 119 Creating a hemline.

line of machine stitching pleats

RS face fabric

seam line

width of block

(Far right) Fig 120 A line of machine stitching to stabilize the position of pleats.

the valance and attached to the welt. Keeping this line just inside the seam line ensures that these stitches are not seen when the valance is finally joined to the welt.

7 Iron. Taking special care to make the hemline very sharp.

8 Using your pleat marker card, re-check all pleats and re-press if necessary. Make sure each pleat is accurately set and sharp.

9 Pin and tack the width of the pleat in place, i.e. 20cm (8in) along the top raw edges of each of the four pleats.

10 Machine a line of stitching *exactly* on the seam line through all thicknesses. Use a matching thread, the long stitch and size 16 machine needle. You are now machining through several layers of fabric (Fig 120).

Joining the Welt to Valance

The valance is now complete and ready to attach to the base of the welt of the completed block top and welt section.

Make a final check by placing the block top and welt section onto the block and pulling it well down into place. Once again, use long glass-headed

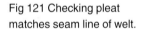

Fig 121 Checking pleat matches seam line of welt.

pins to pierce through the line of piping machine stitching and into the foam at intervals, along each side. This ensures it is well in place.

Using your measuring card for checking the hemline, finally check that the length of the valance from the welt is correct and you have clearance of floor coverings. If necessary, this measurement can be adjusted by taking a slightly deeper seam allowance along the top edge of the valance.

Now remove the completed section from the block in order to attach it to the prepared valance section.

ORDER OF WORK (Fig 122)

1 Place the completed valance section and completed block top section on the table.

2 *Take one section at a time. Note:* It would be necessary if using a patterned or striped fabric that you start with the front welt. This would ensure you had continuity of pattern across the cushion top and down into the front welt.

3 With the right sides facing, place the top edge of the completed valance to the bottom edge of the piped bottom of the welt section.

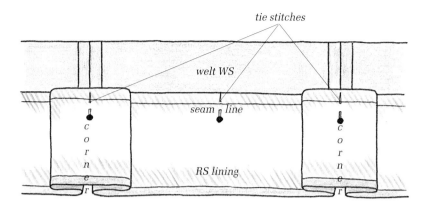

4 Using a pin vertically, pin the centres together.

5 Match each corner.

6 Tie-stitch in place. From the lining side of the valance, pierce the needle into the centre of the pleat on the seam line taking the needle through to pierce into the right side of the centre of the welt seam on the seam line. This must be accurate. Reverse the needle and follow the same route back, the needle reappearing in the same position in the lining seam line.

7 Pull the two facing, right sides of these sections together and tie tightly in place (*see* Fig 122).

8 Turn the work to the right side and, if this is correct, the pleat will exactly match the seam line of the welt. This must be accurate (*see* Fig 121).

9 *Note:* If you have a striped or patterned fabric it will be necessary to make several tie stitches in between, to keep the stripes even and running through and, in a patterned fabric, the continuity of pattern.

10 Follow the same order of work on each section, joining the valance to the welt.

11 Once you have checked that all is even and correct, pin and tack in place all round.

12 Machine through all thicknesses using the longer stitch and stronger machine needles (size 16).

13 Finish off all ends carefully.

14 Zigzag stitch all round to neaten the seam. *Note:* If you adjusted the length of the valance you will have to trim the seam line to the same 1.5cm (½in) level.

15 Press and, if necessary, place the pleat marker into the pleated corners to sharpen up the fold.

16 Place completed cover on calico covered block.

17 Place the boxed feather or foam cushion on top (Figs 123 & 124).

(*Above*) Fig 122 Joining the welt to the valance.

(*Below*) Fig 123 Completed footstool (cushion and base).

Fig 124 Completed footstool.

It is also possible to adjust the machine stitch to its longest length and machine along the gathering line. This again is not always successful as you can only use the thread on your machine and this tends to break when pulling up the gathers on large amounts of fabric, although two parallel lines of stitching considerably helps to strengthen this method.

A more satisfactory and stronger method of gathering by machine can be found by using the zigzag facility by zigzagging over a stronger thread such as bold or buttonhole twist.

Traditionally, the standard method of gathering was done by hand and there may still be occasions when hand gathering may be necessary or easier, for example, a short area or a lightweight fabric such as voile and some silks.

When gathering large lengths of fabric by hand it is necessary to gather in equal sections to keep the gathering even and more manageable, using two rows of small, even running stitches. When using the sewing machine, the fabric is marked into even sections but the gathering can be done as one length of machining (Fig 125).

Whether hand- or machine-gathered the result is always much more successful if two lines of stitches are worked and the lines of stitching are always worked on the wrong side of the fabric. Work two rows of stitches of gathering 6mm (¼in) apart, either side of the seam allowance. The first line is worked just outside the seam line and the second line just 6mm (¼in) inside the seam line. It is important that these lines of stitching are straight and parallel to the edge of the fabric and to each other.

BY HAND: RUNNING STITCH (FIG 125)

These small running stitches are worked from right to left, if right handed. Begin with a double backstitch and leave a

A GATHERED VALANCE

As an alternative you may prefer a gathered valance for your footstool.

Gathering

Gathering fabric can be time consuming and although some of the more sophisticated sewing machines provide attachments, these are sometimes both more complicated and less than satisfactory to use.

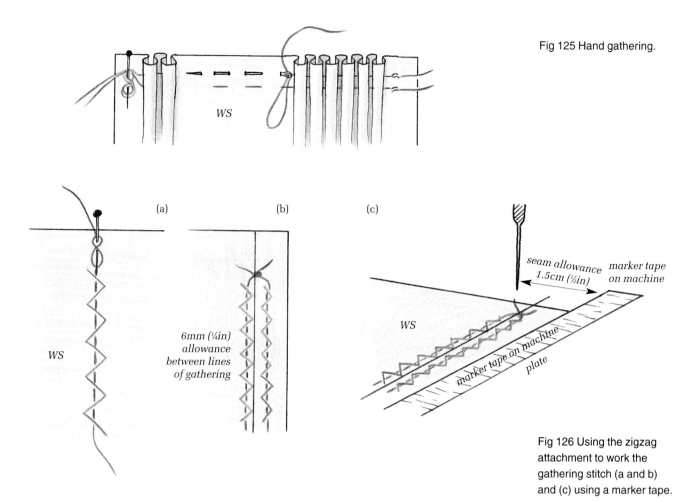

Fig 125 Hand gathering.

(a) (b) (c)

6mm (¼in) allowance between lines of gathering

WS

seam allowance 1.5cm (½in) *marker tape on machine*

marker tape on machine plate

Fig 126 Using the zigzag attachment to work the gathering stitch (a and b) and (c) using a marker tape.

long end. Keep the stitches even and equally spaced along the gathering line. At the end of the lines of gathering, leave long equal ends of thread and, holding these two threads together, gently push the fabric along adjusting the fabric into even gathers to the required amount of fullness. Secure the threads by twisting a figure of eight around a vertical pin. Readjust the gathers if necessary.

MACHINING (FIG 126)

Unless you are very practised or confident with your machining, place a marker tape on your machine plate. Machine just below the width of the seam allowance for the first line. When working the second line of stitching, it is sometimes pos-

sible to use the width of your machine foot against the first line. Check its width or replace the marker strip 6mm (¼in) to be parallel to the first line of machining.

USING THE ZIGZAG ATTACHMENT TO WORK THE GATHERING STITCH

I would suggest that even if you are not immediately using a gathering stitch and in order to keep the build up of skills and techniques, that you have a practice run on a small piece of fabric using this method (*see* Fig 126). This can then be added to your files.

1 Set the zigzag stitch to its narrowest position and the machine stitch length to its longest length.

2 Working from the wrong side of your fabric place a pin in a horizontal position at the beginning of a line of gathering. Using sufficient strong thread to cover the area to be gathered plus about an extra 15cm (6in), hold the thread in place with a figure of eight round the pin leaving a long end (*see* Fig 126a).

3 Lower the machine needle into the fabric on the gathering line and start machining with two or three zigzag stitches. Leave long ends on your threads.

4 Leave the needle in the work and lift the foot. Bring the length of strong thread underneath the machine foot and let it lie against the machine needle. Lower the foot and zigzag over the strong thread the length of the line of fabric to be gathered.

5 Leave a long end on your thread and do not use the reverse stitch.

6 Work a second line replacing the pin and a second length of strong thread 6mm (¼in) inside the seam allowance and follow the same order of work as for the first line. The strong threads held in place by the figure of eight around the pins can now be released from the pins and the ends tied together in a strong knot leaving long ends. The gathers can then be pulled up into even folds using this strong knot to pull against.

Gathering and Attaching the Valance for the Footstool

When gathering fabric the amount of fullness varies according to the project being made and the weight of the fabric being used.

For example, if using a lightweight fabric such as a voile for a project you would need 3 to 3½ times of fabric to the area being covered to give sufficient fullness in the gathers.

For the footstool we are using a medium-weight furnishing fabric, allow twice the amount of fabric to the area to be covered.

The block top is:

46cm × 4 sides = 184cm × twice the length = 368cm (18in × 4 sides = 72in × twice the length = 144in)

3 widths of the 137cm fabric = 132 × 3 widths = 411cm (3 widths of the 54in fabric = 54in × 3 widths = 162in)

Looking at the above sum you have more than sufficient joined-up width of valance in three widths of fabric and once you have accommodated the seam turning – this would give you a generous amount of fullness.

An adjustment to your pattern layout would have to be made, as only three widths of fabric would be needed for this valance.

1 Divide the length of the valance into four even sections and mark positions with a tailor tack (or if preferred, a vertical pin or pencil mark). (*See* Fig 127b.)

2 Adjust the gathers evenly to roughly the size of the four sides of the footstool and hold the two threads together around a vertical pin with a figure of eight (*see* Fig 127c).

3 Mark the centre of each side of the base block top welt along the piping line with a tailor tack (*see* Fig 127a). Placing right sides together, match the tailor tacks (or markings) on each side to the sections of the valance to the marked centres of the bottom edge of the piped welt (*see* Fig 127d).

4 Pin in place with vertical pins and readjust the gathers where necessary as evenly as possible and tack between the two lines of gathering, readjusting the gathering where

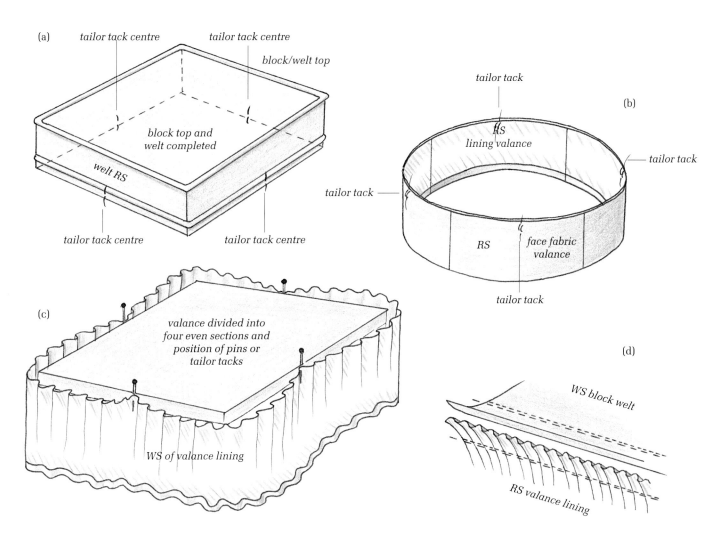

Fig 127 Gathering and attaching the valance for the footstool: (a) the completed base block top and welt; (b) the completed valance; (c) gathers adjusted evenly to roughly the size of the four sides of the footstool; (d) joining the bottom edge of the base block welt to the valance.

necessary. This tacking line will more or less fall on your seam line.

5 Attach the piping foot to your machine.

6 Place a marker tape on your machine plate the width of your seam allowance 1.5cm (½in). Use a stronger machine needle (No 16) with a stitch length on your machine of approximately 3–4.

7 The bulk of your fabric should lie to your left on your machine plate and the folds of the gathers should be kept in even horizontal fold lines. Smooth these into place as you progress with your machining.

8 Machine all round the four sides through all layers. Your machining stitch will lie just inside the first gathering line. Finish ends carefully.

9 The long, strong threads can now be easily removed. Clip the securing knot loose and remove the gathering stitches by pulling through the long strong thread and the zigzag stitches will then pull out very easily.

10 Remove the tacking stitches.

11 The raw edges can now be finished with the zigzag stitch. Remember to readjust your zigzag and stitch length to the correct settings for neatening the raw edges of the fabric.

11 Curtains

For both the beginner and those who have already made curtains, this section of the book is designed to give a basic foundation of curtain making leading to the more advanced hand-headed and interlined curtains. Making curtains for the first time can be a daunting task, but with careful measuring and stage by stage accuracy you will be more than rewarded for your time spent.

You will by now have some basic knowledge of your fabric in making your cushions. Now we are dealing with larger pieces of fabric it becomes more important that we cover each stage accurately. In particular we know exactly how to measure and estimate the amount of fabric needed.

Your track should be chosen and fixed in position before you buy your fabric as the quantity of fabric you will need depends on the length of your track, the length of your curtain and your choice of heading, and you must know the width of your fabric and the length of the pattern repeat, if any.

TRACKS AND HEADINGS

Choosing and Fitting Your Track

Curtains are suspended from tracks or poles and to make a really professional curtain it is essential that the track or pole is of good quality and strong enough to take the weight of the curtains.

Being confronted with a large range of tracks and poles when walking into a shop to select one can be very off-putting. These will vary from corded and uncorded, plastic, PVC and aluminium tracks to a strong metal track with an overlap arm and a built-in pulley system. At the bottom of the range are the plastic tracks; although these are sold in different grades for supporting various weights of curtain I would suggest that these tracks are only used for curtains of less importance. The appearance of the track can be considerably improved either by painting it to match the walls of your room or by covering it with matching curtain fabric.

Poles

You will also find a very wide range of poles in different colours and designs. The basic poles are sold in 22, 30 and 35mm diameters and in natural, beech, teak or dark wood coverings. The 22 and 30mm poles are also available in white. All three sizes come in various lengths. There are brass coloured poles, which are usually made of steel plated with brass. There are also wrought iron and anodized steel poles with decorative finials of different designs.

The poles come in kits, which include rings, finials, brackets, fixing screws and Rawlplugs, and instructions for assembly and installation.

Choosing Your Heading

Curtains are attached to the track or pole by means of a heading. Once you have chosen, *not bought*, the fabric you must decide on the heading.

Heading Tapes

There are many commercial heading tapes on the market in a variety of gathered and pleated styles. These are attached to the curtains by machine stitch. The stitching shows from the right side of the curtain and has an added disadvantage in that when the curtain is stacked back they often look uneven and untidy.

The standard gathering tape is 2.5cm (1in) deep and comes in cotton and synthetic material. It has limited use and should only be used on less important, smaller curtains. It also comes in a 'mini-tape', which can be used on sheer fabrics.

Of the commercial heading tapes, the standard pencil pleat is the most widely used and the 8cm (3¼in) width is quite adequate for most curtains. It is most successful if used under a pelmet or valance because, when the curtain is stacked back, the heading is concealed and the depth of the pleat allows the curtain to appear from under the pelmet or valance in even folds.

The pencil pleat commercial heading tape is reputedly so called because of the narrow, vertical folds, which appear when the tape is pulled up and gathered, appear to be shaped like pencils.

Pencil pleat tape comes in both cotton and synthetic material. Always buy good quality tape. The cotton tape, which may not always be available, does have the advantages of giving a firm pleat when the cords are pulled up and the cords knot and unknot more easily. Pencil pleat tape comes in two widths:

- 8cm (3¼in), with three different levels of pockets in which to place the hooks, and

- 14.5cm (5¾in), with six levels of pockets, but this would only be used on very large curtains or

curtains in a static position or on a valance.

The pockets on the tape are used to attach the standard one-prong hooks to suspend the curtains from the runners. These hooks come in plastic, brass and aluminium. The plastic hooks are used on the plastic runners, but the strong metal hooks should always be used on the metal rails.

The pencil pleated heading tape available with integral loop Velcro is a most successful tape when a heading remains in one position, for example, on a valance attached to a pelmet board with a reciprocal strip of Velcro fixed to the front edge of the board.

Velcro

The word 'Velcro' is derived from velour and crochet. In French 'crochet' means 'hook'.

Velcro is sold in strips 2cm (¾in) and 2.5cm (1in) wide. It is made up of two strips of material, one covered with a tiny soft loop pile and a reciprocal strip with tiny, hard, nylon hooks. These cling together when pressed. It is sold from a reel in various colours and in different combinations.

1 The loop and hook strips both have to be hand sewn onto fabric.
2 Self-adhesive – on which the hook side has a self-adhesive backing and the reciprocal loop side is soft and can be sewn onto a fabric.
3 Hook side only, with self-adhesive backing.

The most successful heading is handmade. This will stack back evenly and no stitching will show from the right side. These are time-consuming to make, but not difficult, and once you have worked through the second curtain project on hand-made headings, you will find the results very worthwhile and rewarding.

Buckram

Hand-made headings are stiffened with curtain buckram made of coarse, woven cotton and heavily sized. It is available in three widths, 10cm (4in), 12.5cm (5in) and 15cm (6in). It can be bought as iron-on, but this is more difficult to apply.

Hand-made headings with French pleats and goblet pleats need a *pin hook* to hang them from a pole or track. The pin hook has a sharp, pointed prong, which is inserted into the back of each pleat. When using a pole with rings, insert the pin hook 1.5cm (½in) below the top of the curtain.

If using a pole, the curtains will be suspended under the poll – termed 'underslung' – and the heading will be totally exposed.

THE PELMET BOARD AND CURTAIN TRACK

- Fixing the track directly onto the wall can be a problem particularly in an older house, therefore it should be attached to a pelmet board of planed and finished pine or deal if at all possible. The wood is a much stronger fixing.

- A pelmet board made from a piece of deal or pine, planed and finished, width 15cm × 2.5cm (6in × 1in).

- The length of the board should be the width of the window plus an allowance either side of the

window known as the stack-back area (*see* page 127).

- Use a metal curtain track with an overlap arm, a top fixing, a built-in pulley system and a spring cord and tensioner and gliders that run smoothly.

- The width of the board and that of the position of the track should allow the curtains to hang correctly in relation to the window sill and the front of the pelmet.

- The track is fixed at least halfway back from the front edge of the board and must finish 2cm (¾in) short of each end of the board.

- If the curtains are particularly thick or heavily interlined it may be necessary to fit the rail further than halfway to the back of the board to give clearance from the pelmet front or valance as the curtains are drawn open and closed.

- In order to have your curtain returning neatly to the wall, insert a screw eye 3cm (1¼in) long into the underside of the board as close to the wall as practicable, level with each end of the track. The ends of the curtains can then be hooked into these eyes so retaining the curtain against the wall.

- Fix strong right-angle brackets 10cm × 12.5cm (4in × 5in) to the underside of the board at either end. It may be necessary to fix one or more evenly spaced, intermediate brackets if the pelmet is very long or the curtains are very heavy, approximately every metre.

- Fix the pelmet board to the wall with strong, long screws of 3cm (1¼in) using appropriate Rawlplugs and using a spirit level to ensure the board is level. Drill holes in the wall. Plug with the appropriate fixing, depending on wall type

- The board is usually placed 10–15cm (4–6in) above the window

Fig 128 The pelmet board.

frame, but this sometimes may vary depending on window treatment or your particular window.

Making the Pelmet Board (Fig 129)

1 Cover the board with matching fabric or lining material.
2 Measure around the board and add 4cm (1½in).
3 Measure the length of the board and add 10cm (4in).
4 Cut out a rectangle of fabric on the straight of grain to these measurements. Bring the short ends together to find the centre of the long edge and mark centres top and bottom.
5 Press over a 1.5cm (½in) seam allowance along one, long edge to the wrong side of the fabric.
6 Mark a pencil line on the board across the centre and another line 2.5cm (1in) from the back edge of the board along the length.
7 Lay the wood onto the wrong side of the fabric and align the long, raw edge of the fabric to the pencil line along the board, matching centre markings and staple the edge of the fabric to the board.
8 Bring the folded edge over the already stapled edge. Staple the centre into position, the two ends, and then along the rest of the board at regular intervals (*see* Fig 129a).
9 Fold the ends of the fabric like a parcel and place a staple across the end (*see* Fig 129b), bring these ends over the ends of the board and fold in the raw edge of the turning and staple neatly into position (*see* Fig 129c).

Note: The top side of the board (i.e. that part which faces the ceiling) has the stapled fabric, so the staples do not show from the underside.

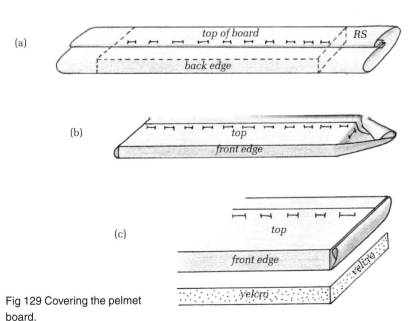

Fig 129 Covering the pelmet board.

10 Attach a self-adhesive piece of Velcro along the front edge of the board and the two side returns. Reinforce this strip with staples.
11 Offer the board to the wall to determine the position of the brackets and mark the position of the holes to be drilled to attach the board to the wall.
12 Now attach brackets to the board.
13 Fix strong, right-angled brackets 10cm × 13cm (4in × 5in).
14 Length of board up to 1.5m (5ft) – 2 brackets are sufficient.
15 Length of board up to 2.45m (8ft) – 3 brackets are sufficient.
16 A bracket is required approximately every metre (3ft).
17 Now fix the track, using a bradawl to mark holes, through the fabric, into the wood.

An overlap arm ensures that the leading edges of the curtain overlap each other and do not part in the centre when closed, showing light or darkness. It also eliminates draughts.

A pulley system means that the track is corded along the top allowing the cord to be pulled from behind the back edge of the curtain. This prevents the leading edges from becoming soiled and worn by constantly pulling them from the centre by hand. A spring cord and tensioner will enhance the arrangement (lead edge is also called centre edge, and back edge called side edge).

Stackback

This is the term used for the area of curtain where the track takes it clear of the edge of the window when it is drawn back. The amount of stackback varies with the width of your curtain in relation to the width of the window and the length of track. It is usually 10–30cm (4–12in).

Estimating Fabrics and Understanding Patterns

Before calculating the amount of fabric, you need to look carefully at the

(Top) Fig 130 Pelmet board showing overarm cording and tensioner.

manufacturer's notes on the selvedge or ticket and write these down.

- Width of fabric (this is from selvedge to selvedge)

- The size of the pattern repeat (PR) or size of the pattern repeat with a half-drop repeat (HDPR)

- Fabric faults. Check for flaws in material. These are usually marked with a coloured thread in the selvedge

LENGTH OF PATTERN REPEAT (PR)

This is the distance from the top of one pattern to the top of the next identical pattern. You can check this by bringing the selvedge to the selvedge across the straightened end of your fabric. If correct, the pattern will match. *Refer to* 'Length of Pattern Repeat', page 41.

HALF DROP PATTERN REPEAT (HDPR)

- In this case the pattern has been printed diagonally. If you bring selvedge to selvedge you will find the pattern does not match and you will have to go halfway into the next identical pattern to make it match. In other words you need one and a half times the length of each identical pattern.

- So when estimating your material you will have to allow one and a half times the length of each pattern repeat to each length of fabric.

EXAMPLE:
If your PR were 35.5cm (14in) for an HDPR, it would become 35.5cm (14in) + 18cm (7in) = 53.5cm (21in).

Measuring Windows and Estimating the Amount of Fabric for Curtains

Once the track is in position the window can be measured.

Draw a rough plan of your window plus the stackback with the track in position, in your notebook.

- Chosen heading

- The finished length of your curtain will be either:

1 Sill length
2 Apron length 10–15cm (4–6in) below the sill
3 Floor length allowing 6mm (¼in) clearance
4 Extra long floor length adding 15cm (6in). This is very much a fashion trend and can look elegant but is not always practical

There is often the problem of a radiator and in this case you must make your own judgement. There should be a minimum of 1.5cm (½in) between the bottom of the curtain and the radiator. It is never a good idea to cover a radiator; you will lose heat and damage your curtains. Night-storage heaters will need even more clearance than this.

Use the rough, drawn plan of your window on which to record measurements. Measure most accurately with your steel retractable measure (never use your soft tape measure, it will stretch). *Take two measurements and always recheck.*

The Measured Width: is the length of the curtain track (not the width of the window) *plus* the returns at both ends *plus* the length of the overlap arm (usually 10cm or 4in).

The Measured Length: is the desired finished length of your curtain, called *drop*, from the top of your track. Take these measurements at both ends and in the centre.

Ring Drop: A second measurement is then taken from the ring of the rail to the desired, *finished* length.

 RECORD IN YOUR NOTEBOOK

Calculating the Width of Fabric

- The *required width of fabric* is twice the measured width recorded to give the required fullness for the commercial pencil pleat heading tape.

- The *required width of fabric* is two and a quarter times the measured width recorded to give the required fullness for the hand-headed curtains using buckram.

- To work out the number of widths of your chosen material, divide *required width of curtain* by the *width of your chosen material* (already recorded in your notebook).

- It is sometimes necessary to add a half width to obtain the correct fullness. Never skimp on your material and if you are more than 30cm (12in) short, buy an extra width.

- These extra widths are always joined to the *back edge* of the curtain, never to the centre edge, called the *lead edge*.

Calculating the Length of Fabric

Take the finished length of your curtain from your plan.
To this add:

- 20–25cm (8–10in) for hems and headings.

- If there is a pattern, add one pattern repeat. Add this amount to *each drop*.

- Multiply this final length by the number of curtain widths required (this is recorded in your notebook).

Write on your plans:

- *Finished measurement*
That is the length and width of your finished curtains.

- *Cutting measurement*
These include allowances for hems and headings.

WATCHPOINTS:

Note: Most fabrics today are 137cm (54in), although some are still 122cm (48in).

Bolts of Material. These are produced in batches so make sure that if you require more than the amount on one bolt you do have the remaining fabric from the same batch of bolts as different batches of fabric may have slight variations in colour. Bolts of material range from 120m to 150m.

- Ask the shop to roll your fabric rather than folding it.

- If you are more than 30cm (12in) short of double the width it will be necessary to buy another width thus adding half a width to each curtain. Remember, all half widths must be added to the outside edge of a curtain.

12 Project 6 – The Basic Lined Curtain

It is better to begin with a small window in making this first, basic, lined curtain using a cotton furnishing fabric to enable you to learn the various new skills and techniques.

Before estimating and buying your material, there are certain considerations that could considerably help you to achieve a really rewarding result from all your hard work.

We all have our own ideas and taste regarding furnishing our homes and some of us are born with more artistic flair than others, as I discussed in my introduction to fabrics. Most of us usually make curtains because we want to freshen an existing room or we have moved house. It is not often we have the luxury of starting from scratch, and creating a whole new look to the room.

Once you have established and considered the window for your curtain project and the possible colour you might prefer for your fabric, a little pre-planning is necessary.

It is worthwhile doing a little research before buying your fabric. Many shops will allow you to take home a length of material. You will have to pay a small deposit but this is worthwhile as the material seen in the shop will often look very different in your own home in both daylight and artificial light.

Although it might appear unnecessary, considering the aspect of your room is worthwhile and it does have a bearing on the overall result of furnishing a room. Most of us know we like a certain colour and style and usually pick our fabrics accordingly.

Whatever room my students choose for this first basic curtain, and after I have given a short talk to them about colour, I ask them to go home and during the following week, notice what happens to the light in their chosen room at each stage of the day, morning, noon and night and in artificial light. Then establish whether their room faces north, south, east or west and what view, if any, they have from their chosen window.

Read again the section on colour in Chapter 1, beginning on page 5.

It is always very interesting to see how many of my students come back the following week and have become quite enthusiastic and adventurous in their possible choice of fabric for this first basic curtain project.

For this next project, 'The Basic Lined Curtain', I have indulged in the luxury of the redecoration and new soft furnishings for my room.

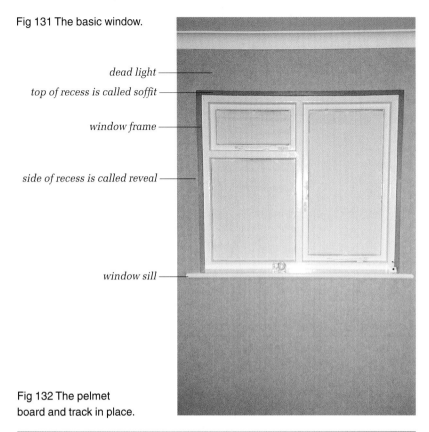

Fig 131 The basic window.

dead light ——————

top of recess is called soffit ——————

window frame ——————

side of recess is called reveal ——————

window sill ——————

Fig 132 The pelmet
board and track in place.

I have chosen a small dark room with a window looking out onto a large surface of brick wall with a little view of trees to the side, and it has a north-east aspect. The only shaft of sunlight comes into the room early to mid morning. Then it becomes cold and lifeless. It is, in fact, a miserable little room and I felt it needed some 'sunshine'.

I have chosen a bright sunshine yellow for the walls and a curtain fabric of yellow, blues and greens, all nature's colours. I am breaking rules in that a small pattern is usually regarded as a better choice for a small room. But I wanted to demonstrate for the purpose of this book the use of the pattern on the material in different colour ways in the cushions and that the photographs of the finished projects would be bright and clear.

It was not necessary to go to the expense of a full-length curtain. Apart from the fact that the size of my pattern in relation to the size of the room would have resulted in an overwhelming appearance, if I had added the extra material necessary for a full length plus the length of my pattern repeat the cost of my curtains would have been considerably increased.

THE WORKED CURTAIN PROJECT

To reinforce and practise measuring curtains I will use this room and window for all considerations and measurements for the worked basic curtain project.

Follow my instructions and adapt to your own curtains. Draw a rough plan of your window with the pelmet board and rail in place and use your metal measuring tape.

Before taking measurements and estimating your fabric the curtain track must be in place, the length of the curtain must be decided and the heading for your curtain chosen.

For my window, the curtain will hang from a metal curtain track mounted on a pelmet board with a top fixing and overlap arm and a built in pulley system and cord tensioner hidden behind the back edge of the curtain.

I have chosen an apron-length curtain dropping 12cm (5in) below the sill using a commercial pencil pleat heading tape. The heading will be covered by a pelmet, which will be attached to the pelmet board with Velcro.

The pelmet board is placed 14cm (5½in) above the recess.

Measure the width.

The length of curtain track is 160cm (63in); add to this the returns on the board at both ends 15cm (6in) times two = 30cm (12in) and then add the overlap arm of 10cm (4in).

The width is:

160cm + 30cm + 10cm = 200cm
(63in + 12in + 4in = 79in)

I have chosen a pencil pleat heading tape, which requires twice the width of fabric.

The width is:

200cm × 2 = 400cm
(79in × 2 = 158in)

Divide this by the width of the fabric which is 137cm = 2.92 widths (*rounds up* to 3 widths)

or

Divide this by the width of the fabric which is 54in = 2.92 widths (*rounds up* to 3 widths)

(Top) Fig 133 Made curtain without pelmet.

(Above) Fig 134 Made curtain with pelmet.

Measure the length (drop).

This is the finished length of my curtain from the top of the track to my chosen, finished length, which is apron length dropping 12cm (5in) below the sill:

Finished drop	= 132cm (52in)
Add heading allowance	= 5cm (2in)
Add double the hem allowance of 7.5cm (3in)	= 15cm (6in)
The total of this is the cutting length	= 152cm (60in)
You must now add the pattern repeat	= 64cm (25in)
The finished estimating drop including pattern repeat	= 216cm (85in)

Take the *finished estimating* drop and multiply this by *the three widths*:

$$216\text{cm} \times 3 = 648\text{cm}$$

divided by 100cm (i.e. 1m) = 6.48m
rounded up = 6½m

or = 85in × 3 = 255in

divided by 36in (i.e. 1yd) = 7.08yd
rounded down = 7yd

Note: The estimation of fabric is only for the curtains. The method for estimating for the pelmet or valance is covered in the Pelmet and Valance chapters, and at this stage in the course we would only confuse the beginners before arriving and working through the following chapters on the Valance and Pelmet.

During the course we made a sample valance and pelmet and I will suggest when we arrive at this chapter you do likewise. It is then possible to visualize and plan with this practical knowledge and experience before planning the window and estimating the fabric as a whole.

For the more experienced, you may prefer to begin the basic curtain and valance or pelmet immediately, but do please read both the chapters on The Valance and The Hard Pelmet before pre-planning and estimating and buying the necessary amount of fabric. Remember, it is important to buy all your fabric from one roll or colour batch.

(Right) Fig 135 The finished drop from the top of the rail.

(Far right) Fig 136 Measuring the finished drop from the ring.

Lining Fabric

The lining fabric is cut 7.5cm (3in) shorter than the face fabric regardless of the depth of hem to be used. When estimating the lining fabric, no pattern match is necessary.

RECORD IN
YOUR NOTEBOOK

Once all the measurements are taken and checked and the amount of fabric estimated and bought, we are now ready to make the curtains.

Pre-planning
Selection of fabric
Fabric content
Width of fabric
Pattern repeat

Copy the plan into your notebook
Amount of face fabric
– Amount needed
– Amount of lining fabric
– Amount of heading tape

Useful information

DEMONSTRATION PROJECT

My selected fabric:
Tulka
Content: 100 per cent cotton
Width 136cm (54in)
Pattern repeat 64cm (25in)

Amount of fabric
– 6m 50cm (7yd)
– Amount of lining fabric (4.4m or 4¾yd)
– Amount of heading tape (4.3m or 4¾yd)

We have found there is some merit in making a large, visual aid 'sample' curtain, although I know that on the whole samples are often termed as rather a waste of time. For those who are real beginners it can be a good confidence-building exercise. This large sample can be used to hang in the position of your proposed curtains on your curtain rail when estimating for the amount of fabric, not only checking your accurate measuring but, hopefully, giving you that added confidence.

This sample curtain has also proved invaluable in learning the skills and techniques before making the first purchase of fabric. Added to this, it does considerably help when measuring your curtains, enabling you to place the hooks into the correct pocket to establish the position of the top of your heading, either covering the track or underslinging (to prevent large amounts of stackback of fabric throwing out the line and fall of the valance or pelmet).

(Far left) Fig 137 Using the visual aid 'sample' curtain to measure the drop.

(Right) Fig 138 Position of the curtain if using the top pocket of the pencil pleated tape on the 'sample' visual aid with the hook in place, the heading tape covering the track.

(Far right, top) Fig 139 Position of curtain if using the second pocket of the pencil pleated heading tape on 'sample' visual aid with the hook in place, i.e. underslung. This is the suitable position if using a valance or pelmet.

(Far right, bottom) Fig 140 Heading in place on the worked curtain, underslung to be covered by the pelmet.

USING THE VISUAL AID 'SAMPLE' CURTAIN

The hook drop is from the position of the ring (glider) on the rail. Using your sample curtain insert a hook so that the position will give you the required drop. This is particularly important when measuring onto a sill or floor.

If measuring a sill or a full-length curtain where the length (drop) of the curtain and any clearance at the sill and floor must be accurately established, it is important to measure carefully. Do remember you must consider the type of carpet or floor covering to calculate the clearance necessary.

If, for some reason, your carpet is not already laid, use a square of carpet at the hemline of the curtain when measuring the drop.

Materials for 'Sample' Visual Aid

- ◆ 1m furnishing fabric

- ◆ 1m lining fabric

- ◆ 2 weights

- ◆ Pencil pleat heading tape and turning allowance

You may, however, wish to start immediately on your first curtains and all the following instructions will be the same as we progress with the work.

13 Preparation for Making Curtains

Additional equipment will be required before embarking on curtain making. *Refer again to* Chapter 2 'Equipment', page 17.

Prepare measuring cards for making curtains (*see* Chapter 2 'Equipment', page 18 for sizes).

The most important piece of equipment is the work surface.

To construct a really professional curtain the sewing machine is only used to join the long seam lengths when joining widths of curtains and lining fabric and the additional interlining if interlining the curtain, and if using one of the commercial heading tapes. Hand-headed curtains, as the name suggests, are done by hand, apart from small lines of machining to set the French and goblet pleats in place.

The curtain should be moved as little as possible while being constructed. You will, of course, have to move it from the work surface to do the machining. But the iron should be brought to the work surface and every stage of the work must be ironed to achieve a really professional finish. A build up of careful ironing and pressing should result in very little, if any, ironing of the finished curtain.

A cordless iron would be a luxury for most of us, the addition of a sound extension lead to the iron will have to be used, but do take care and remember to switch off at all times.

Devoid of the ironing board, an ironing pad must be used when using the iron.

As in each of the cushion projects, pre-planning is very important. Once the fabric is chosen and bought, do remember to ask the shop assistant to roll it onto a cardboard tube rather than fold it. Once creases appear in the fabric, valuable time will be lost ironing it before cutting out can begin. Any creasing across the fabric must be completely removed. Crease lines running down the fabric can be more easily disguised in the folds of the curtain, but the fabric must be ironed, and on the wrong side.

The basic lined curtain is constructed with a face fabric and a cotton sateen lining fabric. For the more advanced, really luxurious classic curtain, an interlining can be added.

Refer to Chapter 1, page 10 'Lining Materials'.

Before embarking on the first curtain it has proved a valuable exercise to understand the construction of a curtain and to prepare a paper visual aid.

Fig 141 The completed curtain.

BASIC LINED CURTAIN

For the purpose of this book I will include the use of *interlining* in italics and a different font. When following instructions for the Basic Lined Curtain, ignore the *interlining* instructions in italics. In a more advanced curtain project, when *interlining* is included, the complete instructions must be followed, including the additions in italics.

Visual Aid for Constructing a Curtain

From the following diagrams and text make a paper visual aid.

Note: The visual aid is made to include *interlining* a curtain. When making a lined-only curtain, remove the *interlining paper.*

Take three pieces of A4 paper. The long edge of the paper will represent the length of the curtain and the short edge the width.

◆ Mark the first piece 'Face Fabric' and RS (right side) and WS (wrong side).

◆ Mark the second piece 'Lining Fabric' and RS and WS.

◆ *Mark the third piece 'Interlining fabric'.*

   Note: *For the interlined curtain:*

◆ *Place the WS of the face fabric paper against the interlining fabric paper.*

◆ *You will now use those two pieces of paper as one piece.*

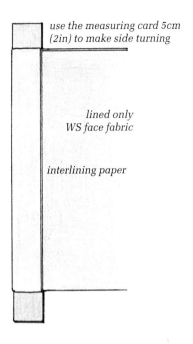

use the measuring card 5cm (2in) to make side turning

lined only WS face fabric

interlining paper

Fig 142 The side turning using the measuring card.

◆ *Place a staple in the top right hand corner of the two sheets of paper.*

The Side Turning (Fig 142)

Place the paper with the WS of the face fabric paper uppermost (*if interlining, interlining uppermost*) with the long edge of the paper on your left (i.e. the length of the curtain). Place the 5cm (2in) cardboard strip onto the paper and align it to the edge. Fold over the card and paper onto the wrong side of the face fabric (*if interlining onto the interlining*) and crease in the fold. This forms the side turning.

The Hem

Use the 7.5cm (3in) card (Fig 143).

Note: a 7.5cm (3in) card is used for a short curtain and a 10cm (4in) card for a full-length curtain.

Place the card at the bottom edges of the paper to form the first fold of the

(Far right) Fig 143 The hem using the measuring card.

hem and align it to the edge. Fold up the paper and the card and crease along the fold line. Leave the card in place and fold up a second turning for the double hem and crease. It is very important that these lines are clear and sharp.

Open out the papers completely (Fig 144).

♦ Turn the first fold of the hem back into position. Fold the bottom left-hand corner of the

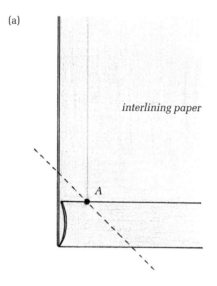

Fig 144 Forming the mitre.

(a)

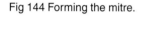

interlining paper

A

papers over at point A (*see* Fig 144a).

This point will be the fold line of the side turning and the raw edge of the single turned hem (*see* Fig 144b). This must be accurate.

Note: Placing the weight in the mitred corner is explained during construction of the curtain (*see* page 158).

Now fold the side turning and the second hem turning back into place (*see* Fig 144c).

(b)

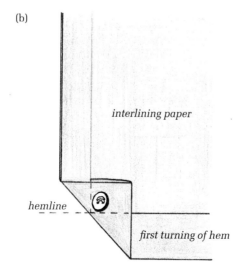

interlining paper

hemline

first turning of hem

(c)

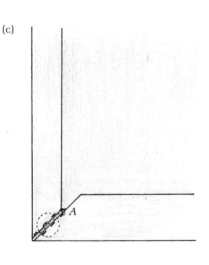

A

You have now formed a mitre at the bottom corner of the curtain. Notice the position of the weight at the corner.

For an interlined curtain only:
Open out the papers still together as one so they are completely flat (Fig 145).

Fold over the corner of the interlining paper to form a triangle to marry up with the side-turning fold line and the first fold line of the hem. Crease in place.

Cut off the triangle of the interlining along this line through (A).

Now cut off the interlining along the fold line of the first fold line of the hem (B).

By trimming away the interlining at these positions it eliminates bulk at the mitred corner and hem line of the curtain.

Refold at the mitre again to its original position, as in Fig 144, making sure it is sharp and even.

The Lining Paper

The cutting length (drop) of the lining fabric for a curtain is cut 7.5cm (3in) shorter than the face fabric.

Remove 7.5cm (3in) from the bottom edge of the lining paper.

Using a 5cm (2in) cardboard strip, fold up 5cm (2in) of double hem as for folding the hem using the face fabric paper.

Note: If making a curtain with a 4in hem make a 3in double hem for the lining and use the 7.5cm (3in) card.

When making the curtain, the hem is machined into place on the lining fabric along the top edge of the fold.

Place the face fabric paper, WS uppermost (Fig 146), on the table (*if interlining – interlining uppermost*). Place the WS of the lining fabric paper against the WS of the face fabric paper (*or interlining*) and staple the papers together at the top right-hand corner. You will notice that the top fold line hem allowance of the lining paper falls on the top fold line of

the hem allowance of the face fabric. This is correct.

You will also notice that the lining drops into place leaving a 2.5cm (1in) margin of face fabric paper below the hemline of the lining paper.

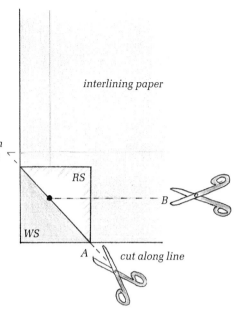

Fig 145 Trimming the interlining from the corner.

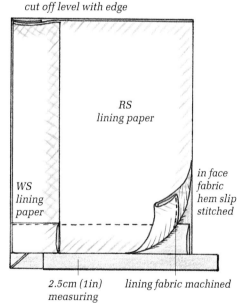

Fig 146 Lining in place.

(Far right) Fig 147 Folding the lining side turning into place.

(Far right) Fig 148 Lining slip-stitched into place. Note the smaller stitches at the corner.

You can align the 2.5cm (1in) cardboard strip along the hem line of the face fabric paper and check that the hem line of the lining fabric paper is even (i.e. the two hemlines are 2.5cm (1in) apart). Let the lining paper fall over the edge of the side turning. You will notice there is extra paper. This will happen when using the curtain lining fabric.

Fold the paper back onto itself and very carefully fold the paper to the finished side edge of the paper and fold in place. Trim off the paper very accurately along this whole line.

Peel back the lining paper and place the 2.5cm (1in) card against the wrong side of the lining fabric paper and crease in the fold line (Fig 147). Let the paper drop back into place over the 5cm (2in) side turning of face fabric. You will notice that it drops into place leaving a 2.5cm (1in) margin of face fabric. This is correct.

At the same time the corner of the lining fabric paper will drop onto the same position on the mitre corner line as the hem lines of the lining fabric paper. This must be correct.

Note: Special care for attaching lining at the corner is explained during the construction of the curtain on page 162.

This visual aid (Fig 148) can now be stored in your file and used when making the curtains and for future reference.

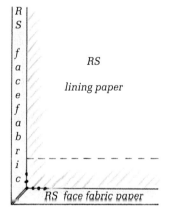

Preparing to Cut Out the Curtains

- Straighten the fabric.

- If using a printed, patterned fabric, check that the pattern is printed straight and if there is a pattern drift, or to what extent. Remember this should be no more than 2.5cm (1in); if the drift is more than this amount, return the fabric to the shop.

- It is essential that if there is a printed pattern on the fabric you must cut the fabric to this pattern line.

- Plain fabrics and woven patterns should be cut to the straight of grain.

The first length (drop) of curtain fabric must now be carefully planned. This is known as the master drop (Fig 149).

When using patterned, checked or a textured pattern fabric the placement of the design on the fabric is important. The hemline of the curtain must be planned.

The complete design should preferably finish at the bottom edge of the curtain after the hem has been turned up. It may be you have to cut a little from the top of the master drop to accommodate the pattern and this is the reason for buying one pattern repeat for every drop.

Use your paper visual aid to help you plan the master drop. Look carefully at the fabric and taking your measurement from your notebook, mark out with pins down the selvedge the first length (i.e. the Master Drop).

1 Place the first pin horizontally through the selvedge 5cm (2in) from the straightened top edge of your fabric. This is the position for the heading.
2 Measure the finished drop. This is the hemline. Check the measurements in your notebook.
   Note: Use coloured, glass headed pins to mark the heading line and hemline so you do not confuse these with the cutting line (use the steel pins).
3 Place a second pin through the selvedge, the hemline.
4 Now mark out the hem turning allowance. Place another pin 7.5cm (3in) below and a second pin 7.5cm (3in) below that. *Note:* If using a 10cm (4in) hem allowance place pins accordingly.

Use your visual aid. Open out your visual aid and check that the pins are in the correct position for the double 7.5cm (3in) hemline. This will establish on your fabric exactly the finished length i.e. the hemline, taking a line across your fabric you can then see exactly where the pattern falls on the hemline. If this is not correct, you will have to move the measurements of the master drop down the fabric until you pick up a pleasing hemline. Once you have established this, recheck all measurements.

Mark out the opposite selvedge in the same order.

Each additional drop of fabric required must now be marked out with pins down the selvedges. It is important that you carefully note where the pattern begins at the top of the master drop and place your first pin in this position in the selvedge.

Mark each drop in the same way as the master drop.

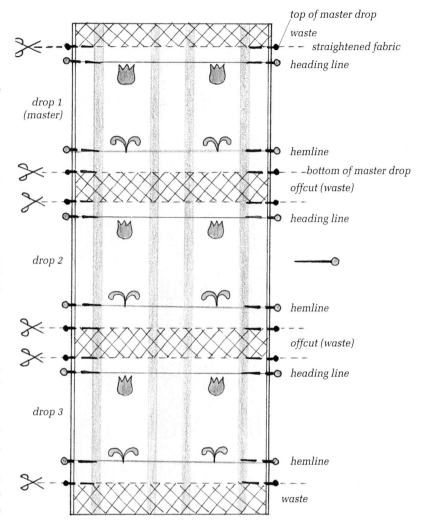

Fig 149 Planning the master drop.

**BEFORE CUTTING
YOUR FABRIC:**

♦ Check each drop matches the master drop.

♦ Check the pins marking down each selvedge.

♦ Re-check all measurements.

The Hemline of the Worked Curtain Project

In planning the hemline for the worked project, bear in mind the size of the room and large pattern on the fabric. To place the large blue motif along the hemline simply brought the eye to a strong block of colour. The overall appearance looked more balanced by using the definite shape of the green leaf pattern as the hemline. Looking ahead to the balance and placement of the pattern along the top heading line would allow the placement of the pattern on the pelmet to look balanced with an even distribution of pattern and colour. It does take a little time to plan this out, but it is time well spent to achieve an overall appearance of your window dressing. You will learn from experience and handling fabric how to make best use of the pattern on your fabric. This planning was first shown in the basic square cushion, where we were able to create two quite different cushions with a completely different design and colour impact. You are doing the same with your curtain planning but on a much bigger scale, by planning the lines before cutting the fabric.

Cutting Out Face Fabric

When cutting out, the most important pieces of equipment are your scissors. Now we are cutting out larger lengths of fabric it is essential that the scissors are really sharp and that you take full advantage of the long blades, and that the scissors are correctly held with the broad blade on top of the fabric and the pointed blade lifting the fabric from underneath. Holding the fabric flat with your left hand, let the scissors do the work and use the whole blade with long, even cuts. For those students who are left handed, special left-handed scissors can be used accordingly (Fig 150).

♦ Using the full length of the table, turn the fabric to allow both selvedges to lie on the table. Using a soft HB pencil and a metre stick join up the line of markings across the master drop of fabric, selvedge to selvedge. Cut along the line using the full blade of your scissors, using long, even cuts. Cut the master drop first and continue cutting each drop in the same way using the master drop to check the accuracy. This is particularly important when using a patterned fabric ensuring the pattern will match up on each joined width.

♦ It is very important that the top of each drop of fabric is marked and numbered as each drop is cut. Clip a small diagonal piece of fabric from the right side of your fabric at the top left-hand corner and pencil on to the selvedge the number (i.e. drop 1, 2 and 3, etc). If using a patterned fabric the offcuts must be marked and numbered in the same way. These offcuts will automatically

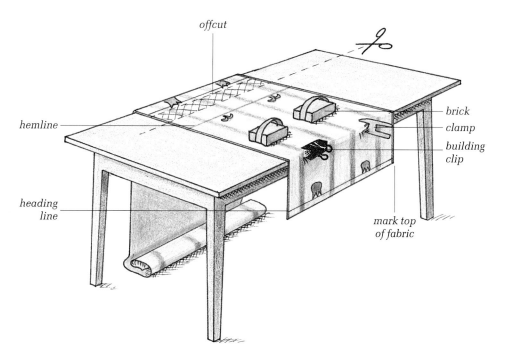

offcut

hemline

heading line

brick

clamp

building clip

mark top of fabric

Fig 150 Cutting lengths of curtain face fabric.

pattern match and depending on the amount of excess fabric, can often be utilized for valances or tie-backs.

The next important consideration is the storage of your fabric. Having already prepared your fabrics and, if necessary, ironed at every stage of the construction of your curtain, you must look after it. If not using the fabric immediately, place all the lengths evenly on top of one another and re-roll them evenly back on to the cardboard roll. If intending to cut out and immediately begin the construction of your curtain, fold the length of fabric off-centre down its length and then make a second fold. These lengths should be left entirely flat if you have the space, or the cardboard roll placed along the width fold and the length of fabric folded in half. Another option is to hang the lengths over a banister rail. It really depends on the space available. At no time must the fabric be folded or indented across its width.

Lining Fabric

The lining fabric is cut 7.5cm (3in) shorter than the face fabric regardless of the depth of hem to be used. Manufacturers fold lining fabric down its centre line with the right sides of the lining fabric to the outside. For this reason the fabric can be cut double. It is essential that you first straighten the lining fabric by aligning the selvedges along the long length of the table and squaring it off along the short edge of the table and making and cutting to the straight weft grain. Each drop can now be measured, pinned out and marked down the length of the fabric. There is obviously no pattern match.

◆ Cut each drop double and mark and number each drop as for the face fabric.

◆ Mark and cut each drop accordingly.

◆ Lining fabric is the only curtain fabric that should be cut double.

Cutting Interlining Fabric

The interlining is cut the same cutting length as the face fabric.

Note: Although less interlining fabric is needed, we do find when interlining curtains for the first time that it is more accurate to work with the interlining cut to the same length as the master drop face fabric, the intention being to use the face fabric and interlining as one while constructing the curtain. In time, when you become more experienced in working with the interlining fabric and understand that the interlining is trimmed away to avoid bulk in the hems and headings, the relevant amount can be deducted from these measurements and the estimation of fabric adjusted accordingly.

The cotton interlining is soft and loses its shape, especially bump. You will also find the loose fluff from the surface of the domette, and even more so the bump, will rub off onto your clothing. Do protect yourself, in particular if wearing dark colours.

Fig 151 Preparing the weight.

The man-made or mixed interlinings do not give as much or deposit the same amount of fluff but there still remains a limited amount.

Preparing to Construct the Curtain

Once all the fabric lengths are cut and carefully stored the next stage is the construction of the curtain. Before beginning the work there are more considerations and preparations to be made.

Lead Weights and Cord Bags

Before beginning the construction of your curtains, prepare lead weights and cord bags. *See* the following instructions.

THE LEAD WEIGHT (Fig 151)

This is used to weight the mitred corners and hemlines of a curtain. The round, flat, lead penny 2.5cm (1in) is the most useful size. Allow one for each corner and one at the base of every seam line on a lined only curtain or interlined curtain.

There are a number of ways of covering lead weights and these weights are available as rectangles, round or the round weight with two holes in the centre like a button. The latter we find very successful. The weights should not sit immediately on the hemline or the corner of the mitre, as they pull the curtain out of shape. It is for this reason that by using the button style the weight can be hand stitched accurately into place. The lead weights should be covered with lining fabric. There are a number of ways of doing this. One successful way is to cut a card 20cm × 6cm (8in × 2½in). Use this to cut the lining fabric, then follow Fig 151.

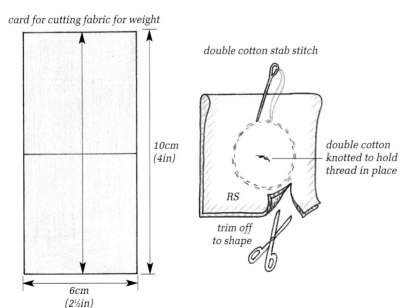

card for cutting fabric for weight

10cm (4in)

6cm (2½in)

double cotton stab stitch

double cotton knotted to hold thread in place

RS

trim off to shape

THE CORD BAG

These small bags allow the cords of a commercial heading tape to be neatly stored at the back edge of the curtain once the heading tape is drawn up. Allow one for each curtain or for a valance, one at each end. Follow Fig 152.

The Selvedge

The question is so often asked, 'Do you leave or remove the selvedges?' This really entirely depends on the fabric you are working with.

Face Fabric

If the fabric frays badly, the selvedge should preferably not be cut off, and some fabrics are woven with a particularly tight selvedge. In both these cases, slash through the selvedges at regular intervals of about 5cm (2in) with evenly spaced short cuts and allow the scissors to face towards the top of the fabric on the diagonal. This means when the curtain is hung, the slash will find its natural place and will lie flat falling towards the bottom edge of the curtain. If the fabric is very light coloured and any markings on the selvedges might show through once the curtain is hung against the light, the selvedges must be removed.

If working with a patterned fabric no selvedge should ever be removed before the pattern match is made and the seam machined

* The selvedges on the lining fabric are not removed or slashed.

* *The selvedges on the interlining fabric are not removed or slashed.*

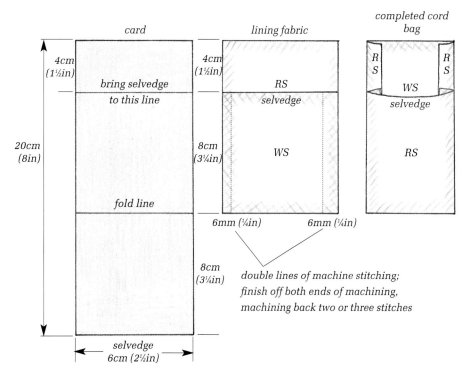

Fig 152 Making the cord bag.

Joining up the Lengths of Fabric

Assemble the fabric. It is important to remember that all half-widths of fabric must be added to the back edge of the curtain and the lead edge must have a full drop. Check each curtain. Any half drops must now be cut in half. To cut half drops, fold the fabric in half lengthways and let the broad blade of the scissors lie inside the fold. Holding the fabric in place with your left hand, slightly pull the blade against the fold line while cutting with long, even cuts. This will give you a sharp and even cut edge. Left-handed students adjust as necessary.

In general a flat seam is used in soft furnishings. When making curtains, the flat seam needs a seam allowance of 2cm (¾in) and no stitching is seen from the right side of the curtain. Less often a French seam is used when using sheer transparent fabrics and, in some cases, silk fabric.

Flat Seam (Sometimes Called Plain Seam)

This is the seam that is most often used when making soft furnishings. When making curtains a seam allowance of 2cm (¾in) is used for the flat seams, although if pattern matching, you may find you need to take a wider allowance to accommodate the pattern match. This is then cut back to 2cm (¾in) after the seam line has been machined or if using a heavier fabric such as velvet, you may need a slightly wider seam allowance and the selvedges should be left on (Fig 153).

Fig 153 Flat seam (a), and finishing the seam edges using a zigzag attachment (b).

French Seam

There will be occasions when a *French seam* is used on sheer, transparent and lightweight fabrics. This narrow, double hem neatly contains all raw edges, which is self-neatening. A French seam can only be worked on a straight edge. It gives a neat finish with no stitching showing on the right side of the fabric:

1 With the wrong sides of the fabric facing, tack the edges together along a seam line with a 2cm (¾in) seam allowance (Fig 154a).

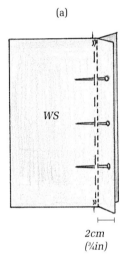

(a)

WS

2cm
(¾in)

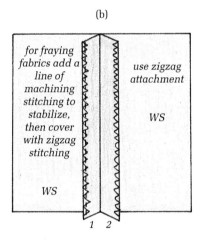

(b)

for fraying fabrics add a line of machining stitching to stabilize, then cover with zigzag stitching

WS

use zigzag attachment

WS

WS

1 2

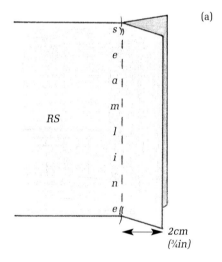

(a)

s
e
a
m
l
i
n
e

RS

2cm
(¾in)

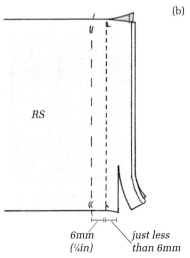

(b)

RS

6mm
(¼in)

just less than 6mm

1 With the right sides of the fabric facing and the edges level, pin the two layers together, placing the pins horizontally at right angles to the edges down the seam line.
2 Tack the length of the seam line 2cm (¾in) from the edge.
3 Machine a straight line of stitching immediately beside the tacking line, not over it. Use your reverse stitch at the beginning and end to secure the machining. With experience, you should be able to machine over the horizontal pins, thus eliminating the tacking line.

(Far right) Fig 154 French seam (a & b).

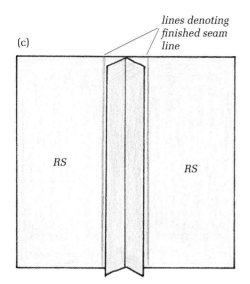

(c)

lines denoting finished seam line

RS

RS

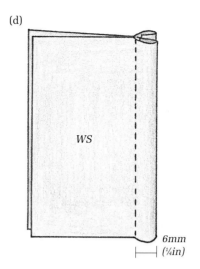

(d)

WS

6mm
(¼in)

Fig 154 French seam (c & d).

2 Machine a line of stitching 6mm (¼in) parallel to the tacked seam line (Fig 154b).

3 Trim off the selvedges or raw edges outside the line of machining to just less than 6mm (¼in).

4 Remove tacking stitches.

5 Press open the trimmed seam allowance (Fig 154c) with a firm fabric finger press or use the toe of the iron – test the heat of the iron particularly if you are working with a man-made or mixed fabric. This will give a neat finish to the seam.

6 Fold the seam back onto itself, creasing sharply along the pressed first line of stitching so that the right sides of the fabric come together and the seam line lies flat, and tack through all the layers.

7 Machine a second seam 6mm (¼in) *away* from the folded edge, enclosing the raw edges (Fig 154d).

8 Remove tackings, press the length of the seam, then press it flat onto the wrong side of the flat fabric.

Machining Widths Together

It is important when machining curtain lengths together, that the stitch on your machine is correct and that the fabric is not held too tight as this can cause the fabric to pull and pucker and the curtain will hang badly. A blunt needle will have the same effect. A longer machine stitch must be used and use a new machine needle. Use a scrap of matching fabric and check the correct stitch. Adjust the stitch length to 3½–4. Use matching thread and use a number 90/14 machine needle.

Make sure you have matching reel and bobbin threads for both face fabric and lining fabric and fill a bobbin for each and ensure the thread is applicable to natural or man-made fabric.

Equally important is that the lines of machining should be straight and exactly parallel to the edge of the fabric. If you are unsure of your machining as a beginner, and there are no marking lines on the plate of your machine, place a piece of freezer tape across the width of your machine plate. Carefully check the measurement from the position of the needle in its down position to the width of the seam 2cm (¾in) and use this as a guide until you gain confidence in machining in straight lines.

Take care to finish off both ends of machining.

Another question so often asked is the difference between ironing and pressing.

To iron really means smoothing the flat plate of the iron backwards and forwards over your fabric.

Pressing is more about understanding your iron and using it to advantage, and more to the lifting up and down of the iron applying the appropriate amount of pressure. You can use the full plate of the iron or the toe (front) or the heel (back edge) to enable you to eliminate over pressing and marking through tacking stitches or hemlines onto the right side of the fabric and to ensure clear, sharp, seam lines.

Throughout the construction of the curtain each stage of the work must be carefully ironed or pressed as appropriate. For the final finished curtain, little or no ironing should be necessary. Only the main body of the curtain may need to be ironed to give it that crisp, finished look. Care should be taken not to over press hems, turnings and stitches or you will mark these lines through onto your finished curtain.

Test the heat of the iron on a scrap of fabric and adjust the iron to the correct setting. Take particular care when using man-made fabrics as many of these fabrics do not tolerate great heat; some fabrics can melt under heat, in addition to causing problems in marking the plate of the iron.

PRESSING A FLAT SEAM

Remove any pins or tackings and leave the seam turnings in the same position with their right sides together and facing. Press and iron the whole length of the seam to bed in the machine stitches.

◆ Lay the fabric wrong side uppermost on the table and open out the seam and run

the toe of the iron down the seam line to sharpen the line. Then use the flat sole of the iron to give a final iron.

Some heavier fabrics can indent the edges of the seam allowance through to the right side of the curtain, therefore care should be taken not to over press. Should you mark the fabric, lift the seam allowance and re-iron the single layer of curtain fabric along the mark to remove the line. To avoid the same problem you can run a piece of brown paper under the seam turning and press the seam open over the seam allowance and paper.

The Lining

A flat seam is used to join the lining fabric using the same seam allowance of 2cm (¾in).

When placing the right sides of the fabric together check that you have the shinier side of the lining fabric facing; this is the right side and it is sometimes difficult to see the difference between right sides and wrong. Place it over the back of your hand and hold it up to the light. You will be able to see the difference more clearly. No selvedges are cut off the lining fabric. The lining fabric is bought in the same widths of fabric as the face fabric and the seam lines on the two fabrics should lie on top of one another. This is particularly important in lined-only curtains. This avoids too many joined lines hanging against the light when the curtain is in place.

There may be occasions when you have to slightly adjust the width of the lining fabric seam allowance to match the face fabric seam allowance. This can happen if perhaps you have to cut away more of the face fabric selvedge to remove the markings of a light coloured fabric or perhaps the width of the face fabric is a more unusual width. This should be checked when joining curtains of two and a half widths or more.

The Seam Line

1 Pin, tack and machine, using matching thread, the widths of lining together using a 2cm (¾in) seam allowance. Make sure you place any half widths to the back edge of both curtains to marry up with the face fabric.
2 Removed tackings and iron and press the flat seam open, as for the face fabric.
3 The hem turning is now made on the lining fabric.

The hem on the lining fabric is made 2.5cm (1in) less in depth to the face fabric. Use a 5cm (2in) measuring card if working a 7.5cm (3in) hem on the face fabric and a 7.5cm (3in) measuring card if working a 10cm (4in) hem.

Use the visual aid and visual aid diagrams to make the double hem.

Tack in place. Once you become more practised, it is sufficient to hold the hem in place with vertical pins and carefully machine over the pins with the wrong side of the lining fabric uppermost. Machine a line of stitching very close to the top edge of the top of the first fold of the hem, along the whole width of lining.
  Remove tacking. Iron and set aside.

If interlining, an overlapped seam is used to join interlining.

FACE FABRIC

If the material you are using is patterned you must now pattern match. The professional curtain maker can do this without tacking, but as a home curtain maker, and to ensure accurate machining, it is better to tack your fabric in place using slip-tacking stitch (*see* diagram of Slip Tacking, page 65).

After slip tacking, the lengths of fabric can be folded with the right sides together and machined on the tacking line. If pattern matching it is important you do not trim off any selvedge until after you have machined the drops together. Use a 2cm (¾in) card to trim off seams when the machining is complete.

If interlining the seam lines of each of the face fabrics, lining and interlining should lie on top of one another.

ORDER OF WORK FOR MAKING A BASIC LINED CURTAIN (CHECKLIST)

◆ Assemble all necessary equipment.

◆ Notebook with all planning and measurements.

◆ Position the table centrally so that it is easy to work from both long sides.

◆ Preparing to cut out.

◆ Check fabric for flaws.

◆ Straighten fabric and check for pattern drift.

◆ Plan master drop – if using a patterned fabric establish pattern placement.

◆ Mark out each drop – recheck all measurements.

◆ Cut lengths (drops) of face fabric.

◆ Mark top of each drop.

- Store drops carefully – set aside.

- Cut drops of lining fabric – set aside.

- *If using interlining, cut drops of interlining fabric (domette or bump).*

- Cover necessary weight.

- Make bags for cords.

- Using 2cm (¾in) flat seam, tack and join widths of face fabric.

- Pattern match if necessary. Do not cut off selvedges until the pattern match is complete.

- Set aside and store carefully.

- Tack and join width of lining fabric using a 2cm (¾in) flat seam.

- Set aside and store carefully.

- *If interlining, tack and join width of interlining fabric using a 2cm (¾in) overlapped seam.*

- Check machine stitch on a scrap of face fabric. Use a new size 14 (90) machine needle.

- Machine face fabric.

- Machine lining fabric.

- *If interlining, machine interlining using a zigzag stitch.*

- Trim back seams on face fabric. If necessary, and after pattern matching, trim seam back to 2cm (¾in). Use your 2cm (¾in) measuring card for accuracy.

- Do not remove selvedge from lining fabric.

- *If interlining, set aside interlining.*

- Press seams of face and lining fabrics.

- Remove all tacking stitches. With the seams still in the machining position and right sides together, press using the flat sole of the iron to embed all the stitches.

- Open out the seam and using the toe of the iron, press along the seam line.

- Finally, press the seam in this position but lightly with the sole of the iron so as not to imprint the edges of the seams through to the right side of the fabric.

- Store all lengths of fabric carefully to avoid creasing.

It is now time to begin the construction of your curtains. The following order of work is applicable to the worked, sample visual aid or for those who are starting to make their own curtains immediately.

Beginners, until you gain more self confidence and skills, the taking of extra care in tacking and a strict order of work will considerably speed up the work and result in a well-made curtain. Once you become familiar with this construction you will be able to replace some of the tacking with pinning.

Order of Work

- Machine face fabric using a flat seam and if necessary pattern match.

◆ Machine lining fabric. Do not remove selvedge from lining fabric

◆ *Machine interlining using a zigzag stitch.*

◆ *Set aside interlining.*

◆ Press to embed seams on face fabric and lining fabric.

◆ Press all seams open.

◆ Carefully fold lining fabric and set aside.

Follow the instructions for the basic lined curtain. Use the visual aid and visual aid diagrams to make the double hem.

◆ Place the prepared face fabric on the table wrong side uppermost with the length of the fabric running down the length of the table.

Obviously, when working with the small sample curtain this may sound unnecessary, but it is important that you follow a routine when making curtains as this does save a lot of time.

Lockstitching

If interlining, the interlining must first be locked to the face fabric with a lockstitch. These are long, loose stitches, which help the two fabrics to hang as one in the fold lines of the curtain as they hang from the curtain rail or pole. At the same time they stabilize the two fabrics enabling you to work the next stages of the curtain as if one fabric.

NUMBER OF LOCKSTITCHES

It will be necessary to use lockstitching a second time when the cotton sateen lining fabric is worked into the curtain. Additional lines of lockstitching are used when locking the interlining to the face fabric. This is because of the bulk and weight of the interlining.

Fig 155 Denoting the lines of lockstitching for interlining fabric and lining fabric.

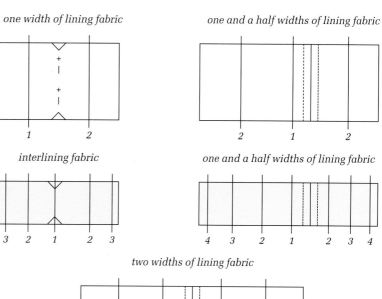

one width of lining fabric

interlining fabric

one and a half widths of lining fabric

one and a half widths of lining fabric

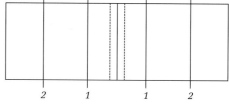

two widths of lining fabric

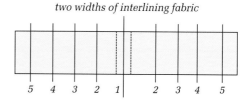

two widths of interlining fabric

If interlining (Fig 156 overleaf):

◆ *Find the centre of the face fabric by folding in half, lengthways. Clip a V on the fold line at the top and*

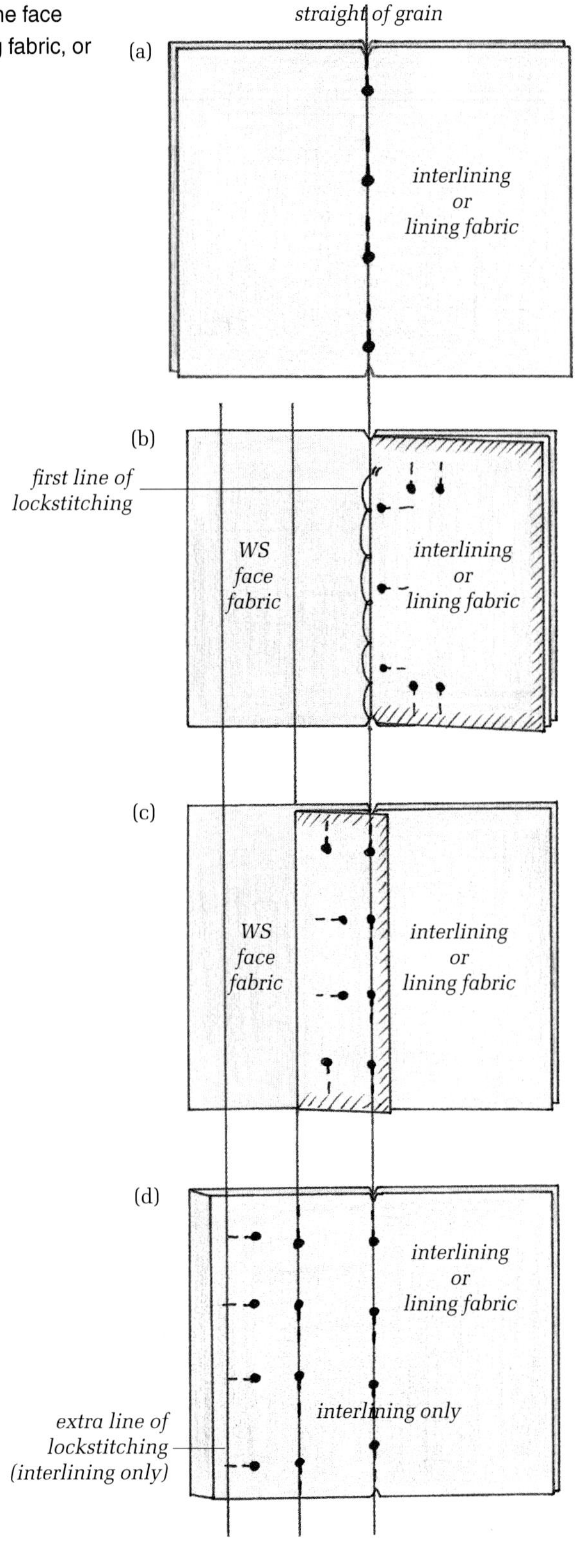

Fig 156 Preparing the face
fabric and interlining fabric, or
lining fabric.

bottom edges of the curtain (see *Fig
156a*).

♦ *Repeat on the interlining fabric.*

♦ *Place the face fabric WS uppermost
onto the table, the selvedge running
the length of the table.*

♦ *Place the interlining on top of the
face fabric.*
   Note: *If using a man-made
interlining place the fluffy side of the
interlining against the wrong side of
the face fabric. Match the notches
top and bottom and pin in place with
the pins in the vertical position. It is
very important that this first line
should lie on the straight of grain of
both fabrics.*

*The following test is applicable to all
lockstitching:*
Smooth the interlining/lining up to the
top and down to the bottom edges with
the flat of your hands to ensure the correct position and add a minimum number of extra pins down this straight grain
line. If this is not correct you will
destroy the hang of the curtain and the
fabric will twist.

Fold the interlining/lining (*see* Fig
156b) over onto itself along this pinned
line making sure it is correct and that the
fold lies even at the top and bottom edges
of the curtain. This must be accurate.
Place pins through all layers on a horizontal position away from a folded edge.

The correct placing of the pins is very
important when lockstitching. Once
again, minimal pins are used but correctly placed following a planned order.
With practice this will become an auto-
matic routine and will save considerable
time, while ensuring the interlining/lin-
ing lies in place on the curtain, straight
and even.

You are moving, smoothing and pinning the fabric towards the side edge of the curtain, and placing pins in a horizontal position, at the same time smoothing the fabric up towards the top edge and down towards the bottom edge, placing pins in a vertical position. Note that the pins follow the directions of the smoothing actions.

First Line of Lockstitching for Interlining or Lining Fabrics

Thread a straw or darning needle with a single thread matching the face fabric (Fig 157). The length of the thread should be about one and a half times the length of the curtain. This unusual length of thread is necessary, as the thread must not be joined when making these long, loose stitches. Thread the needle straight from the reel, by doing this it is less likely to knot.

Begin stitching 20cm (8in) from the top of the curtain if lining only.

If interlining, begin stitching 30cm (12in) from the top of the curtain.

Finish all lockstitching 20cm (8in) from the bottom edge.

Attach the thread to the *interlining* or lining fabric with a small double backstitch leaving a long end of thread. Take the first stitch down through the lining/*interlining* with the needle in a horizontal position and pick up a single thread of face fabric keeping the thread under the needle. Do not pull this stitch too tight or you will indent the right side of the fabric. It is essential that the stitches do not pull or show from the right side of your curtains. Let the thread fall over the back of your left hand, this will ensure you do not pull the stitch too tight and do be careful you do not catch any rings on your fingers.

Make the next lockstitch and carefully

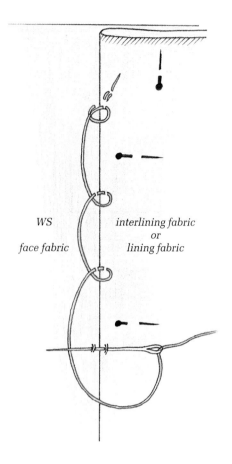

WS

face fabric

*interlining fabric
or
lining fabric*

Fig 157 Lockstitch.

remove your hand leaving a loose loop of thread. Continue the lockstitching to the hem edge of your curtain stopping short of the bottom raw edges by 20cm (8in). Backstitch off on the *interlining*/lining fabric and leave a long end – this end will fall into the hem.

Note: If lining curtains, the lockstitching is not used until later in the construction of the curtain. But the following order of work will then be applicable for both lined and interlined curtains when the linings are put into the curtains.

(a) Let the *interlining*/lining fall back into place over the face fabric and place a minimal number of pins down the line of lockstitching through both layers. This will stabilize the stitches while moving on to the next line of lockstitching (*see* Fig 156).

(b) Continue smoothing and moving the *interlining*/lining fabric to the top, bottom and side edge following the same direction with your pins.

(c) After 40cm (16in), once again fold the *interlining*/lining back on to itself and pin in place with horizontal pins as before. This fold line should be parallel to the first line of lockstitching. Check that this is correct by measuring the 40cm (16in) to this centre line. Repeat the line of lockstitching. Continue folding, pinning and lockstitching the necessary lines of lockstitching.

(d) *When interlining a curtain you must add an extra line of lockstitching 15cm (6in) from the raw, side edges of the fabrics. This strengthens and holds the two fabrics together to ensure accuracy when making the side turning of the curtains.*

Continue order of work for the basic lined curtain, following text in italics if interlining the curtain. *Include interlining visual aid paper when interlining.*

Use the visual aid and visual aid diagrams throughout.

1 *If interlining, place the prepared face fabric with the locked-in interlining and face fabric now as one piece of fabric, continue the order of work.*

2 Side Turnings. *Side 1*. Left-hand side wrong side uppermost, using your 5cm (2in) measuring card.

3 With the ironing pad placed under the fabric and the iron on the extension lead.

4 Place the edge of the 5cm (2in) card to the raw edge (*if interlining, the two raw edges of the face fabric and interlining will be lying on top of each other*) and fold both card and fabric over onto the wrong side of the face fabric (*if interlining, the interlining*).

5 Press along this fold, moving the card and ironing pad down the length of the fabric and repeat where necessary. Take care where you put the iron and turn it off. The pressed turning should be sharp and it should not be necessary to pin in place.

6 Tack in place. Tack top to bottom but finish 25cm (10in) from bottom edge. When tacking curtains a slightly different tacking stitch is used, by using the conventional tacking stitch for two stitches then a long tacking stitch before the next. This speeds up the tacking considerably on the long stretches of turnings and hems.

Use a back stitch to start and finish your tacking, making sure you leave long ends at both the beginning and end. It is sometimes necessary to loosen some of the tacking stitches while still maintaining continuity in other areas. By leaving these long ends on the backstitch it is easy to remove, allowing you to keep the long piece of thread complete for replacing any necessary tacking after completion of this stage of work. It sounds unnecessary, but in the end it does save time.

The tacking on the side turning is worked along the centre of the 5cm (2in) turning. This is because the stitching used to secure the side turnings can easily be broken when removing the tackings, in particular with Serge Stitch, which is used to secure lined-only curtains, where only a single thread of face fabric should be picked up or the stitches would show on the right side of the curtain.

The raw edge of the turning is now serged to the face fabric (Fig 158). Once again, stop short of the 20cm (8in) at the base. Back-stitch off on the right side of the face fabric turning and leave a long end. These stitches will be completed once the hem is in place.

For the interlined curtain, it is necessary to take a larger stitch to secure the interlining (Fig 159). As the interlining lies between the face fabric and the right side

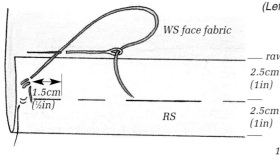

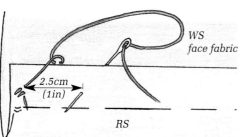

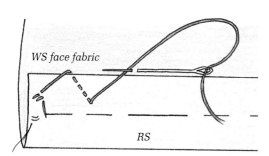

(Left) Fig 158 Serge stitch, used for lined-only curtains.

(Below) Fig 159 Herringbone stitch, used for interlined curtains.

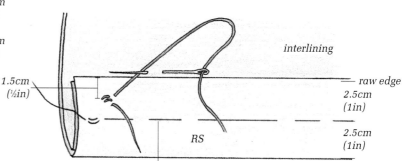

tacking stitch down the middle

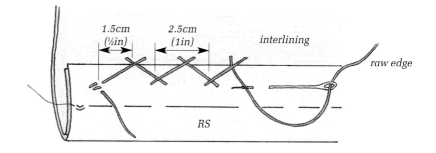

Fig 160 Rolling the curtain to its new position for side 2.

of the curtain, the larger stitch (i.e. herringbone) makes the interlining, which is a heavier fabric, more secure.

Begin your herringbone stitch 30cm (12in) from the top and finish 20cm (8in) from the base. The reason you leave 30cm (12in) at the top is because, when making interlined curtains, the fabric will have to be opened out to work the hand heading.

Roll the completed edge onto itself (Fig 160), onto the table and roll the fabric over the table until the opposite side of the curtain raw edge lies along the opposite edge of the table. Go round to the other long side of the table and with the curtain in position, follow Order of Work as for Side 1.

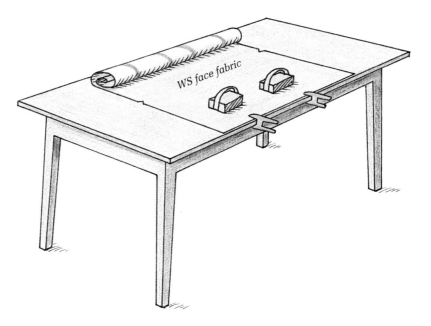

Making the Hem (Fig 161)

Use the visual aid for making the hem (see pages 139–40).

Carefully turn the curtain with the hemline running along the long edge of the table. Clamp or weight in position to ensure it is even. Then move the clamps or bricks to the other side of the table and secure fabric in position.

Use a 7.5cm (3in) measuring card (*note:* 10cm (4in) if a long, full-length curtain).

If interlining, use interlining and face fabric as one.

Align the measuring card along the raw bottom edge of the curtain. Fold up the hem allowance.

1 Press in place.
2 With the card still in place, fold the fabric once again to make a double fabric hem.

This must be accurate and sharp, particularly at the corners. Making this

Fig 161 Curtain in position for making the hem.

double fabric hem may seem a little extravagant but it does result in a heavier hemline and the extra weight makes the curtain hang really well.

3 Move the card along the hem.

If interlining, peel back the face fabric to the first turning line (see Fig 145).

Trim off the interlining along this line. This is to eliminate some of the bulk of the interlining.

Fold the hem back into place.

Pin or tack the hem into place leaving 20cm (8in) free at each side.

Mitring a Corner

Use the visual aid for mitring the corner (see pages 140–1).

The correct placing of the weight is important. Do not place it at the very base of the mitre for two reasons:

◆ A weight too near to the point can result in pulling the curtain corner down.

◆ When stitching the mitre in place it is difficult to get a neat finish at the base point if the stitches are restricted by the thickness of the weight.

◆ Stitch the weight onto the front face of the loose piece of curtain fabric formed by the mitre. Set it slightly up from the corner point.

◆ *If interlining, place weight underneath the loose piece of face fabric formed by the mitre. This is because the underside is padded against the face fabric by the interlining.*

Ladder stitch mitre. The ladder stitch is worked from the top of the mitre down to

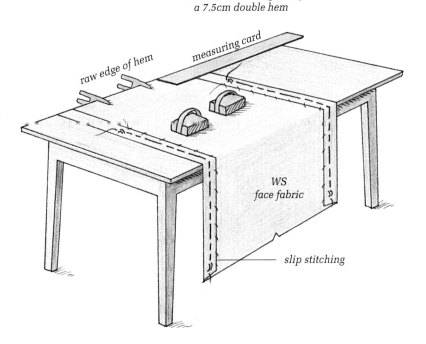

7.5cm (3in) measuring card for
a 7.5cm double hem

raw edge of hem

measuring card

WS
face fabric

slip stitching

the point of the mitre. This is important as it means fastening on your thread can be larger and firm and will be hidden once the lining fabric is in place. The point of the mitre will be neat.

◆ Begin your double backstitch at point A (*see* Visual Aid). Use a small ladder stitch, along the folded crease lines of the mitre. Do not pull the stitch too tight or you will pucker the fabric.

◆ Bring the last stitch out of the fold exactly at the point of the mitre. Very gently ease your thread, pulling it along the fold line of the mitre to even out the ladder stitches. Then run the needle back along one folded edge behind the stitches, making sure you do not go through to the right side of the curtain, towards the top of the mitre and backstitch off with a small stitch. This stitch will be hidden by the lining fabric.

◆ Complete the tacking on the side turning of the curtain and complete the serge stitching (*if interlined, use herringbone stitch*) down to the top of the mitre – finish off ends carefully. The mitre and side turning are now complete.

Go to the other side. Repeat the procedure at the second corner and side.

Stitching the Hem in Place

You might find it easier to place a minimal number of vertical pins into the already pressed in hem turning if you have a wide curtain.

◆ Tack the hem into place through all layers using the curtain tacking

stitch, placing the line of tacking just off the edge of the fold line to be stitched. This must be held in place accurately and if you tack down the centre of the hem turning, the edge will not be held in place correctly. This sounds fussy again, but in the end it is time saving.

◆ Remember, we are not professionals and with practice you may cut back on some of your tacking, and replace with vertical pins but, while you are learning, it does add up to accuracy and a rewarding end-piece of work.

The hem is stitched into place by hand using a slip hemming.

Slip Hemming (Fig 162)

Slip hemming is used to hold the hem invisibly in place. The stitch should not be pulled too tight or it will indent the hem on to the right side of the curtain. Fastening threads on and off when hand sewing must be neat and secure. It is not a good idea to use a very long thread about (50cm or 18in is long enough) or it knots and breaks. Thread from the reel cutting your thread at an angle.

Fold back the top of the hem edge and begin by slipping your needle inside the fold about 2.5cm (1in) from the starting point and fasten the thread to the underside with two small backstitches leaving a long end on your thread. This end must be snipped off later. The diagonal fold line above the top of the mitre must be left loose, if this is stitched you will indent the line on to the right side of your curtain.

Working from right to left (if right handed) slip the needle between the fold of the hem edge bringing it out at the corner. Pick up one thread close to the folded edge and take a tiny stitch catching the flat fabric, then slip the needle through the folded edge as close as possible to this first small stitch and bring it out about 6mm (¼in) to the left. Make these stitches in one movement pulling the thread through the stitches firmly, but not too tight, or again you will indent the fold line of the hem onto the right side of the curtain. Repeat the stitches, alternately between the flat fabric and fold of the hem, all the way along to the opposite end of the hem. The thread must be securely fastened off underneath the hem edge and the end of the thread run thorough the fold line. Slip the needle along through the fold 2.5cm (1in) and fasten off with a small double backstitch on the edge of the fold and run off the thread through the fold. This end will be snipped off later.

◆ Remove the tacking stitches and press the hemline again. Take care not to over press the line of stitching or the weight or you will indent these on to the face fabric.

Fig 162 Slip hemming.

Lining the Curtain

Use the visual aid for lining the curtain (see pages 141–42).

If interlining, the lining is put into the interlined curtain in exactly the same method as for lined-only curtains.

Follow all lining instructions.

Turn the curtain to run the length of the table with the face fabric *wrong* side uppermost (*if interlining, interlining uppermost*).

1 Fold the face fabric in half (*if interlined, face fabric and interlining as one*) lengthways and mark the centre of the curtain at the top edge with a clipped V and mark the bottom of the completed hemline with a vertical pin 1 (Fig 163).
2 Repeat these markings on the lining fabric.
3 Place the lining fabric with the *right* side uppermost on top of the face fabric with the wrong sides facing (*if inter-

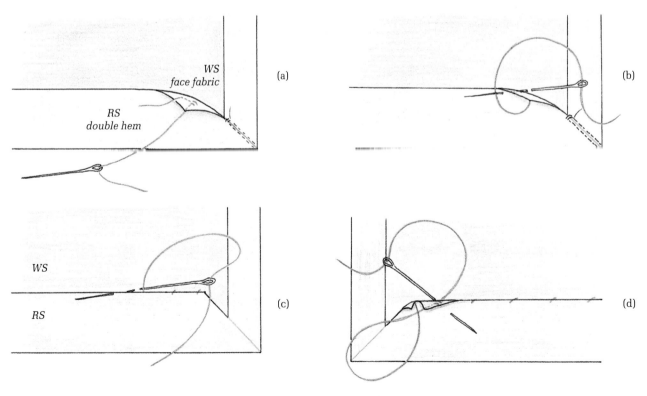

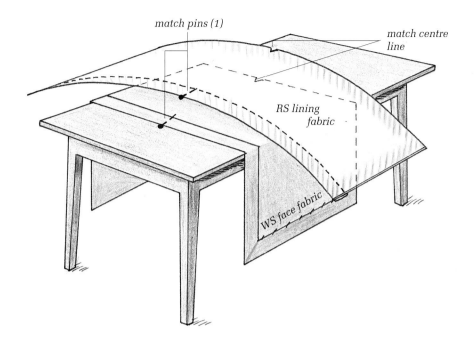

match pins (1)

match centre line

RS lining fabric

WS face fabric

Fig 163 Placing the lining into place on the face fabric.

lining, onto the interlining).

4 Place the hemline of the lining 2.5cm (1in) above the face fabric hemline, at the centre point and position of the pins. The pins will lie in a vertical line with the lining pin above the face fabric pin. If this is correct the line of machining on the lining fabric will lie over the line of slipstitching on the curtain. You can check this is even by using your 2.5cm (1in) measuring card.

5 Pin in place down the centre straight of grain line of the lining fabric and curtain.

6 Smooth out the lining fabric towards the top of the curtain and match the two clipped Vs of the face fabric and lining. This must be flat and even. Pin through both layers of fabric (*if interlined all layers*) up this vertical line from hem to heading. The lining is now attached to the face fabric (*if interlining, to the interlining*) by lines of lockstitching (*see* page 153).

Note: Follow the diagrams for lockstitching and order of work on pages 153–4.

Use your 2.5cm (1in) marker card at all times along the hemline to ensure the hemline of the lining falls exactly 2.5cm (1in) from the bottom of the curtain hem. Particular care must be taken at the corner.

To Complete the Lining at the Side Turning of the Curtain

Use the paper visual aid and Figs on page 141–2.

1 Let the lining fall into place over the curtain fabric with the lock stitching in place. Stabilize this position by putting pins through all thicknesses of fabric 15cm (6in) from the finished side edge of the curtain fabric.

2 Smooth out the lining fabric towards the edge of the finished, side turning of the curtain and pin in place with horizontal pins.

3 Turn back the lining fabric onto itself and iron a sharp line to finish exactly at the edge of the curtain turning outside edge.

4 Cut off the excess lining fabric. Do take care you do not catch the edge of the curtain with the scissors.

5 Peel back the lining from the curtain and align the 2.5cm (1in) measuring card to the wrong side edge of the lining fabric. Fold lining fabric and card over and press in a sharp line.

6 Remove the card and let the ironed-in edge turning of the lining fabric drop into place on to the completed side turning of the side curtain. If this is correct, it will drop into place exactly on the diagonal line of the mitred corner and leave a 2.5cm (1in) border of face fabric along the hem and side turning.

7 Pin and tack into place.

8 This side is now completed by slip stitching the lining to the curtain. Care must be taken at the corner.

SPECIAL CARE ATTACHING LINING TO THE CORNER (Fig 164)

◆ At the corner make three small stitches; the corner stitch must be spot on.

◆ Complete the slip stitching, remove the tacking and press the finished work.

Roll the curtain with the completed side turning to position the other side turning along the opposite long edge of the table. Walk round to the other side of the table and repeat the order of work.

Measuring the Finished Length (Drop) of your Curtain

To stabilize your fabric and hold the lock stitching in place while the finished length of the curtain is marked and the chosen heading worked, a stabilizing line of tacking is put across the whole width of curtain.

For lined curtains this is one hand span from the top edge (about 20cm or 8in).

For interlined curtains this is 30cm (12in) from the top edge.

◆ Turn the curtain to have the top edge of the curtain running down the long edge of the table (Fig 165).

◆ Run a line of curtain tacking stitch along the whole width of the curtain, commencing and finishing with a backstitch, leaving long

Fig 164 Slip stitching the lining with special care at the corner.

(a)

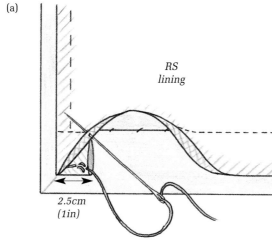

RS lining

2.5cm
(1in)

(b)

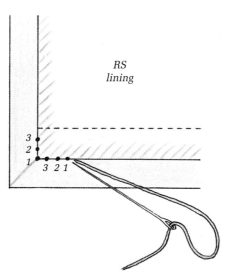

RS lining

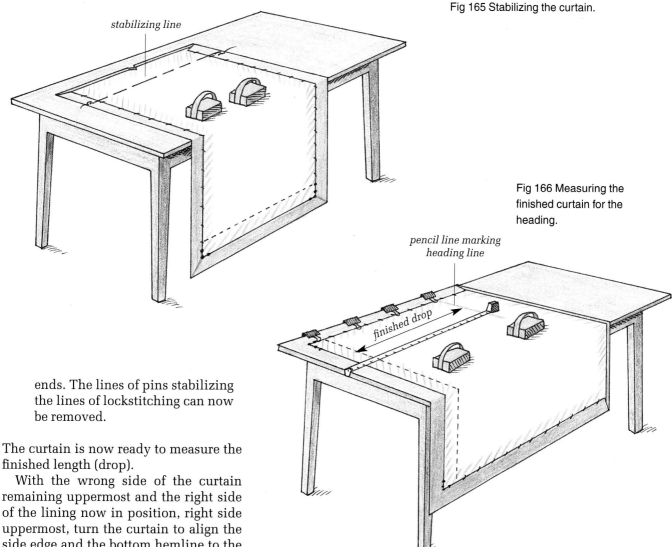

Fig 165 Stabilizing the curtain.

stabilizing line

Fig 166 Measuring the finished curtain for the heading.

pencil line marking heading line

finished drop

ends. The lines of pins stabilizing the lines of lockstitching can now be removed.

The curtain is now ready to measure the finished length (drop).

With the wrong side of the curtain remaining uppermost and the right side of the lining now in position, right side uppermost, turn the curtain to align the side edge and the bottom hemline to the two sides at the corner of the table (Fig 166). This must be accurate.

Clamp or brick in position. It is a very obvious advantage to have clamps, two bricks will suffice but to be honest you do need four bricks.

A cheaper alternative to clamps is bulldog clips, large enough to clip onto your table.

No doubt you have realized by now what an important role clamps and bricks play in stabilizing your fabric. This is particularly evident when making large curtains.

Measuring the Finished Drop

Measure the correct, finished drop, and make a pencil mark at intervals of 30cm (12in) across the width of the curtain.

Turn the curtain with the heading running along the length of the table. The curtain should be lying flat with the right side of the lining uppermost. Using a metre stick, join up the pencil markings along the heading width of the curtain. The curtain material and lining are folded along this line onto the right side of the lining fabric.

If your original measurements were correct, the heading allowance of 5cm (2in) will be correct. Use your 5cm (2in) measuring card to check this depth. Do not worry if this is not exact, as this turning will be covered by the heading tape. The heading is worked according to your choice of heading, either commercial heading tape or hand heading using the buckram.

Heading Tape (Fig 167)

The turning is now mock mitred at each side end (a) and pressed. This will eliminate some of the bulk from the side edges where the ends of the tape must lie flat. It is important that the heading tape is placed along the top edge of the

curtain correctly, so ensuring that the final made up curtain is finished and hung in the most professional way.

Establish the right and left curtains. Any half widths must go to the outside edge, i.e. the back edge, and the full drop goes to the centre edge, i.e. the lead edge of the curtain. The heading tape is positioned just below the top of the fold of the prepared heading of the curtain and machine stitched into place. The stitching must run in the same direction to avoid twisting the tape and the machining along the top and bottom edges of the tape must be parallel.

The amount of heading tape needed is the width of the finished curtain plus 20cm (¼yd) for each curtain. This probably sounds extravagant but, with experience, you will be able to reduce this amount.

The pencil pleat heading tape is 8cm (3¼in) wide with three cords, which are pulled up to form pleats. The cords are pulled from the back edge of the curtain and adjusted to the curtain measurement. These cords can so often be untidy and restrictive when finally hanging the curtains on the track. There are various ways of anchoring and storing these cords and all are correct. We have, over the years, found the following method to be both neat and satisfactory and these guidelines will help you.

Attaching the Heading Tape

1 Make sure you have the right side of the heading tape uppermost. The pockets where the hooks are attached must be on top.

2 Make sure the ends of the tape are squared off.

3 Starting at the left-hand side pull out 10cm (4in) of cord from the wrong side of the tape. Knot all the ends separately but very firmly. Tie the three

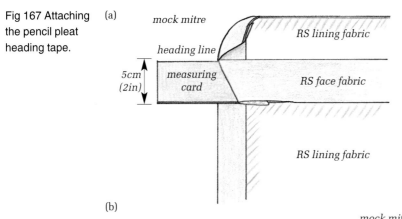

Fig 167 Attaching the pencil pleat heading tape.

(a)

mock mitre

RS lining fabric

heading line

5cm (2in)

measuring card

RS face fabric

RS lining fabric

(b)

A

knotting cords

mock mitre

B

lead

edge

D

E C

edge

stabilizing line of tacking

bag for cords

RS

lining fabric

ends together with a strong knot, which gives the cords extra strength.

4 Cut back the now uncorded tape to 4cm (1½in) and fold it over the knot and encase the knotted cords underneath the tape. This must be correct, as these cords must be anchored by the machining to give them added strength.

5 Place this folded end under the mock mitred and turned down 5cm (2in) of heading, making sure the top edge of the tape is just below the top edge of the curtain and the folded end is just behind the side edge. The tape should not show from the right side of the curtain.

6 Pin in place along the heading with vertical pins.

Begin your tacking with a double backstitch over the left-hand side edge of the curtain. This will ensure the folded end of the tape stays in place and does not show from the right side of the curtain (Point A, Fig 167). Tack to within 10cm (4in) of the right-hand side of the curtain and let the tape run another 20cm (8in) beyond. Once again uncord the tape from the wrong side to just beyond the edge of the side of the curtain, and knot the cord. Trim off the uncorded tape to 4cm (1½in) and tuck the end under the mock mitre. Continue tacking to the end of the tape and finish off with a double backstitch over the side edge of the curtain, leaving a long end of thread. Do not tack down the short end of the tape.

Go back to the left-hand side of the curtain and tack a second line along the bottom edge of the tape.

Tuck the prepared pocket for the cords under the tape to the level of the top of the bag, i.e. the selvedge of the bag, and place it level with the slip-stitched edge of the lining on the side turning. Continue tacking along the bottom edge, finishing with a backstitch over the right-hand-side edge.

MACHINING

Use a size 110/16 machine needle. Test stitch using matching thread. It is essential that the tape is machined very accurately on the edge of the tape. Lower your machine needle into point A; use your reverse stitch, then machine along the top edge of the tape to point B.

Pivot your needle at a right angle and continue machining down the short end, at the same time machining through the cords. This is important as it strengthens this point. Finish your machining at the bottom of the short end with the reverse stitch (C).

Go back to the point where you began machining, A, use the reverse stitch, then machine down this short end, once again through the cords to Point D. Pivot your needle and machine along the bottom edge of the tape through all the layers, so attaching the bag. Finish off the stitching at the other end (Point E) using your reverse stitch accurately covering the last few stitches. These are weak points and it is important that they are secure.

You may find with experience that you are able to pin and adjust the tape and knot the cords while machining the tape into place. As beginners, and probably beyond, it is essential that the tape is first tacked into place.

Repeat for the second curtain.

Note: The second cord pocket must be placed at the opposite end, i.e. the back edge of the second curtain.

The curtains are now compete. Little ironing should be necessary. The curtain is now drawn up from the position above the cord bag, which is why it is so important that the cords are well anchored. By drawing up the cords from this position, it gives the tape neat folds at the end of the curtain, eliminating the added bulk of cords hanging immediately on the back edge of the curtain.

Note: The much used and traditional method is to leave these cords at the back edge free and to pull the cords from the back edge of the curtain. This is done by leaving the cords knotted, but loose, on the face of the tape and not folding them underneath and anchoring with the machine stitching through the tape at the back edge. This means that you pull up the curtain from the very edge of the side turning, so adding bulk at this point.

1 Draw up the curtain to half the width measurement (recorded in notebook).
2 Once adjusted for size, the cords are knotted together, placed in the bag and neatly stored under the return edge of the pelmet board.
3 Place a metal hook every fourth pocket and one at the end. Put these in after the curtain is drawn up.
4 Pull the runners into the closed position and check the number of rings on the rail. Match the number to the number of hooks on the curtain. The lead edge goes to the centre of the window.
5 The first two hooks are placed on the overlap arm. Do not place these into the arm until you have secured the remaining hooks in place or you will strain the arm with the weight of your curtain. Continue attaching the hooks to the rings to the end of the rail, i.e. the back edge. Place the last hook in the screw eye at the back of the pelmet board. Finally, place two hooks in the overlap arm.
6 Repeat on the second curtain.
7 Draw the curtains backwards and forwards, adjusting the heading if necessary and allowing the curtain to fall into even folds to the hemline.

DRESSING THE CURTAINS

Once the curtains are complete they should be dressed. This means that you set the curtains in even folds ensuring that when the curtains are opened and closed they always fall neatly into position. This is called 'dressing a curtain'.

To set these folds into a permanent position dressing bands are used. These bands can be made from unused off-cuts of fabric or from lining fabric, and stored for future use.

For full-length curtains you will need five bands; three for sill or apron-length ones. Cut the bands on the straight grain 10cm (4in) deep across the width of the fabric. Fold in half along the length and iron.

1 With the right-hand curtain open to its full extent, stand in front of the lead edge.
2 Open your left hand and place your fingers behind the curtain and your thumb in front, with the lead edge in the V of the thumb and forefinger.
3 Keeping your right hand on the face of the curtain fabric and your fingers straight, push the curtain back towards the window creating a fold. Continue folding by sliding one hand alternately over the other, the left hand pushing the fold away from the window and the right hand pushing towards the window. This should make all the pleats equal. The back edge of the curtain must be towards the window. If this is not the case, restart, adjusting the length of the fold.
4 Place the first band around the curtain to hold the folds in position and pin in place. Care should be taken that the dressing bands are not too tight or you will indent the fabric. Work down the curtain from top to bottom placing the bands in relevant positions.
5 Leave these dressing bands in place for several days.
6 Repeat for the left-hand curtain using opposite hands.

14 Valances and Pelmets for Curtains

Valances and pelmets serve not only to cover up the curtain headings and conceal the tracks and fittings but at the same time they add a professional and decorative finish to your curtains.

The words 'valance' and 'pelmet' can sometimes be confusing when reading books and magazines, and to make things more difficult, there are certain parts of the world where the word 'valance' is used for both valance and pelmet.

In the main, I think you will find that a valance is thought of as something short and gathered or pleated and may be regarded as a short curtain with a softer finish than a pelmet. A pelmet, on the other hand, is a flat piece of material held rigid with pelmet buckram or, more commonly today, with hardboard or plywood, to give a much more tailored and formal appearance.

Before making any valances or pelmets, there are certain general considerations to be aware of which are described below.

The length (drop) of a valance or pelmet, at its shortest point, must be long enough to conceal the top of the window (soffit) and the top of the window frame; but it must not eliminate too much light from the window. You must also take into consideration any opening doors and other windows.

The valance or pelmet is attached to a pelmet board which has a 2cm (¾in) hooked strip of self adhesive Velcro stuck (and reinforced with staples) along the narrow edge of the front and the return edges of the board. The board is usually set 10–12cm (4–5in) above the window.

There are also various curtain rails on the market incorporating a smaller rail from which the valance can be hung. Or you can buy a special valance track that is hooked on to the main curtain rail. The major disadvantage of these rails, apart from being more expensive, is that they are open at the top and light can sometimes show through. I prefer to use the standard pelmet board.

FACE FABRIC

The amount of fabric needed for a valance varies according to your choice of heading, but it should be fuller than the curtains you are covering.

The first full drop of the face fabric should be placed in the centre of the valance or pelmet and all additional widths added equally at either side. This is particularly important when making a pelmet where there is no fullness to disguise the joins. If there is a

Fig 168 Valance with contrasting band.

pattern repeat in your fabric it must be matched.

When making a pelmet and using a patterned fabric, the pelmet and curtain matching patterns must lie one on top of the other in the same position at the top of the curtain or you will lose the continuity of the pattern of your curtains.

When making a valance, it is not generally essential that you match the pattern with the curtain, as the fullness of the valance will disguise any mismatch. However, there may be occasions when you might have to consider this, for instance if you are using a particularly large pattern or there is a strong, dominant colour in the overall pattern of your fabric. In more advanced valances where you might hand head the valance, more care and consideration is necessary in choosing the position of the pattern in the valance in relation to the curtain.

When making a valance it is sometimes possible to use the off-cuts from your curtain fabric after pattern-matching the curtains. If you are short on valance length, a solution may be to add a contrasting band at the hem or heading, or even both, thus creating an interesting feature. Plain chintz is a good choice for this as it is produced in a range of many colours. The glazed surface of chintz can be reversed if it is used with unglazed cotton furnishing fabrics, but do remember that your choice of contrasting fabric must be of the same weight as your face fabric. Do not be tempted to trim with a coloured lining fabric as this can be of lesser quality and in many cases will fade more easily.

LINING FABRIC

The lining fabric for your valance/pelmet should match the colour of your curtain lining. When making a valance, the width of the lining fabric should be the same as that of the face fabric. This will ensure that the seam lines of the face and lining fabrics lie on top of one another and that the centre drop of the lining fabric lies in the centre of the valance with any necessary extra widths added equally on either side.

The lining for the valance is cut 5cm (2in) shorter than the length (drop) of your calculated face fabric length, but it has the same number of widths.

INTERLINING A VALANCE

It is not strictly necessary to interline a valance, but there are many advantages in doing so and I prefer to interline all valances.

The interlining gives your valance a softer appearance and allows it to hang with more body. At the same time it acts as a shield against seams, turnings and hems as the valance hangs in the window against the daylight.

The lightweight interlining Domette must always be used if you interline a valance. It is essential that if you interline a curtain, you also interline the valance, but that must be done with the lighter Domette, even if the curtains are interlined with the heavier 'bump' interlining.

You may alter the colour of a light-coloured face fabric if you place the unbleached, cream Domette behind it. In this case you should use the bleached, white Domette. You can then use the same coloured lining sateen as chosen for your curtains to line the valance. Always hold the layers of fabric up to the light before making a final decision.

HEADING A VALANCE

There are various ways of heading a valance and, as the valance is really a short curtain, care should be taken to select a heading that does not reveal too much of the machine stitching on the right side of the fabric. One of the simplest headings for a valance is to use the commercial pencil pleat heading tape.

With the added fullness necessary for the valance, the tape forms tight pencil-shaped folds, which conceal most of the machining. The introduction of this tape, incorporating small spot-shaped Velcro (integral loop Velcro heading tape), has considerably simplified its use.

To attach the valance to the board, it is only necessary to pull-up the cords in the tape, adjusting the valance to the length of the board and returns, and to press the

Fig 169 Valance using integral loop Velcro.

valance in place with the tape, which incorporates the loop Velcro spot onto the hooked Velcro strip, already stapled along the front edge and returns of the board.

The commercial heading tapes, which pull up into a variety of headings, should be avoided, as the lines of machine stitching will show.

Like curtains, a valance can be hand-headed with French or goblet pleats.

15 Project 7 – The Valance

The next project will be a simple valance using the commercial integral loop pencil pleat heading tape. You now have the option of making a valance or a pelmet to complete the curtain project.

In order to have continuity from curtain to valance or pelmet, my students make their own choice for a worked project. For some a pelmet is more suitable for their curtains and they therefore go straight to the pelmet for their worked project.

In order to keep the continuity of this course and for those students choosing to make a pelmet to complete their curtain project we have, once again, found merit in making a small sample valance with an interlining. This introduces the handling of interlining for the first time, involving new techniques and stitches. This also makes a good practice run for the hand-headed, interlined curtains.

Materials for a sample valance:

1. 0.5m (½yd) of printed cotton furnishing fabric
2. 0.5m (½yd) or of sateen lining fabric
3. 0.5m (½yd) of Domette interlining fabric
4. Depending on width of fabric, pencil pleat tape and turning allowances

The following order of work is applicable for those wishing to make an *interlined valance for their curtains or a sample valance.*

Bearing in mind that the valance must look well proportioned and balanced and that it must be long enough to cover the top of the window without eliminating too much light, it is important to get the correct depth. It is therefore essential that you make a pattern.

TO CALCULATE THE DEPTH (DROP) OF THE VALANCE/PELMET

Make your finished valance/pelmet length one sixth of the finished length of your curtains. Obviously there can be slight variations to this proportion and you should be guided by your own window and circumstances. If you take this measurement as a rough guide you will not go far wrong with the overall look.

Example:

If the curtain drop is 60 units (inches or centimetres):

Divide 60 by 6 = 10, which will be the finished drop of the valance.

A slightly longer valance will be achieved by making it one fifth of the curtain length:

Divide 60 by 5 = 12 to give the finished drop of the valance.

Add to the finished drop length 5cm (2in) for the heading and 4cm (1½in) for the hem.

TO CALCULATE THE WIDTH OF THE VALANCE

To calculate the width of fabric you need for your valance, you must measure the length of the board or valance rail plus the two returns and multiply by the amount of fullness you require. The fullness will depend on the type of heading you have chosen.

For the worked project using a pencil pleat heading tape, the width of fabric will be three times the length of the board plus the two returns.

Now make a *flat* paper pattern of the depth required and of the length of the board and returns.

Attach this pattern with drawing pins to the front and return edges of the board and live with it for a while before estimating, buying and cutting your fabric.

Do remember, as for curtains, you need the depth of the pattern repeat to calculate the amount of material that you need. When you actually *cut* your length, the measurement will be the *finished* drop plus the amount for headings and hems.

Now calculate the amount of fabric you will need to make your valance using the same method as for calculating your curtain fabric.

Note: It is important that you buy all your fabric from one bolt. Calculations of amount of fabric for your curtains and valance or pelmet must be done at the same time.

CUTTING OUT FABRIC

◆ Cut the face fabric calculated drop plus 5cm (2in) for the turning at the heading and plus 4cm (1½in) for the hem.

◆ Cut lining 5cm (2in) shorter than the face fabric.

◆ Cut interlining 4cm (1½in) shorter than the face fabric.

FACE FABRIC: ORDER OF WORK

1 Place the widths of face fabric on the table right side uppermost.
2 Assemble the lengths of fabric, making sure you have a complete panel in the centre.
3 Using a flat seam and a seam allowance of 2cm (¾in) and with right sides facing, pin, tack and machine each drop, joining all the pieces into a long strip.
   Note: If necessary, pattern-match using the same method we used in matching patterns for curtains, remembering not to trim off any selvedges before pattern-matching. Then trim back to the 2cm (¾in) seam allowance.
4 Press seam open.

Set aside.

LINING FABRIC: ORDER OF WORK

1 With the right sides facing and using a 2cm (¾in) seam allowance, pin, tack and machine the lining fabric into a long, continuous strip. The length should be the same as your face fabric.
   Note: No seams are cut off lining fabric, and check that your seam lines match the seam lines of your face fabric.
2 Press the seams open.

Set aside.

2cm (¾in)

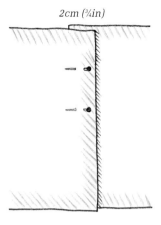
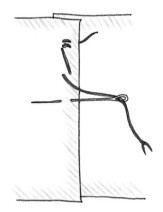
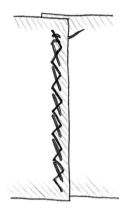

Interlining Fabric (Domette)

When joining interlining an *overlapped seam* is used.

OVERLAPPED SEAM (FIG 170)

Place the edge of the first width of the fabric over the next width by 2cm (¾in) and pin in place. Interlining fabric has a nasty habit of moving when being tacked and machined and in order to stabilize the fabric it must be line tacked into place.

The line-tacking stitch (Fig 171) is the same as basic tacking except that it is done vertically down the length of fabric. Begin your tacking with a backstitch. Take the first stitch down the overlapped seam and tack in the usual way from right to left. Continue tacking down in this manner for the whole length of the seam and then backstitch off.

The seam is now machined down (Fig 172) the centre using a large zigzag stitch. Set the machine to this stitch and test on a doubled piece of Domette. Then machine the seam using the zigzag stitch. It is not necessary to press the seam.

I suggest students making their project valance use a small piece of Domette and, following the above instructions, make a sample for their file.

Set aside.

Joining the Lining Sateen to the Face Fabric

1 Place the right side of the lining fabric to the right side of the face fabric along the raw bottom edges of the valance.
2 Pin, tack and machine using a 1.5cm (½in) seam allowance along the whole length.
3 Press the seams open.
4 Fold the face fabric and lining together bringing the wrong sides together and matching the long raw edges of both fabrics along the top edge of the valance. This will create a 2.5cm (1in) width of face fabric below the seam line you have just stitched.
5 Press this firmly into place. This will now mark the hemline of the valance.

Inserting the Domette into the Valance (Fig 173)

1 Open out the face fabric and the lining fabric and lay them flat on

(Far left) Fig 170 Overlapped Seam.

(Middle) Fig 171 Line tacking.

(Above) Fig 172 Interlining machined with the zigzag stitch.

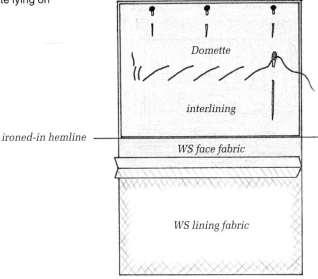

Fig 173 Domette lying on hemline.

the table with the wrong sides uppermost.

2   Place the Domette on top of the face fabric so that the bottom raw edge lies on the ironed-in fold line of the hem.

3   Pin in place with vertical pins and run a line of large line-tacking stitches down the centre along the whole length of the strip through the Domette and the face fabric.

4   Using the bottom hemline ironed fold as a guide, reverse the lining fabric to face the right side of the face fabric,

with the Domette tacked to it, and match the top raw edges and the two side raw edges evenly together (Fig 174).

5   Pin and tack these edges together using the long curtain-tacking stitch along the top edge, or just pin vertically into place.

6   Tack the side edges into place and machine down the two raw side edges 1.5cm (½in) from the edge, through all layers, and use a reverse stitch to finish off both ends.

7   Press and embed the stitches flat and trim back the Domette to the machine stitching on the seam line.

8   Trim off both corners – not too close.

9   Remove the tacking stitches from the side edges and the pins or tacking along the top edge.

10 *Do not* remove the line-tacking *between* the *Domette and the face fabric.*

11 Turn the valance to the right side.

12 Press the completed valance strip, taking particular care to press the side edges evenly and firmly into place.

Attaching Heading Tape to Valance (Fig 175)

1   Using the 5cm (2in) measuring card, iron the turning for the heading to the wrong side, as in the basic curtain.

2   Open out the fold and carefully trim back the Domette to this indented line. Take care at the corners where the Domette has been trimmed back to the machine line.

3   Refold the heading line along the top of the valance.

4   Place the pencil pleated, Integral Loop Velcro Heading Tape incorporating the Velcro spots along the top edge, making sure it does not show from the right side of the valance.

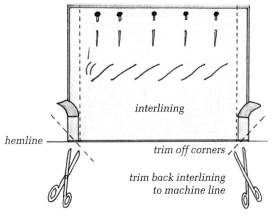

Fig 174 Machining the raw side edges and trimming back the Domette.

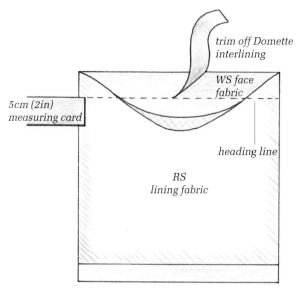

Fig 175 Preparing the heading for attaching the heading tape.

5 Pin, tack and machine into place using the same order of work attaching the heading tape as for the basic curtain.
6 Add a bag for the cords at *each* end to allow the extra lengths of the cords to be evenly distributed at both ends of the valance.
7 Remove the line-tacking stitches and iron the completed valance.

Hanging the Valance

◆ Re-check the measurements of your board front and returns from your notebook.

◆ Pull up the cords on the heading tape from each side to give even, tight pencil pleats to a total length of that measurement.

Attach the valance to the Velcro on the edge of the board using the Velcro spots on the heading tape, adjusting the pleats into even folds, and finally store the ends of the cords in the two bags.

Fig 176 Attaching the valance to the board.

16 Project 8 – The Hard Pelmet

It was clear when I chose my fabric for the curtain and pelmet that, like the cushions and footstool, for the purpose of this book I would be able to use the fabric to advantage when planning my pelmet.

My chosen room for the worked curtain and pelmet is small. I felt the small drop was sufficient but it could stand a little extra length at the sides. As I have both motifs and a striped effect in the fabric, I felt it was better to cut angular lines which will marry up with the striped effect.

If using a patterned fabric, the pattern on the pelmet should marry up with the pattern on the curtain hanging underneath the pelmet. You must consider the pattern on your fabric when you pre-plan the first drop of your curtain and at the same time you must look for the placement of your pelmet. Fabric for both pelmet and curtains must be estimated and bought together to ensure it is cut from the same roll (bolt).

Like the valance, the centre panel of your pelmet must be complete and any extra width must be added equally to either side. Equally important is the join of the extra width, which must be perfectly matched and inconspicuous. There will be a fair amount of tension on the fabric as it is pulled over the board, and the stitching lines will take some strain. In order to keep these lines firm, reduce the stitch length on your machine to about No 2. Test this on a piece of your chosen fabric.

The pelmet is upholstered on a piece of hardboard 3mm or ⅛in thick. This is sold in various widths and lengths. Buy a piece of hardboard nearest to the dimensions of your planned pelmet, erring on the large size. *Note:* the rough side of the hardboard will eventually be the front side of the pelmet.

Making a pelmet for the first time involves many new techniques. We have found making a small sample pelmet has been considerably helpful before tackling the pelmet for the curtains.

The following instructions are applicable to either a sample or a worked pelmet to your own window dimensions.

The dimensions of the worked sample are written for your use on Fig 182.

MEASURING

◆ Check the size of your pelmet board (this would be recorded when measuring for curtains).

(Opposite) Fig 177 The pelmet.

Fig 178 Measuring the drop for the pelmet.

◆ Once you have established the right position, you can now add shape. You could bring some depth to the sides of the pelmet.

Make a rough sketch of a pelmet in relation to your fabric and window. The measured drop of a pelmet is the shortest point of your pelmet drop. This, you have just calculated and recorded. You can add depth at the sides of your pelmet with angular and curved shapes. I do suggest that you keep this first pelmet fairly simple. As you gain more experience you can become more venturesome with various shapes.

Many interesting shapes can be observed in department stores, show houses and magazines, etc.

MAKING A PATTERN

Make a paper pattern including returns and mark these accurately on the paper pattern.

Cut a rectangle of brown paper the length of your pelmet board plus returns and the drop of the pelmet to its deepest point (at the corner of the return).

In order to get an accurate and balanced shape of both sides of the pelmet, fold the pattern in half marking the fold CF (Centre Front). Hold together with a pin while you sketch on the desired shape.

◆ Calculate the drop of your pelmet at the shortest point in relation to the length of your measured curtain, using the same measuring calculations as for your valance.

◆ Hang the metal measuring tape onto the top of the pelmet board and lock the tape to the calculated drop.

◆ Stand back and check that you cannot see the top of the recess or the top of your window frame.

1 Mark in the measurement of the two returns and cut out the folded pattern.
2 Open the pattern out and fold in the returns along the marked line.
3 Pin the paper pattern in place with drawing pins along the front edge of your pelmet board and the two return edges.
4 Check that the length and shape are correct.

Fig 179 Curtain pelmet *(left)* and in place *(below)*.

CUTTING HARDBOARD PELMET SHAPE

1 Remove the paper pattern and lay it onto the *smooth* side of the board.
2 Put a few spots of glue onto the paper to hold it in place, being careful to keep this to the minimum.
3 Press into place and draw a very accurate line on the board around the pattern shape with a soft pencil (HB).
4 Set pattern aside and mark on it PATTERN NO 1. FINISHED SIZE OF PELMET.
5 Using a jigsaw, cut out the shape. Do be careful if using the saw yourself. Better still, persuade a DIY friend to do it for you.
6 Mark off the returns and cut these off.

Set aside.

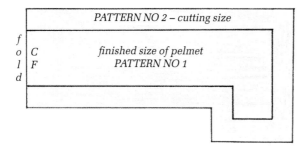

Fig 180 Patterns nos 1 and 2.

1 Using PATTERN NO 1 as a guide, make a second paper pattern adding on a turning allowance of 4cm (1½in) all round. This paper pattern is now used to cut the width of lining and face fabric if using a patterned fabric, this larger pattern will help you to place your pattern accurately.
2 Mark: PATTERN NO 2. CUTTING SIZE. Fold in half, mark *centre front* and clip a V top and bottom, and then mark onto the pattern the 4cm (1½in) seam allowance all round.

Note: In order to give the face of the pelmet a more pleasing and softer appearance the hardboard is first covered with wadding or heavy bump. I prefer the wadding, but you have a choice.

CUTTING FABRICS FOR PELMET

Note: Cut widths of wadding/bump, lining fabric and face fabric. Use the full width of your pattern and the longest drop point. Wadding is a synthetic fabric made of bonded fibres.

Wadding/Bump

Using PATTERN NO 1 (the pelmet finished size pattern), cut sufficient widths of wadding/bump to cover the length of your board. When joining wadding/bump, no seam allowances are necessary as the fabric is butted together to avoid the bulk of a seam. The excess wadding/bump is then trimmed away to the shape of the pelmet once it is attached to the board.

Set aside.

Using PATTERN NO 2 – The Cutting Size, for the *lining* and *face fabric,* cut as rectangles.
Note: Once the widths of lining fabric and face fabric are machined together into the correct lengths, the joined widths of fabric are folded in half to mark the centre and to ensure the centre panel is accurate. The folded paper pattern is then replaced on the folded fabric and the correct shape cut to the paper pattern. Remember to use PATTERN NO 2 cutting size.

Lining Fabric

Cut sufficient widths of lining fabric to cover the width of the board. Remember a full width must go to the centre. If joining fabric at either side you will have to allow 2cm (¾in), that is 4cm (1½in) for each join.

Repeat for a second lining.

Set aside both linings and carefully mark lining 1 and lining 2.

Face Fabric

Using paper PATTERN NO 2 to establish and check the position of a patterned or striped fabric, fold in and crease the turning allowance at the top and bottom of your paper pattern. It makes it visually easy to see exactly where your pattern will fall in relation to your curtain. Remember that it is very important that the first drop is centralized.

Open out the pattern and cut the necessary widths of rectangles of face fabric.

Note: If using a patterned fabric and adding extra fabric either side, you will have to go down to the next identical pattern and mark out the drops as for curtains.

Set aside.

JOINING WIDTHS OF LINING AND FACE FABRIC

Lining Fabric

◆ Pin, tack and machine all necessary widths of lining fabric using a 2cm (¾in) seam allowance. Press seams open. If necessary, iron lining again.

◆ Repeat on the second lining following the same order of work.

Set aside both linings.

Face Fabric

◆ Pin, tack and machine all widths of face fabric together.

◆ If using patterned fabric, pattern match. This must be done accurately. Remember you must not trim off any selvedges until the machining is complete.

◆ Trim back seams to 2cm (¾in).

Replace the folded paper pattern onto the folded lining (repeat for lining 2) and face fabrics. These should be folded down the centre front (CF) line and cut accurately to the shape of the pelmet. Remember to use PATTERN NO 2.

Set aside face fabric and the two lining fabrics.

PIPING

If using piping along the bottom edge of the pelmet, prepare sufficient crossway strip to cover the length of the board plus returns.

◆ Make up piping.

1 The ends of the cord must be encased in the crossway to make a neat end (Fig 181).
2 Cut the short end of the crossway straight and place the cord onto the centre of the wrong side of the crossway and fold over the 2cm (¾in) of the straightened end of the crossway to cover the end of the cord. Then bring

Fig 181 Enclosing the ends
of the cord in the crossway.

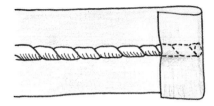

PREPARING AND MAKING THE HARDBOARD PELMET

◆ Cut four rectangles of lining fabric or calico the depth of the board at the return point and 10cm (4in) wide. Fold in half down the drop length and clip a V top and bottom. These strips of fabric will now be used to form hinges for the front corners of the pelmet.

The rough side of the hardboard will eventually become the right side of the pelmet, i.e. the face fabric side.

the two side raw edges of the cross-way to meet. Tack in place and continue tacking along the full length of piping required. Leave a little extra piping cord and crossway to adjust length if necessary when piping is attached to the bottom edge of the pelmet. This end will be encased when the final measurement is complete.

3 Machine along the full length in matching thread, taking care to keep the piping foot close to the cord. Stop short by about 4cm (1½in). Leave ends unfinished, and leave long ends on your thread.

Set aside.

ORDER OF WORK

Lay the hardboard, smooth side uppermost on the table and place the sawn off pieces of board (the returns) butted up against the front piece of pelmet (Fig 182a).

This diagram includes measurements for those students wishing to make a sample pelmet. The measurements are not applicable for individual projects.

1 Mark the centre of the board down the drop length.
2 Mark off 5cm (2in) at each end of the board, down the drop length.
3 Mark off 5cm on the butted up end of the two returns, down the drop length.

(a)   (b)

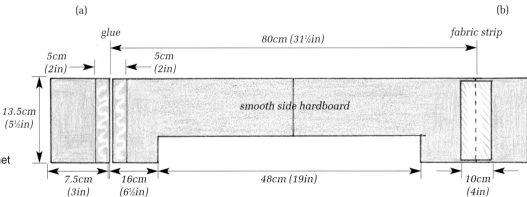

Fig 182 Marking the pelmet
board and applying the
fabric strips.

Fig 182c Making the hinge.

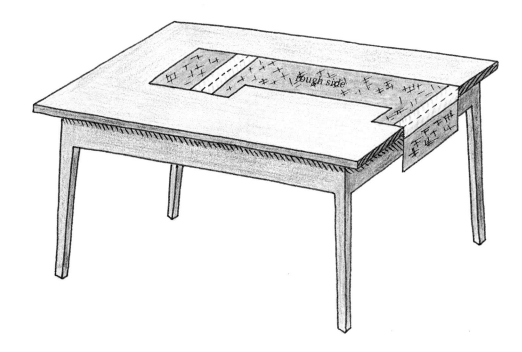

4 Apply a strip of Copydex onto each marked off 5cm (2in) area. Do be careful with the adhesive. It is important that you do not apply too much and it is spread out to ensure full coverage of the area with no excess glue. Use a circular movement with the nozzle of the adhesive.

5 Take the strip of lining and match the centre top and bottom **V** to the butted-up line of pelmet and returns. Press evenly into place (Fig 182b).

6 Repeat at the other end of the board.

7 Allow to dry.

Carefully turn the board over so the rough side is uppermost and create the hinge at the corner (Fig 182c).

SIDE ONE

1 Mark off 5cm (2in) as in (Fig 182) in the same position on one end of the front board and return.

2 Apply a strip of adhesive to one end of the board and the return.

3 Apply the prepared lining strip and smooth down.

4 Before the adhesive becomes too dry, carefully move the whole pelmet along to the edge of the table allowing the return end to drop over the edge at right angles to form a corner. Run your thumbnail along the point of the join, backwards and forwards. This will relax the fabric a little, then work the hinge up and down, which will have the effect of creating a loose hinge.

5 Move the pelmet back onto the surface of the table and you will notice a small, loose ridge of material has appeared along the joint, which forms the hinge. This is necessary to make the hinge work.

SIDE TWO

Repeat the procedure as for side one.

APPLYING THE BUMP/ WADDING TO THE BOARD

With the completed pelmet board remaining in position with the rough side facing, apply the bump/wadding to the face of the board. Apply a little adhesive to the board being careful not to use too much, and smooth it out.

⬩ Place the strips of bump/wadding to the face of the board. It does not matter where the joins lie. Take the first piece of wadding and place it to the end and sides of the board. Press in place. Take the second piece of bump/wadding and butt it up to the first, down the drop length. Do this very accurately, ensuring that the join is flat and even. Press into place and continue along the board until it is completely covered. Allow to dry and then trim off any excess to the shape of the pelmet board.

Set aside.

LINING: ORDER OF WORK

Lining Fabric No 1

Look carefully at the diagrams on the opposite page (Fig 183).

Place the first piece of lining, wrong side uppermost, on the table and iron-in the 4cm (1½in) fold along the top, sides and flat, unshaped bottom return edge. Iron-in the mitre at all four corners (*see* Fig 183a).

Open out the folds. Turn over the pelmet board and place it on top of the lining allowing the bump to lie against the wrong side of the lining with the edges of the board lying on the ironed markings of the lining. Making sure the centre markings on the board and lining fabric follow through. This must be accurate.

1 Fold over the turning allowance over the top edge of the board. Check this line is accurate. Staple the *centre* in place. Use a staple size of ½in crown, ³⁄₁₆in leg. Add more staples either side but leave sufficient room to bring the mitre over the corner (*see* Fig 183b).

2 Make the first fold in the mitre across the corner and staple in position (*1*). Then fold the complete mitre and staple again (*2*). Complete the stapling along the top edge.

3 Repeat at the opposite end.

4 Fold the lining over the side edge of the board. Work the joint up and down and complete the mitre at the bottom corner in the same way and fold and staple the first flat section of the bottom of the board into place (*3*).

5 Repeat at the opposite end.

6 Now go back to the centre and line up the straight of grain on the lining and the board and make sure the lining is falling flat and even along the bottom edge of the board (*see* Fig 183c).

Depending on the shape of your board, you will now have to slash the lining to any curves or angled corners as in the case of the sample pelmet board slashed at point *3* (*see* Fig 183d).

7 Slash into each corner (*3*).

8 Now complete the centre section by bringing the remainder of the fold up and over the edge of the board and staple it into place to the end of the slashed piece of fabric.

9 Complete the corner using another mitre.

10 Now complete the rest of the bottom edge towards the outside corner.

11 Repeat at the opposite end.

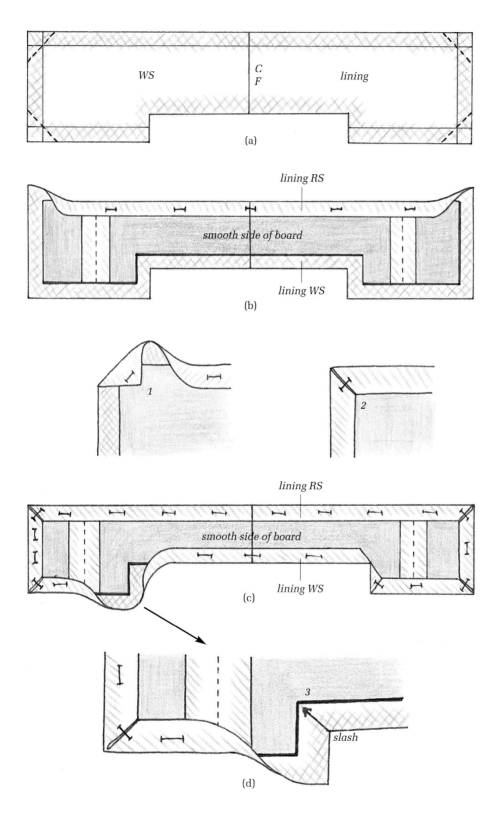

WS

C
F

lining

(a)

lining RS

smooth side of board

lining WS

(b)

1

2

lining RS

smooth side of board

lining WS

(c)

3

slash

(d)

Fig 183 Applying lining fabric No 1, slashing the corners and completing the bottom edge.

SECOND LINING

Lining Fabric No 2

Place the lining fabric on the table, wrong side uppermost.

1 Iron over the turning along the top edge 4cm (1½in).
2 Iron-in the side turnings but make these turnings 4.5cm (1¾in) – this ensures that the edge of the lining does not show from the front of the pelmet. There is no need to mitre these corners,

just make a neat fold.
3 Turn lining to right side.

Velcro

Place the Velcro onto the right side of the lining over the folded edge line. Pin and tack into place.

◆ Machine top and bottom edges of Velcro through all layers

Note: re-adjust the stitch length of your machine to a larger stitch after using the smaller stitch for seaming up the lengths of lining and face fabric.

Face Fabric

Iron-in all turnings to the wrong side and mitre the corners as for lining No 1.

ATTACHING THE FACE FABRIC AND LINING No 2 TO THE UPHOLSTERED, LINED BOARD

Look at the diagram *(left)* placing the face fabric in position (Fig 184).

1 Place the pelmet board on the table smooth side uppermost, upholstered side lying on the face of the table.
2 Place the face fabric, right side uppermost on the table above the board (*see* Fig 184a).
3 Open out the folds on the face fabric and place the top edge of the face fabric along the top edge of the board over the stapled, folded edge of the lining. Take care this is accurate and that the ironed fold line of the fabric is lying exactly on the edge of the top of the board.

Fig 184 Attaching the face fabric and lining to the board.

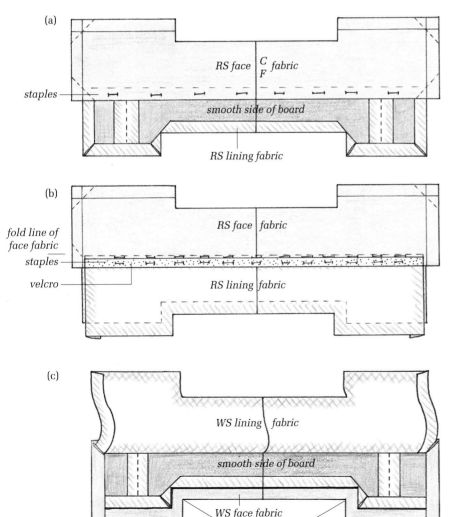

Match the centre markings on the face fabric, lining fabric and board centre-drop line. Put the first staple in place through all the layers. Staple either side of this along to each side edge, stopping short of each corner by 7cm (2½in).

Attach Lining No 2

With the right side uppermost, place the lining with the Velcro strip, already machined into place, over the turning allowance of the face fabric at the top of the board, along the ironed-in fold line of the face fabric (*see* Fig 184b).

Match all centre markings and set the top of the Velcro just on this line to ensure the lining does not show from the right side of the pelmet. Staple the centre into position, continue stapling into place towards the two side edges, stopping short of each corner by 7cm (2½in) as for face fabric.

Eventually, this will be neatened.

Lift the board off the table and allow the face fabric to fall over the front of the board. Now place the face fabric and board back onto the table with the face fabric lying flat and under the board and pull neatly down into place (*see* Fig 184c).

Complete the Corners

Fold the lining up and out of the way and go back to the edge of the board and complete the mitre on the face fabric at the top and bottom corners and staple the fold into place along the side and short length of the bottom edge. Work the joint up and down (*see* Fig 184c).

Repeat at the opposite end.

Complete the whole of the face fabric lying along the bottom edge of the board in the same order of work as for lining fabric No 1 (see Fig 183c).

Now drop the lining into place over the completed face fabric and complete the stapling of the Velcro along the top edge. Repeat at the opposite end.

Because we allowed the extra width of turning at the side edges, the lining will drop into place leaving a small margin of face fabric. This will ensure that the lining does not show from the right side of the finished pelmet. *Do not staple this edge.*

Once again, fold the lining fabric up and out of the way.

PIPING (Fig 185)

At this stage, if piping is to be added to the edge of the board, it must be worked into place.

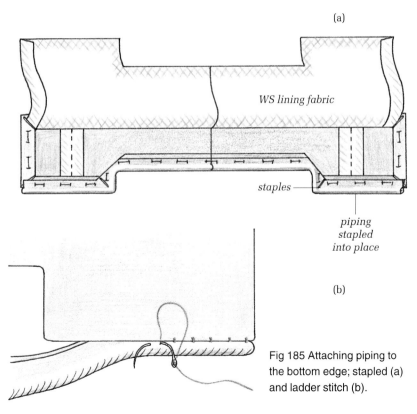

(a)

WS lining fabric

staples —

piping stapled into place

(b)

Fig 185 Attaching piping to the bottom edge; stapled (a) and ladder stitch (b).

Take the completed, machined piping strip and place the finished end at the base of the corner with the covered cord edge lying along the bottom edge of the board and the raw edges of the crossway strip lying on the face of the board.

Keeping this position, accurately staple the piping into place, moulding and slashing where necessary (*see* Fig 185a).

Fig 186 Completing the lining on the pelmet board with slipstitch.

Or, more professionally, ladder stitch into place for a better result, and you will have to clip into the piping for corners and curves as you go, where necessary (*see* Fig 185b).

Complete the stapling or ladder stitching and finish off the end of the cord, encasing the end of the cord with the crossway using the same method as in commencing the piping.

Allow the lining to drop back into place over the completed work.

The side turnings are already ironed into place and should fall onto the sides just short of the edge of the board. Pin in place with horizontal pins (Fig 186a).

Carefully turn the board over with the finished right side of the face fabric uppermost and ease the fabric accurately into place along the bottom edge making sure the straight of grain follows through at the centre.

Slash into the corners (or shapes). Do take care not to slash too close to the piping (Fig 186b).

Turn the board with the right side of the lining now facing and the face of the board on the table.

- Fold the lining fabric back to the seam line.

- Place the slashed points evenly into position and mitre the corners and hold the lining in place with vertical pins (Fig 186c).

- Slip-stitch the lining into place down the sides and along the bottom edge (Fig 186d).

The pelmet is now complete. Take the pelmet to the pelmet board and position it accurately along the top of the board and press hard into place onto the Velcro strip which is stapled along the front edge and side returns of the board.

(a)

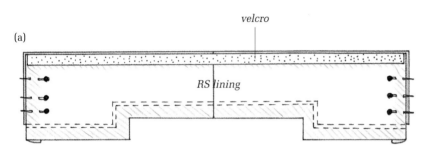

(b)

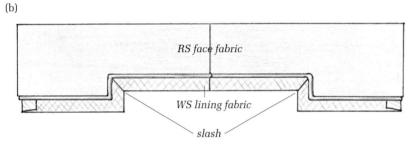

(c)

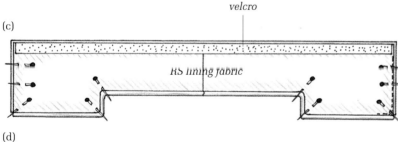

(d)

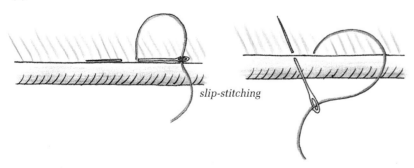

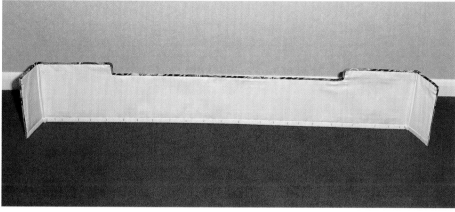

Fig 187 The completed pelmet from the wrong side *(above)* and the right side *(right)*.

Fig 188 The completed pelmet and curtain.

(Above) Fig 189 A French-pleated curtain.

(Right) Fig 190 The fabrics used. Face fabric: Doulton, a printed chintz fabric. Interlining: Domette, bleached white. Cotton lining: Sateen, cream.

17 Project 9 – Interlined and Hand-Headed Curtains

INTERLINED CURTAINS

The fabric used in the photographs to illustrate the hand headings of French and goblet pleats is a chintz fabric, *Doulton*, width 134cm (54in) with a pattern repeat of 41cm (16in).

Chintz is a traditional and much used fabric in soft furnishings. It is of medium weight and easy to work with and is a plain-weave cotton fabric, usually printed with patterns of bird or flower motifs. This traditional fabric originated in India, *chintz* being the Hindu word for spotted or variegated, and was originally hand painted.

A chintz fabric is usually glazed, which gives the fabric some lustre and protects against dust and dirt. The original glaze washed out, but today manufacturers have produced a resin treatment that is more permanent. Although dry cleaning is recommended on small items such as cushions, it can be washed with care and a spray starch will restore much of the lustre.

At the top of the range of the classic curtain is the hand-headed, interlined curtain. Although interlining adds to the cost of the curtain, at the same time, it improves the finished look of the curtain, improving its drape and its lifetime.

Interlined curtains can be hand headed such as a French or Goblet pleat or a commercial heading tape can be used. There are a variety of these commercial tapes on the market which, like the pencil pleat tape, can be pulled up with cords to form French pleats, goblets, boxed pleats, etc. The disadvantage of these is that they do not stack back well and you will see the lines of machine stitching on the face of your curtain. Added to this, to have a really professional finish, the heading must be tailored to fit the rail or pole to size. The pencil pleat commercial heading tape still remains the most successful, suspended from a rail underneath a pelmet or valance, and if desired, an interlining can be added to the curtains.

The basic foundation of curtain making, already worked through in the lined curtain using the pencil pleat commercial heading tape, established skills and techniques.

Fig 191 Fabric for Doulton curtain.

and fuller finish. So I would suggest that if hand heading a curtain you do use an interlining. For the average curtain domette is sufficient and for a slightly fuller look, the lightweight bump. When interlining silk, which should always be interlined, the light- or medium-weight bump does enhance the silk and protect it from sunlight and rotting. You must always use the bleached bump as the small particles of cotton fibre can give a rough surface and can work their way through into the silk fabric.

POLES

Poles are used to hang curtains with French pleats. These hand-made headings with NO stitching seen on the right side of the curtain can be shown off to advantage, displaying a tailored professional finish

Poles with finial ends are supported by brackets and extend into the stackback area of 7.5–30cm (3–12in) beyond the window at each end or depending on the position of the window in relationship to wall space.

Position screw eyes in the wall immediately behind the ends of the poles to make returns.

Poles *must* be in position before taking curtain measurements.

It is important that the pole is fixed far enough above the top of the window to ensure no daylight is seen between the top of the curtain and the pole and that NO hooks are visible from outside the house.

Measuring

Always take three measurements – one at each end and one in the middle. This will determine if the floor is even. If it is not, take the shortest measurement.

◆ Follow all instructions for the lined-only curtains and include the instructions for interlined curtains given in *italics* and a different font.

HAND-HEADED CURTAINS

Hand-headed curtains, where the heading is exposed, are generally most successful if suspended from a pole.

The most popular hand heading is formed with triple pleats (French pleats) which stack back evenly in elegant folds. A goblet pleat can also be used but this is much more successful if it is used in a static position, i.e. where the curtain heading remains in one position when the curtains are drawn back into elegant full drapes. Or, both French pleats and goblet pleats can hand head a valance over a pencil pleated curtain hanging from a rail.

The hand headings are worked on a stiffened strip of curtain buckram, which is placed between the interlining and the lining, thus giving the face fabric a softer

Drop   Measure from floor (or finished curtain position) to where the large ring joins the ring for the curtain hook plus 6mm or ¼in. By adding the 6mm or ¼in it ensures that the curtain heading will cover the screw end. It is always difficult to stop the ring swinging round as you measure. Ask someone to hold this ring in place while you measure the drop.

Width   Measure length of pole between finials plus returns at each end.

◆ Estimating the fabric is done in the same way as the basic curtain but you must allow two and a quarter times the amount of fabric.

FASCIA BOARD

There may be times when you will prefer to suspend the hand-headed curtains from a track. The hand headings look extremely elegant when closed and the heading shows up to advantage. The big disadvantage is that when the curtains are drawn back the track is exposed, which detracts considerably from the overall appearance. The advantage is in having the track with the overlap arm and the pulley system, which in general is not possible with a pole, although there are now available very specialized, top-of-the-range poles with which this feature might be included. But they are either unsatisfactory or very expensive. A solution to this is to cover the track with a fascia board attached to the front of the pelmet board and covered with a fabric to match your curtains.

Use a corded metal track with top fixing and an overlap arm. The track is attached to the underside of the pelmet board, which in turn is fixed to the wall with angle brackets in the same way as previously described for the basic pelmet board. But there are various considerations to be taken into account:

◆ The board is not as wide as the board used for suspending curtains, which has a valance or pelmet in place, as the track must be placed flush up to the fascia hardboard and immediately behind the fascia board attached to the front edge of the board.

◆ The depth of the fascia board should be 5cm (2in) and just cover the metal track but reveal the runners, the edge of the overarms and the metal ends of the curtain rail housing the pulley system. The depth of the fascia board may need slight adjustment to accommodate this requirement.

◆ The ends of the track must finish flush with the ends of the board. A piece of Velcro is attached to the 10cm (4in) return ends of the board and the reciprocal piece of soft Velcro sewn to the last 10cm of the curtain at the back edge, to enable you to return the curtain to the wall. To add extra strength at this point, the screw eyes inserted at the back of the underside of the board at each end must be inserted level with the runners and at right angles to the end of the track.

Pelmet Board with Covered Fascia

◆ Pelmet board: buy planed wood, 10cm (4in) wide and 2cm (¾in) thick, the length of the required board

◆ A piece of very thin hardboard, 5cm (2in) wide, the length of the finished pelmet board

◆ Metal curtain track with top fixing, overlap arm and corded, to the same length as the board

◆ Fixing materials, i.e. brackets, screws, Rawlplugs, wood glue, etc.

◆ 30cm (⅓yd) of Velcro 2cm (¾in) wide, with self-adhesive hook and reciprocal loop soft side

Fig 192 Covering the fascia board with fabric.

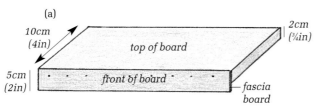

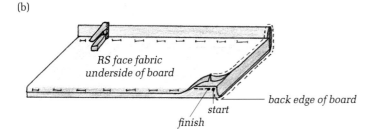

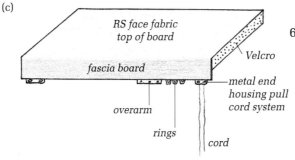

ORDER OF WORK

1 Fix the brackets to the underside of the pelmet board, temporarily offer the board and brackets up to the wall at the correct height, ensuring the board is level. Mark, drill and plug the wall; fix the board to the wall with the brackets and check that it is level. Remove the board from the brackets, leaving the latter in place (Fig 192).

2 Following the instructions for use of the glue, apply it to the front 2cm-(¾in-) thick front edge of the board and to the top 2cm on the back side of the fascia hardboard if appropriate, and stick the fascia to the board, ensuring that the top edge of the fascia is flush with the surface of board. Reinforce with a few panel pins.

3 Cut a piece of matching face fabric on the straight of grain 38cm (15in) wide and of a length equal to that of the board. Add to this measurement 2.5cm (1in). Mark the centres of both the board length and the fabric.

4 Iron a 1.5cm (½in) turning to the wrong side of the fabric at both ends and another along one length edge.

5 Run a little glue along the back edge of the board and place the raw edge of the fabric in place along the edge of the board, matching the centre markings. Having turned in the two side edges these should now be level with the two return ends of the board. Staple the centre in place and add a few more staples to reinforce.

6 Firmly and evenly bring the fabric over the top of the board and down and over the hardboard. Tuck the fabric neatly into the right-angle point at the back of the fascia board where it joins the base of the board. Smooth this well in place. Push the front edge of a staple gun right up into the right-angled position of the fascia board and pelmet board

and staple a line of tacks to reinforce and stabilize the fabric in this position. Keep these even and straight. The top fixing of the track will cover these staples when it is screwed into place.

7 Continue smoothing the fabric evenly over the underside of the board to bring the folded end over the back edge of the board covering the fabric already stapled into position. Staple in the middle and at either end and then evenly in between.

8 Attach the self-adhesive Velcro to the return ends and staple to reinforce.

9 The curtain track is now fixed in place and the board fixed onto the brackets again.

Measuring the Pelmet Board with Fascia

Drop   Measure from floor (or finished curtain position) to the top of the fascia (pelmet) board plus 3mm (⅛in). By adding the 3mm it ensures that the top of the curtain just marginally clears the top of the board when hanging.

Width Measure from one end of the track to the other end. Add on the returns and overlap arm.

Buckram

Hand-made headings are constructed and stiffened using a curtain buckram made of coarse woven cotton, which is heavily sized. It is available in three widths:

10cm (4in)

12cm (5in)

15cm (6in)

There are two kinds of buckram:

- The standard buckram which is soft and easy but time consuming to work with.

- The iron-on, fusible type which is more rigid.

These hand-made headings with French pleats and goblet pleats need a pin hook to hang them from the pole or track. The pin hook has a sharp pointed prong that is inserted into the back of each pleat.

The obvious advantage of the fusible buckram is – time. But you do have to be very accurate in marking out its position before ironing it into place. It does have a tendency to form a more rigid pleat, which some may prefer.

In working with my students we have used both the non-iron and the fusible buckram and the general opinion seems to be that for beginners the non-iron buckram is easier to handle. During my research for this book, I did ask for advice at department stores and soft-furnishing shops and it was abundantly clear that customers had found the iron-on type difficult to cope with. For the purpose of this book and for the benefit of the more advanced students, I will of course work through the instructions for both standard and fusible buckram.

One of the disadvantages for the beginner is that it is not possible to tack the fusible buckram into position, as the resin in the material coats the thread, making it impossible to pull the stitches through. It is also so rigid that it is almost impossible to pin in place. So if fusing the buckram into place, every stage must be set accurately before ironing it into place. In many ways, using the standard, non-iron buckram on your first curtain and tacking it into position can act as a practice run of the placement of the buckram before planning to use the iron-on.

During the course we do make a sample curtain out of a metre of fabric. This allows us to work with the interlining and, like the 'Basic Sample Worked Curtain', it forms a valuable aid when positioning and measuring curtains on poles and tracks with fascia boards. At the same time, we work the heading using the standard non-iron buckram to make a triple

mitre ironed into place

mitre ironed into place

trim off interlining

heading buckram

Fig 193 Marking the mitre and positioning the heading tape.

pleat and a goblet pleat in order to learn the techniques and acquire the skills of construction of each of the pleats. You may wish to do this for yourselves following my instructions, or you may prefer to use the instructions for an interlined curtain. The order of work is the same.

- ◆ Follow the instructions for lined-only curtains and include the interlined curtain in *italic* and include checking the measurements and marking the finished drop of the curtain. The heading is now constructed using the buckram for hand heading.

- ◆ Once the heading allowance is ironed into place with the 5cm (2in) marker card, peel back the

lining fabric and trim the interlining level to the fold line of the face fabric (*see* diagrams of interlined valance on pages 173–4). Reset the face fabric turning allowance with the measuring card to sharpen the fold line. Allow the lining fabric to drop into place over the heading line and then re-iron the heading line of the lining fabric, reversing the fold line with the wrong sides of the facing and at the same time allow the fold to become 6mm (¼in) below the face fabric heading line. In other words, the 5cm (2in) fold allowance now becomes 5.6cm (2¼in). This ensures the lining does not show from the right-hand side of the curtain when it is slip stitched into place.

Marking Position for Buckram (Fig 193)

- ◆ Check the heading turning allowance using your 5cm (2in) card and iron the mitres into place at the corners.

- ◆ Place the buckram along this line the finished width of the curtain: add 5cm (2in) buckram each end – this is turned back to form a double layer at each end.

- ◆ Tack in place (Fig 194).

- ◆ Herringbone stitch into place (Fig 195).

Complete the Lining

Allow the prepared lining to drop into place over the buckram. Pin and tack into place. Complete the slip-stitching up from the stabilizing line on one side and along the heading and down into the second side to the stabilizing line.

Attaching Fusible Buckram

Follow the same order of work up to Fig 193.

Place the buckram in place. Using small bulldog clips, hold in place (Fig 196). *It is important that this is spot on.*

Bring the iron and ironing pad to the work table. You must take great care to be very accurate and not move the curtain around too much at this stage as the buckram is held very lightly in place. You must not allow the iron to touch the surface of the buckram or you will mark your iron surface with the glue.

Work from the edge of the heading where the 5cm (2in) turning allowance is in place. Using only the toe of the iron, press a spot every 4cm (1½in) along the heading line and through the face fabric, melting the glue in the buckram. Work the toe of the iron round and round on the spot in little circular movements putting pressure on the iron. Follow along with the bulldog clips to hold in place and set the glue while it cools.

Lining in Place

Allow the prepared lining to drop into place and secure with vertical pins into the face fabric between the spots of fused buckram. Take care you do not disturb this weak point of fusing. As for the standard buckram, follow the same order of work, completing the slip stitching making sure the mitred corners are neat.

Once the lining is slip stitched into position and pins removed, the moment has arrived to really fuse the buckram into place by pressing it firmly through the lining fabric.

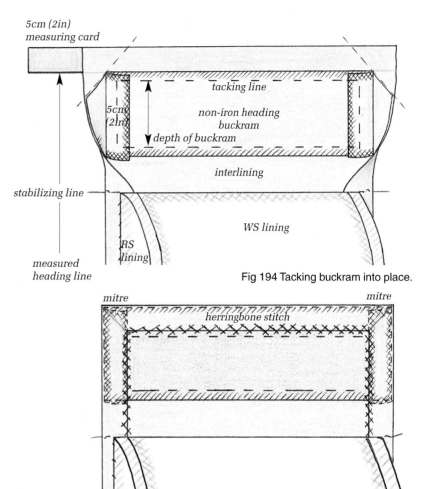

Fig 194 Tacking buckram into place.

Fig 195 Herringboning the buckram into place.

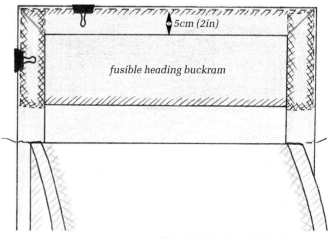

Fig 196 Attaching fusible buckram.

Turn the curtain with the right side uppermost and iron once again through the face fabric.

The stabilizing line remains in place until the curtain is completely finished.

Calculating Pleats and Spaces

Once the curtain is finished and ready for the pleats to be constructed, a little pre-planning will prove to be a valuable exercise. Calculating the pleats and spaces must be accurate and their appearance well balanced. We have once again found making a paper pattern a worth while exercise, enabling the overall effect and size to be checked against the pole or rail before working on the curtain.

Measuring for Making Pleating Paper Pattern

In making the pair of curtains the easiest and most accurate method is to work on the basis of one curtain only, so we must first divide the pole or rail in half.

Fig 197 Making a paper pattern for planning the pleats.

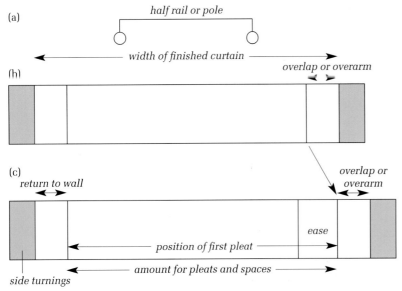

(a)

half rail or pole

width of finished curtain

overlap or overarm

(h)

(c)

return to wall

overlap or overarm

ease

position of first pleat

side turnings

amount for pleats and spaces

POLE

Measure the length of the pole between the two finial brackets and return to wall and divide by two.

Record this measurement.

Curtains suspended from a pole butt up at the lead edge; in order to allow an overlap at this point, add 5cm (2in). Then add to this point 7.5cm (3in) of *ease.*

Track on Pelmet Board with Fascia

Measure the length of the track and the two returns to the wall and the overlap arm of 10cm (4in). Record this measurement and divide by two. Add *ease*

EASE

The reason you add ease is to allow some movement in the curtain as it hangs to find its natural place, otherwise it appears too strained on the rail or pole. Although you measure the correct distance it will spring back into this place due to the gaps in between the pleats. As the curtain is *in situ*, the gaps in between should face inwards towards the wall giving a neat, unified finish.

Note: If using a hand heading for a valance or a static heading, you do not add the ease as the spacers remain flat to give a tailored, straight line and the pleats in a rigid position.

Spaces and Pelmets

Cut a 15cm (6in) wide strip of brown paper to the length of the width of your finished curtain. Add to this the two side turnings (Fig 197).

In general, the amount of fabric required for a French or goblet pleat is about 12–15cm (4¾–6in) and there are usually four pleats per width of fabric.

The spaces between the pleats are generally 10–12cm (4–4¾in). Never alter the length of spaces. Adjust any extra, or less, fabric into the pleats.

Making a Paper Pattern for French Pleats`

◆ Mark the paper LHS curtains.

◆ Mark off two side turnings.

◆ From the left-hand side, mark off the distance of the return to the wall for a pole or 10cm (4in) for a track suspended from a board with a fascia.

◆ At the other end of the paper mark off the overlap for the pole or the overarm of the rail plus ease.

Look carefully at Fig 197c, the amount left for pleats and spaces. The spaces constitute half the length of the track or pole plus the ease. The pleats are constructed from the remaining amount of fabric in one curtain. Subtract the half length of the rail plus the 7.5cm (3in) of ease from the amount of paper left marked 'pleats and spaces'. This will give you the amount of fabric left to work into pleats. Working on the assumption that you allow four pleats to every width of fabric as, for example, if you have used one and a half widths of fabric, six pleats, or two widths of fabric, eight pleats. Divide the amount left over by the amount of pleats required.

Remember, the width of the space is never altered. Any extra, or less, fabric is put into pleats.

◆ Make a measuring card for the spaces. This can be stored in your file.

◆ Make a second measuring card the calculated width of your project pleat. This card will have to be replaced to suit the pleat measurement on your plan for each new project. Mark out the strip of paper from your calculated measurement. Using the pleat markers space or pleat.

◆ Starting from the markings on either end of the paper pattern, return and overlap or overarm. Mark off first pleat at either end.

◆ Continue marking off the spacing and pleating. If your calculations were correct this should work out.

◆ Fold the pleat width to form the pleats and pin in place.

◆ Fold in the two side turnings. Take the pattern to the pole or fascia board and mark the centre (i.e. half the track or pole plus overlap or overarm) and check the size of the pattern (remember it will be 7.5cm or 3in longer, which is the ease). Once you are happy with the measurements make the curtains.

Constructing the French Pleat (Fig 198)

Divide the width of the pleat marking card into three equal parts.

1 Using the card, pin out each marked space along the top of the curtain pleat using vertical pins. Once again you will find it easier if you replace the pins with a single thread. Tailor tack at each of the four pin heads. Pins wriggle out and get in the way when machining.
2 Repeat markings for each pleat.

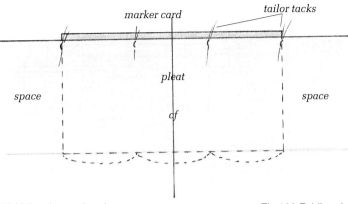

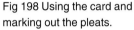

Fig 198 Using the card and marking out the pleats.

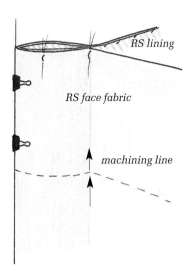

Fig 199 Folding the pleat.

Fig 200 Machining the pleat.

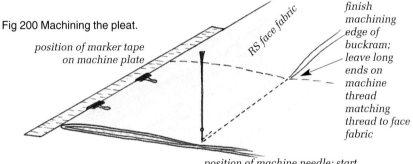

6 Take the curtain to the machine and very accurately machine a parallel line the depth of the buckram. Start your machining 3mm (⅛in) from the top edge of the curtain. Use the reverse stitch. Finish your machining at the very point of the bottom of the buckram. *Do not* use the reverse stitch and leave very long ends of thread (approximately 25cm or 10in).

3 The next stage is machining the pleats into position. You will find it easier to fold and work each pleat one at a time. Change your machine needle to size 16/110 and test your stitch through a scrap of curtain material with a piece of buckram encased. Fold the pleat in half bringing the two wrong sides together, matching the tailor tacks at the two side ends of the pleat and keeping the top edge of the curtain even (Fig 199). This must be spot on.

4 Use small bulldog clips or strong clothes pegs to hold the pleats in place along the centre fold line.

5 Place a marker tape on the machine plate the width of the folded pleat up to the machine needle (Fig 200).

Setting the Pleats in Place (Fig 201)

1 Hold the centre fold of the pleat and push it down onto the line of machining in the centre. This will automatically form three pleats. The French Pleat (or triple pleat) and the tailor tacks will correctly drop into place along the top of the curtain heading. Clamp into place into sharp folds, making sure the centre pleat does not protrude. At the base of the pleat pull the long threads through to the right side and thread a needle with double thread. Pierce the needle back where the threads emerge and bring it out at

the base fold between pleat one and two, then in and out of pleat two and then two and three. Return the needle where the thread emerges from the base of pleat three and retrace the stitches to where you began.

2 Stab stitch along the base of the pleats just under the edge of the buckram, with three stitches (Fig 202). End 3mm (⅛in) from the front of the pleats. Run the thread back and finish off with a small backstitch then run the threads off through the side of the pleat 2.5cm (1in) and clip off the ends.

3 Repeat on each of the French pleats.

Like the basic lined curtain, the hand-headed curtain must now be dressed.

It is important that both the lead edge and back edge of the curtain face towards the inside, i.e. the window, and that the spacing is even and inward facing, and the pleats face outwards. This must be correct – if it is not quite even, return and face the lead edge and re-pleat. Place the dressing bands in place and leave in position for two or three days. The curtains when opened and drawn should fall into neat folds.

The Goblet Pleat (Fig 203)

The goblet pleat is constructed in much the same way as the French pleat but with the following adaptations.

1 No ease is added to the paper pattern (i.e. fabric), as the pleats will be used in a static position, either as a valance or curtains in a static position on a pelmet board.

   Note: If using a French pleat for valances or static heading, the ease on the paper pattern (i.e. fabric) should be omitted (*see* Fig 204 overleaf).

2 The goblet pleat is marked with tailor tacks at each side of the pleat marker.

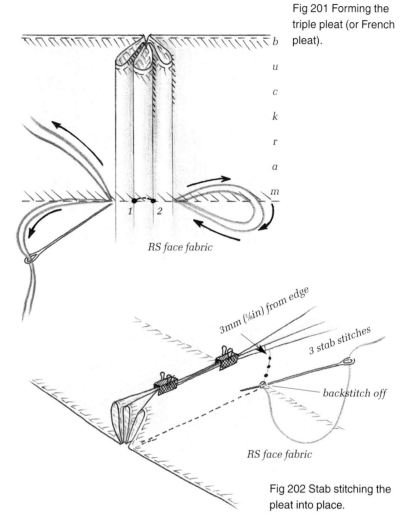

Fig 201 Forming the triple pleat (or French pleat).

RS face fabric

Fig 202 Stab stitching the pleat into place.

3mm (⅛in) from edge

3 stab stitches

backstitch off

RS face fabric

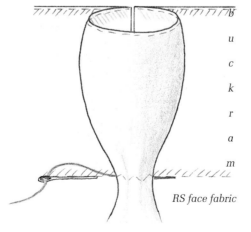

RS face fabric

Fig 203 The goblet pleat.

the thread follows the same route as the triple pleat, but no stab stitches

(Left) Fig 204 Paper pattern used for goblet pleats in a static position.

(Above) Fig 205 Cording and knotting using a figure of eight.

3 Follow Figs 199 and 200 but do not crease in the pleats; leave the pleat as the name suggests as a goblet. Follow the same procedure of securing the pleats at the base of the buckram but *omit* the *stab stitch*. Backstitch off your thread and run the threads through the side of the pleat and snip off the ends.

4 Fill the goblet with small pieces of interlining wadding and shape into the goblet. Or, for a more rigid effect, cut a piece of pelmet buckram slightly less than the depth of the pleat, so it cannot be seen at the top edge and 7.5–10cm (3–4in) wide. Roll it into a tube and place in the goblet and arrange the shape.

5 The base of each Goblet pleat can be finished off by adding a small, matching button at the base, or a more dramatic effect can be achieved by cording the pleats (Fig 205).

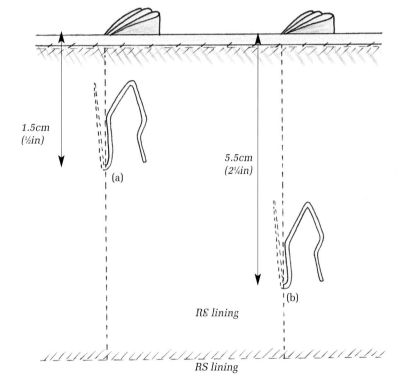

1.5cm (½in)

5.5cm (2¼in)

(a)

(b)

RS lining

RS lining

Fig 206 Position of pin hooks in fabric for pole and fascia board.

(Right) Fig 207 Position of pin hooks for fixing on a pole (a) and fascia board (b)

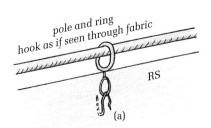

pole and ring
hook as if seen through fabric

RS

(a)

hook as if seen through fabric

fascia board   *RS fabric*

(b)

(Left) Fig 208 Goblet pleats in static position.

(Above) Fig 209 Triple pleats on pole.

6 Adjust knots and attach them to the base of each Goblet pleat with double matching thread and a series of stab stitches.

Poles with rings – inset the pin hook 1.5cm (½in) below the top of the curtain (Fig 206a).

Fascia board – insert the pin hook 5.5cm (2⅛in) below the top of the curtain (Fig 206b).

WATCHPOINTS:

1 Each pair of curtains must have the same number of pleats.

2 The second curtain must be the reverse of the first pattern. As beginners, I suggest making a second pattern to ensure this is correct. As you gain experience it is sufficient to reverse the same pattern.

Fig 210 The dressed curtains.

18 Project 10 – Tie-Backs

(*Top*) Fig 211 Fabric used.
Fig 212 Tie-backs: cords twisted into formal ends incorporating loops (*opposite, top right*); rope tie back with tassel (*opposite, below right*); and classic-shaped tie back (*above*).

These are sometimes referred to as Tie bands. To most of us the tie-backs have a definite and practical purpose. That is to draw the bulk of the curtains off the window, hold them neatly and securely and allow maximum light through the window when the curtains are opened.

Usually the tie-back holds the curtain fairly loosely in an angular position and should never be so short that it holds the curtain too straight causing it to be restrained. This destroys the draped effect and makes it look creased and untidy when it is drawn or released. Allow it to drape into soft folds. Curtains may be drawn back with a heading remaining in a static position.

Hooks to receive the tie-back and keep it in position are normally made of metal in plain and more ornate designs. Do make sure you buy one of good quality, in particular with heavy curtains.

For an elegant and classical appearance there are many lovely ropes and cords. Some of these have tassels, others have cords twisted into formal ends with incorporated loops to hold them in place on the decorative receiving hook. These tie-backs are not restrictive and allow the curtain to fall into soft shaped folds with a fuller look. They can be expensive, although good department stores carry a very good range and many of them are reasonably priced. They are made from both natural and man-made threads and many are coordinated with matching, smaller cords and braids for trimming tie-backs, pelmets, valances and cushions. At the really expensive end of the market it is possible to have these cords and trimming made and dyed to your own specifications and colour, sometimes using silk threads.

Large, heavy, interlined curtains are bulky when stacked back and the weight of the curtain against the tie-back sometimes spoils the shape of the leading edge of the curtain and the form of the tie-back. In such a case or where a formal or 'period' look to the curtain may be desired, a rigid commercial hold back may be employed. These are very decorative and ornate and strong and are made of metal or wood resembling arms.

Knobs can be used as an alternative to tie-backs. The lead edge of the curtain is tucked behind the knob and the curtain held in place in soft folds while the rest of the curtain, to the back edge, hangs loosely in vertical lines. These knobs may be bought in different materials and some have the facility to be covered with curtain fabric.

THE CLASSIC SHAPED TIE-BACK

These tie-backs are made in matching curtain fabric or a contrasting fabric of equal weight. They are much less costly than the commercial tie-back but there are important factors to be considered before making them. They are time consuming to make and the appropriate style and weight of the interfacing must be taken into account.

The tie-back is interfaced with a stiffened hessian known as pelmet buckram. Hessian is a coarse, strong cloth, plainly woven and used for sacking. The buckram is single starched or double starched and comes in different widths, the most used width being 46cm (18in).

The single-starched buckram should only be used for a smaller, lined only curtain of up to a width and a half. Double-starched buckram must be used for any curtain interlined with bump, or the weight of the curtain will spoil the shape of the tie-back.

Piping gives a structural shape to the work and defines the outline and can add colour and contrast. Alternatively, the edges can be finished with cording. Braiding or braiding with tassels along the bottom edge is an alternative and frills and pleats are also possibilities. Current fashion will probably dictate the extent of the decorative feature.

All interfaced, stiffened tie-backs should be lined with a face fabric. This can be done using the same face fabric or contrasting fabric. Whatever your choice, it must be of equal weight to your face fabric. Plain chintz is a very good choice to pick out one of the colours in the face fabric. It comes in a range of many plain colours and the chintz surface of the fabric can be reversed if used in conjunction with unglazed cotton furnishing fabric.

Do not use sateen lining fabric for your piping. Far better to use a cheap chintz and use it for both lining and piping.

MEASURING THE TIE-BACK

A material tie-back should never be made before the curtains are hanging in position. They should be correctly dressed and the dressing bands left in place for several days before taking any measurements. When the curtains are released they will fall into natural folds enabling you to visualize the position of the tie-back in relation to the window and the amount of light and shape required. Usually the tie-back is placed about two thirds down from the top of the curtain, but several different effects can be achieved by placing it either at the mid-point, above or below.

Using a soft tape measure, loosely measure around the stacked-back curtain at approximately the height you want the tie-back to be. Arrange the curtain into folds and shape in relation to the window you are dressing. Do not hold the tape measure too tight or it will destroy the draping of the curtain. As the shaped tie-back will hang in a curve, let the tape measure fall into a downward shape to a point where the lead edge of the curtain may be drawn into a pleasing shape. Hold the ends of the tape at the back edge of the curtain at the point where the position of the receiving hook will be fixed. Use a strong clothes-peg and secure the tape measure at this length round the curtain, or ask someone else to hold it for you, and stand back to visualize the overall effect. Once you are happy with the length and position of your tie-back mark the position of the receiving hook on the wall.

POSITION AND LENGTH OF THE TIE-BACK

Having established the length of your tie-back, a brown paper pattern must be made and tested around the curtain before cutting the fabric. It is important that the depth of the tie-back is in proportion to the length of the curtain. Too wide a tie-back will spoil the drape of your curtain. On average for a sill-length curtain, the tie-back should measure 7.5–10cm (3–4in) at its deepest point, which is the centre front, at the lead edge of the curtain. For a floor-length curtain, the tie-back should be 12.5–15cm (5–6in) deep. In addition to this, you must remember that if piping or cording the tie-back, this too will add to the width and must be taken into account.

A sample template, which can be kept in your file, has proved most successful for those finding it difficult to make a curved shape. This template can then be used to adapt measurements and shapes for future use.

Cut a rectangle of brown paper approximately 15cm × 25cm (6in × 10in). Looking at the diagram below (Fig 213a), from the bottom edge at point A, the centre front, sweep a curve with your pencil to point B at the outer end of the rectangle. Allowing the tie-back to be 7.5cm (3in) deep, draw another curve from C to D parallel to the first line. Round off the ends of the lines at the outer ends with an even curve. You now have a basic shape. Now cut out the template from the basic shape.

Fig 213b illustrates the use of the template to adapt the tie-back pattern for a

Fig 213 Sample template (a), and adapting the sample template (b).

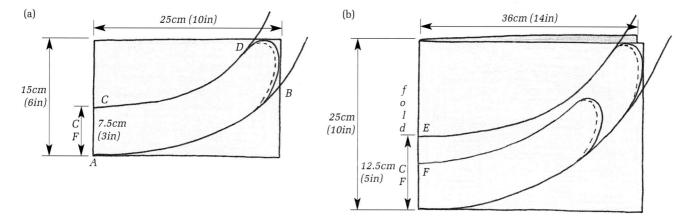

full-length curtain. Cut a piece of brown paper the length of your measured, flat tie-back allowing a little extra. As the depth of the tie-back will be 12.5cm (5in) the depth of the pattern must be twice this to accommodate the upwards sweep (i.e. 25cm or 10in). Fold the pattern in half at the centre front and pin together. Place your template at the bottom edge of the folded pattern as shown in Fig 213b. Extend the depth of the tie-back to 12.5cm (i.e. to point E) on the folded CF edge and mark its position. With the template in place on the pattern, extend the basic shape of the bottom edge to the corner of the pattern. From point E draw a curved line up to the corner of the pattern and adjust the end shape as preferred. Now cut out the pattern and test the size and shape round the curtain and make any adjustments necessary to its length or depth. If adjusting the length, adjust from the centre front fold so that you do not lose your shaped edge.

The shape can now be adapted to your preferred shape. Do not make it too narrow, as the ring, which will secure the tie-back to the receiving hook, must be hidden under this narrow end.

CALCULATING THE AMOUNT OF FABRIC

The amount of fabric needed can roughly be estimated from the rectangle of the brown paper pattern. But there are extra considerations to note:

- If using a patterned fabric you must take into consideration an overall balance of small and large motifs and an even distribution of colour and you will need a little extra material to allow for this.

- If you are piping the tie-back, extra will be required, either for your face fabric or a contrasting fabric.

- Face fabric used for a tie-back must be cut from the same bolt of fabric as the curtains, although you may have offcuts from your curtains that you may be able to use.

Having used fabrics in several projects you should now be able to make your own judgement in estimating the amount of fabric for the tie-back.

Before cutting your final paper pattern (Fig 214), there are certain considerations to be noted. It is essential that the rings attached to each end of the tie-back and looped over the receiving hook to hold the curtain, should not be seen from the front when the tie-back is in place. The ring attached to the visible end of the tie-back in place in front of the curtain, must be set back under the end of the tie-back. The ring at the other end of the tie-back will be attached to protrude beyond the edge. This will have the effect of moving the visible mid-point (centre front) and deepest part of the tie-back slightly to the left or right of the true centre front and therefore must be taken into account when making the paper pattern. Mark the paper pattern right side and wrong side. With the right side uppermost, fold the pattern along the centre front line. Mark on to the wrong side of the pattern the positions and sizes of the brass rings. Fold the pattern so that the positions of the rings are superimposed on one another and re-crease what will now become the new centre front as shown in Fig 214. Turn the paper pattern with the right side facing and fold it at the new

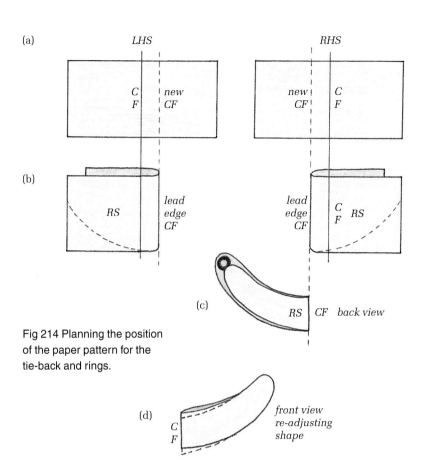

Fig 214 Planning the position
of the paper pattern for the
tie-back and rings.

centre front, and you will notice that the shape of the two halves is slightly uneven. Reshape the paper pattern so that the edges match.

In order to avoid confusion when cutting a left and a right tie-back, and to assist you when placing the patterns on the face fabric, cut two identical paper patterns. Carefully fold these patterns into a right-hand side pattern and a left-hand side pattern and mark them accordingly. Then on each, mark the right side and wrong side and check that these are correct. These will be the finished size of the tie-backs. Mark these patterns No 1.

A second set of patterns must now be made for the cutting size. Allow 1.5cm (½in) seam allowance all round. Place the patterns onto a larger piece of brown paper and a very accurately mark in the seam allowance. Mark both these patterns in the same way as patterns No 1 and call them patterns No 2 (cutting size patterns). Carefully check that both sets marry up.

Before estimating the fabric for your tie-backs, different options must be clarified. The face fabric can be used on both the front and back of the tie-back. Alternatively, you may wish to face the back of the tie-back with a contrasting fabric.

Note: if using the face fabric on the reverse side of the tie-back, it is not important where you place a particular motif or colour. If you are going to pipe the tie-back you may do so in matching fabric or with a contrasting fabric either on its own or to marry up with the contrasting back facing fabric. Make these decisions before estimating your fabric.

MATERIALS

- Face fabric for both sides of the tie-backs – matching or contrasting.

- Fabric for piping.

- Piping cord.

- Buckram – single or double, depending on the size of the tie-back and the weight and size of the curtain. If the curtain is interlined, use the heavier weight buckram.

- Interlining – bump or domette for one side of the tie-back. It really does improve the look of a really classical shaped tie-back if you place interlining on both the front and back of the buckram. This is an operational extra, but I do prefer it.

- Curtain lining sateen fabric – cream or ecru for one side of each of the tie-backs.

- 4 brass rings = 1.5cm (½in) diameter.

- Matching thread

Finally, cut a rectangle of brown paper to the longest and greatest depth on the flat shaped tie-back. This can be used to estimate your fabric and as a cutting pattern for the interlining (bump or domette).

Cutting the Face Fabric

Use Pattern No 2 (cutting size).

A little time and consideration is necessary in placing your pattern in the correct position.

Using a Plain Fabric

- Make sure you place the pattern accurately on the straight of grain down the warp thread line.

- Remove the paper patterns.

- Mark right and wrong side of the fabric.

- Mark the right-hand side and left-hand side tie-backs.

Set aside.

Using a Patterned Fabric (Fig 215)

Careful planning is very necessary to obtain a balance in size of motifs and colour in the fabric. This should appear in similar positions on each of the tie-backs (*see* Fig 215). Once you have established a balanced effect, check the straight of grain. Follow the same procedure as for cutting out the plain fabric tie-backs and *set aside*.

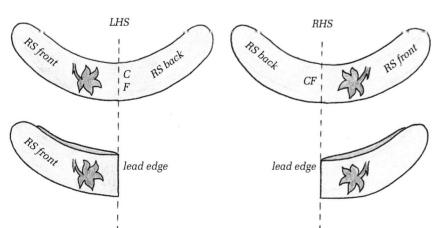

Fig 215 Planning the position of the motif or colour.

Face Fabric for Backing the Tie-Back

If using the matching face fabric for backing the back of the tie-back, cut two more pieces of face fabric. If using a contrasting fabric, cut two pieces.

Note: The motifs on the backing fabric do not have to be matched and the flat pattern can be used on the two layers of fabric. This will automatically give you a right-hand side and a left-hand side.

Place the pattern on the straight of grain. Mark these and *set aside*.

Cutting the Buckram

Using Pattern No 1 (finished size), cut out very accurately using your paper-cutting scissors, as the buckram will blunt your material-cutting scissors. There is no right side or wrong side. Mark left-hand side and right-hand side, and give both of them a right side and a wrong side to identify when constructing.

Set aside.

Lining fabric: cotton lining sateen

Use paper Pattern No 2 (cutting size).

You can cut the two lining pieces from a double piece of lining fabric. You will automatically have a left-hand side and a right-hand side but do make sure that the straight of grain follows through.

Remove the pattern and carefully identify each piece.

Set aside.

Interlining Fabric

Use the rectangle of brown paper you used to estimate your fabric.

The interlining is cut as rectangles and once it is attached to the buckram it is cut back to the shape of the finished tie-back.

Cut four rectangles of interlining to cover both sides of the buckram.

ORDER OF WORK: FACE FABRIC

Piping

Make up sufficient piping to pipe all round the edges of both tie-backs, plus a little extra for the final join.

Before placing the piping in place on the tie-back face fabric, encase the cord into the crossway in the usual way and tack in place. Machine close to the piping using matching thread, leaving space unmachined at either end to complete the final join.

Attaching the Piping to the Tie-Backs

At this stage the piping is attached to the face fabric. This must be very accurate or you will lose the line and shape of your finished size of face fabric.

Place the face fabric on the table right side uppermost. If making two tie-backs, place both face fabric pieces in their correct position, i.e. left-hand side and right-hand side.

Using paper pattern No 1 (finished size), note that when making the final join in the piping the final join should lie on the bottom edge of the back of the tie-back midway between the mid-point (CF) and the ends. Mark the position on both pattern pieces.

Replace the patterns onto the face fabric pieces making sure the 1.5cm (½in) seam allowance is even all round. Pin in place.

Mark with a sharp HB pencil the shape of Pattern No 1 and mark the point for the piping final join. Remove the pattern and replace the tie-backs in the correct position on the table.

Attaching the Piping (Fig 216)

The piping is attached to the edges of the tie-backs in the same way as for the basic cushion, with one exception. The piping cord is already machined into the cross-way. This enables you to use the line of machine stitching to exactly cover, pin and tack onto the pencil marking line on the tie-back. Use the unmachined end to begin your tacking, positioning the piping in the same way as for the basic cushion. At the rounded ends of the tie-backs it will be necessary to slash and mould the piping as for the basic round cushion. The final join will be done in the usual way.

Once the piping is tacked and joined, machine close to the piping all the way round, following the first line of machining.

Set aside.

Attaching the Interlining to the Buckram

Assemble the interlining and buckram. Fill a spray bottle with warm water and check that the nozzle is set to a light, even-spraying position.

It is important at this point that care is taken with your iron and ironing surface. Protect the ironing surface with a tea towel or a small piece of cotton fabric.

Take one piece of buckram and, holding it over the sink, lightly spray the surface on one side. Place the buckram on the ironing surface with the damp side uppermost. Place the rectangle of interlining over the buckram and, using a hot iron, the heat of the iron will melt the starch into a glue form, which will fuse the buckram and interlining together. Do take care that your iron does not touch the raw edge of the buckram otherwise you will cause a problem with starch on the plate of your iron, which is difficult to remove. It is a good idea to cover the interlining and buckram with another piece of cotton fabric and press through all the layers. Let the buckram dry and trim back the bump or domette to the shape of the tie-back.

Repeat on the second tie-back buckram. Then repeat on the second sides of

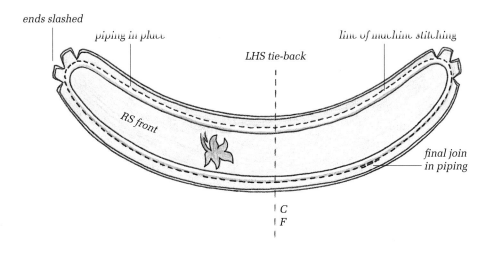

ends slashed

piping in place

line of machine stitching

LHS tie-back

RS front

final join in piping

C
F

Fig 216 Attaching the piping.

both tie-backs. Trim back the interlining and allow the prepared tie-backs to dry thoroughly. Re-mark right-hand side and left-hand side.

Set aside.

Attaching the Lining to the Buckram Covered with the Interlining (Fig 217)

Place the lining fabric on the table wrong side uppermost and check that the right-hand side and left-hand side are correct.

Place the buckram onto the wrong side of the lining fabric, centralizing the shape. Carefully line tack right down the centre of each tie-back. It is difficult to get your needle through the buckram, especially when it is double starched, but as a beginner and beyond it is worthwhile because it then allows an even seam allowance to appear all round the edge of the tie-back. Use doubled thread or Bold.

With the interlining uppermost and the wrong side of the seam allowance protruding along the edge of the buckram, bring the edge of the seam allowance 1.5cm (½in) over the edge of the buckram. Tack into place through all layers using a double thread or the stronger bold thread. Tack as far away from the edge of the buckram as possible because this tacked seam allowance acts as an anchor to secure the face fabric at the next stage.

Carefully slash the rounded ends and any other necessary areas up to near the marked line, but do not slash right up to the line. Now remove a V shape of fabric to remove the bulk as for the basic round cushion.

Repeat on the second tie-back, but remember to check that it is the left-hand side or right-hand side and place your fabrics in the relevant positions.

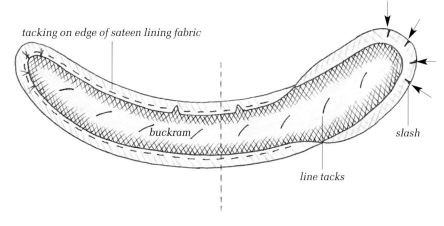

tacking on edge of sateen lining fabric

buckram

slash

line tacks

Fig 217 Attaching the lining to the buckram.

Attaching the Face Fabric to the Lined and Interlined Buckram (Fig 218)

Lay the prepared, piped face fabric wrong side uppermost on the table.

Place the lined side of the tie-back to the wrong side of the face fabric. If the machining of the piping was correct the prepared buckram should fit exactly into the shape. Repeat the tacking process, but this time use the secured lining seam allowance to anchor the seam allowance of the face fabric, including the piping seam allowance. Tack only into the lining seam allowance and not right through to the front face of the tie-back.

Both lines of tacking remain in place inside the tie-back and will not be seen

Fig 218 Attaching the face fabric to the lined and interlined buckram.

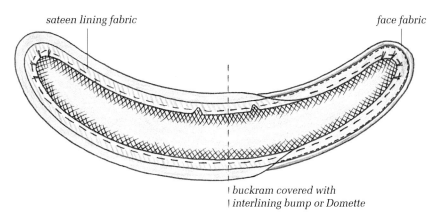

sateen lining fabric

face fabric

buckram covered with interlining bump or Domette

when the tie-back is complete. Use the doubled cotton or bold.

Completing the Tie-Back
(Fig 219)

The rings to hold the tie-back in place on the receiving hook must now be attached and the face fabric backing fabric slip stitched into place.

Setting the Rings in place

The diagram (*see* below) is for a right-hand-side tie-back.

Ring No 1: this lies at the back edge and behind the curtain. This ring should protrude with half its diameter beyond the edge of the piping.

Ring No 2: this lies at the back edge and in front of the curtain. It is hidden underneath the piped edge.

The rings are set in place and secured with a row of tight blanket stitches covering the bottom half of the brass ring. Use double cotton or bold. The stitching must be neat and secure. Repeat for the second tie-back, placing the rings in the opposite positions. The rings can be placed under the backing fabric (*see* Fig 219a) or on the top (*see* Fig 219b).

Preparing the Face Fabric Backing

Mark the seam line using Pattern No 1 (finished size) with a pencil on the wrong side.

You will find at the rounded corners and curve of the tie-back that you will have to slash to the shape. Do be careful to make straight slashes and not too close to the marked pencil line.

Finger-press and mould the shaped ends into place to the wrong side along the marked line and continue finger-pressing all round the edge.

Place the tie-back with the wrong side uppermost, and place the wrong side of the prepared backing fabric on top, matching the straight of grain at the CF. Pin in place with vertical pins.

Let the shaped ends fall into place over the attached rings or attach the rings in the correct position on the top of the facing fabric. The folded line of the seam allowance should drop onto the line of machine stitching holding the piping in place. Pin in place with vertical pins all round and slip stitch the backing fabric into place using matching thread.

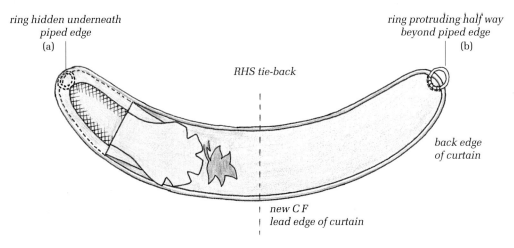

ring hidden underneath piped edge
(a)

ring protruding half way beyond piped edge
(b)

RHS tie-back

back edge of curtain

new CF
lead edge of curtain

Fig 219 Attaching the rings and the face fabric backing.

19 Project 11 – Roman Blinds

The next worked project will be a Roman blind using striped cotton fabric and lined with blackout lining material. It will be mounted inside the recess of the window.

The Roman blind in today's form is no less than in times gone by when the blinds were used in aiding privacy and controlling light in rooms.

In certain circumstances blinds have advantages over curtains. They are extremely economical in the amount of fabric needed as this flat blind covers only the window area. Blinds can be used in conjunction with curtains, under pelmets and valances or under a fixed heading where curtains remain static. They lend themselves well to windows where there may be interesting architraves which enhance the window itself, rather than covering them by curtaining. In modern furnishing interiors they can give a crisp and classical appearance. Bay windows can be enhanced if several blinds are hung. It can be a useful window dressing for bathroom windows where screening is necessary or where curtains may interfere with damp surfaces, as indeed may be the case in kitchens.

There are considerations to be taken into account before buying your fabric and to achieve a really professional, tailored finish; great care will have to be taken at each and every stage of your work.

Measuring must be very accurate and the blind must fit really well. The fabric must be cut exactly on the straight of grain of your fabric. It is therefore very important that you check that the fabric of your choice is printed accurately and there is no pattern drift. The weight, pattern and weave of your fabric must also be considered. To have a really good result the blind must appear crisp and tailored and fold into neat folds when pulled up. Loosely woven fabrics are not suitable and very large patterned fabrics should be carefully considered and probably avoided. Woven patterned fabrics of stripes or checks are a good choice as their weave ensures that the straight of grain is correct. Do check the widths of uneven stripes and the effect a checked fabric would create when the blind is folded up. Firm textured fabrics are a good choice. These again are woven in such a way as to ensure the straight of grain.

Read the list of definitions and equipment on pages 233–4 before making your blind.

A blind always looks better if it is longer than the width. The maximum width should not be much more than approximately 2m (2yd 6in) or it will look overwhelming. It is better to break the window space with several blinds. As with valances and pelmets, it is important that you centralize your first drop of fabric and any extra fabric is equally distributed at either side. If there is a pattern repeat, this must be pattern-matched.

The blind is fixed to a timber batten that is covered with lining or face fabric and the blind is attached to the batten

with Velcro. Commercial tracks are available with Velcro and rings incorporated but these are more expensive than making your own and can sometimes let daylight in at the top.

The Roman blind is raised and lowered by a cord system. Drawn up, the blind falls into neat horizontal folds and lowered, it becomes a neat, tailored, flat, rectangular piece of fabric covering your window area. Channels are made in the lining fabric of the blind to accommodate doweling rods which structure the blind, adding weight and holding the fabric in sharp horizontal folds when drawn up. Fine nylon blind cords are threaded through a vertical line of rings stitched to the edge of the doweling lining channels from the bottom of the blind to the top and then through screw eyes which are screwed to the underside of the batten. This then channels the cords to the side of the blind where they are made into drawstrings.

LINING THE BLIND

It is not usual to interline blinds, but they should be lined as this will protect the blind from sunlight and add a little insulation. A blind is usually lined with the cotton sateen lining fabric. The temptation to line with a coloured lining should be carefully considered. As with your curtains, you must think of the outside appearance of your window and the coloured lining could substantially alter the colour of your face fabric. But as always, rules are made to be broken and it may be you are using a dark fabric and may wish to have a coloured effect from the outside. Do hold the two fabrics together to the light before making a decision.

In addition, the lining on the blind accommodates the channels for the rods and hides the hems and turnings of your

face fabric giving a neat overall finish in appearance from outside your window.

As an alternative, use blackout or thermal linings. These firmer linings lend themselves well to the folds of the blind when they are pulled up. The blackout lining fabric can be particularly useful for children's rooms or in rooms where

Fig 220 The raised Roman blind.

maximum cutting out of light may be necessary. In the same way, you could use one of the thermal linings to add insulation.

Do note that, with both the blackout and thermal linings coming in close contact with the glass of your window, they can cause condensation. So, once again you must make your final judgement to accommodate the particular window you are covering.

To make it clear when the word 'recess' is used, in the following project the correct words for a window recess are as follows:

- The sides of the windows are the reveals.

- The top of the reveals is known as the soffit.

The batten is fixed up into the soffit (Fig 221).

On the whole, Roman blinds are more successful and tailored if fixed onto the soffit of the window so that it fits exactly into the recess. This is why it is so important that your blind is a good fit and that the clearance between the edges of the blind, as it is lowered and raised, is minimal in order to avoid a margin of light each side.

There are, however, circumstances when it may be necessary to mount your blind outside the window frame. You would then have to fix your batten to the face of the wall using metal angle brackets:

- In the case of a very small window where maximum light is needed, the blind should be mounted above the window allowing in as much light as possible when the blind is raised.

- If the recess is so shallow that the blind will fall directly onto the glass, causing condensation on the glass to mark your blind.

Note all relevant information on equipment on pages 233–4 for mounting outside the recess.

Before taking your final measurements for your Roman blind, the timber batten from which the blind will be hung must be covered in lining fabric and in place on the soffit (top of recess) of your window.

You will need a timber batten 5cm × 2.5cm (2in × 1in). This adequately supports a lined, medium-weight, fabric blind, but as always, there are circumstances that might dictate otherwise, such as a very small window or a very shallow recess. In this case you might reduce the size of the batten to 2.5cm × 2.5cm (1in × 1in).

My choice of window for the worked project blind is a small cloakroom where there is opaque glass and a deep recess.

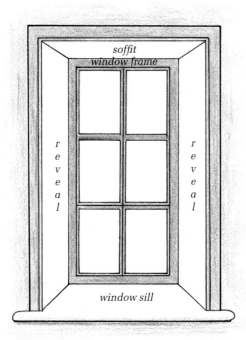

Fig 221 Names of the recess of a window.

The blind will hang inside the recess.

All preplanning, measuring and order of work will be for this worked blind.

Make your own choice of window and follow all these instructions carefully, adjusting and recording your own measurements where necessary.

Width of Blind

You must take the exact measurements inside the recess and do check that this is constant all the way down, particularly in older houses.

Whatever the width of the recess you must deduct 6mm (¼in) from this measurement. There are two reasons for this:

1 In covering the batten with fabric it will bulk out at the ends where the fabric is folded to cover these ends.

2 It is also necessary to have a clearance at either side of the blind to avoid any restrictions as the blind is raised and dropped and to allow it to hang in a straight line.

The final FINISHED width of the blind will be the width of the COVERED batten.

Length of Blind

As the worked blind hangs inside the recess, the measurement taken will be from the top of the recess (soffit) to the bottom (window sill).

Initially this measurement should be taken and recorded.

The FINISHED drop of the blind will be from the top of the batten just onto the window sill. It will, in fact, more or less be the initial measurement, but this must be rechecked once the batten is in place.

All measurements should be taken and recorded before making the batten, but once the batten is in place these must be re-checked and adjusted before making the pattern for your blind.

 *RECORD IN YOUR NOTEBOOK*

◆ Draw a rough plan of the window
◆ Position of batten – inside recess
　　　　　　　– re-check after making the batten

Width of recess	62cm (24½in)
Length (drop) of recess	99cm (39in)

Cutting width of batten = width of recess – 6mm (¼in)

　　　　　　= 　62cm – 6mm = 61.5cm

or　　　　　= 　24½in – ¼in = 24¼in

PREPARING TO MAKE A ROMAN BLIND

Making and Covering a Batten for the Worked Roman Blind

Cut the batten to the relevant length 61.5cm (24¼in) for the worked blind. Smooth the ends of the batten with a little sandpaper or file. Mark out the batten in the following order (*see* Fig 222 overleaf):

1 Mark the front and top of the batten.
　Note: The top of the batten is the wide face;
　The front of the batten is the long, narrow face.

2 Draw a vertical pencil line across the centre of the top face of the batten and another line along the centre front.

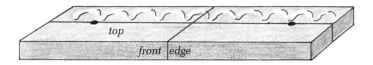

Fig 222 Marking the front and top of the batten and showing the glue in position.

3 Mark two points 12cm (5in) from both ends of the batten on this horizontal centre line.

4 Drill two holes through the batten at these points to accommodate the screws, which will fix the batten to the soffit. This will leave sufficient space at the ends of the batten to accommodate the screw eyes for the cording system to lower and raise the blind. These will be put into the batten once it is covered.

ORDER OF WORK: COVERING BATTEN WITH FABRIC

1 Measure around the batten and add 7.5cm (3in).

2 Measure the length of the batten and add 20cm (8in).

3 Cut a rectangle of lining fabric to this measurement on the straight of grain of the fabric. Mark the centre of the length with a small **V** top and bottom.

4 Iron in a 1.5cm (½in) fold along one long edge to the wrong side.

5 Run a little multipurpose glue along the top of the batten behind the marked centre length line. Take care to spread the glue evenly and sparingly by making round movements with the nozzle of the glue. Spread the excess glue with an old knife to even it out.

6 With the right side of the fabric uppermost, place the raw edge of the lining fabric along the marked pencil line matching the centre markings and gently press into place. Run

your fingers along to ensure it is even. Let it dry.

7 Staple the centre and add one more staple at each end. Take care when using the staple gun.

8 Wrap the remaining fabric around the batten bringing the ironed-in, folded edge over the stapled raw edge, matching centres. Keep this taut.

9 Staple at the centre and then both ends and at intervals in between.

10 Neatly fold both ends of the lining fabric as if making a parcel and place a staple in the short ends of the batten at the bottom base point to strengthen.

11 Bring these short ends over the staples and over onto the top of the batten. Keep the fabric taut and hold this in place with another staple.

This is the top of the batten and goes up onto the soffit.

Attaching the Velcro to the Front Edge of the Batten

Cut a strip of Velcro the length of the front edge of the batten plus 5cm (2in).

The adhesive hook-side of the strip of Velcro is now placed along the front edge of the batten. Reinforce with staples at about 7.5cm (3in) intervals.

The Velcro is cut 5cm (2in) longer than the front edge of the batten. This enables the Velcro to be taken neatly round the corners at each end onto the short return edges by 2.5cm (1in). This allows an extra staple to be placed in the return edge so strengthening the Velcro in position.

Carefully set aside the corresponding soft loop side strip of Velcro. This will be machined to the heading of the blind to enable the blind to be attached to the batten.

Marking Position for the Screw Eyes on the Batten (Fig 223)

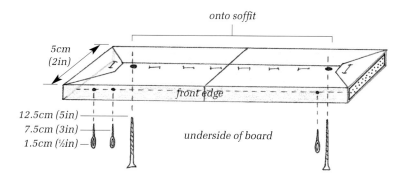

Screw eyes are positioned on the underside of the batten through which the cords on the blind will be threaded. One screw eye is positioned above every vertical line of rings, which are attached to the edge of each dowel channel to enable the blind to be raised and lowered by the cord system. One extra screw eye is placed at one end approximately 1.5cm (½in) from the end of the batten to accommodate the line of cords, which will be formed into a pull cord.

The appearance from outside the window can look unsightly if too many cords and rings are visible. It is sufficient to place one at each side of the blind.

If the blind is more than 100cm (40in) wide, place an extra screw eye in the centre along the same line as the two side screw eyes. This will accommodate the extra line of rings needed on the wider blind.

1 Decide which side you want the draw cord to fall.
2 Mark the position for the screw eyes on the underside of the batten with a sharp pencil point.
3 The screw eyes are set slightly towards the front edge of the batten. All screw eyes should run in a straight line set back approximately 2cm (¾in) from the front edge of the batten.
4 The two side screw eyes should be exactly 7.5cm (3in) from the edge of the short, return ends of the batten.
5 Mark the additional screw eye which will take the draw cord approximately 1.5cm (½in) from one short, return end of the batten. When you have checked all markings are correct, pierce through the fabric into the wood with the bradawl and mark the hole for the

screw eyes and re-establish the position of the drilled holes in the batten by piercing through the batten and into the underneath fabric covering.

Note: When using a bradawl, do take care you do not pull the fabric, twist gently while making the holes in the fabric.

6 Screw all screw eyes into place so that the cords will thread through from side to side.

Position of the Batten

The question is often asked, 'Where is the batten set on the soffit?'

This really depends on the depth of your recess. Care must be taken that it is not set too close to the window glass or you will create condensation. Normally, fit the batten a little nearer the front than midway between the front edge of the soffit and the window frame.

1 Mark position for front edge of batten on the soffit.
2 Place the completed batten with the drilled holes now marked through the fabric and, with the bradawl, mark a corresponding mark onto the soffit.
3 Remove the batten and drill the holes in the soffit. Fit Rawlplugs and tap them home.

Fig 223 Screwing the screw eyes into the batten.

4 Screw the batten up into the soffit. Take care when you tighten the screws through the fabric. It can twist if you make the screws too tight.

PREPARING TO MAKE THE BLIND

The next important consideration is the final measuring and estimating of your fabric. *Re-check* all the measurements in your notebook and adjust where necessary.

- The finished width of your blind will be the width of the covered batten.

- The finished drop of your blind will be from the top of your covered batten onto the window sill.

I know this may sound like time wasting but I have found through experience with my students that if we make up a blind in paper first, we get excellent results. There are three reasons for this:

1 By taking your paper pattern to your window it is easy to note how much light is available, how the balance of the blind appears and that it fits well Into the recess of your window.
2 When calculating the folds on your blind, they can be easily marked out in the paper and once again checked against your window.
3 The paper pattern for the lining fabric can be marked with the channel casing lines. These can then be folded into place on the paper and the corresponding marks for the folds on the face fabric checked against them. It is very important that these points are accurate.

The amount of face fabric and lining fabric can be estimated from the patterns.

The width of the pattern is not so important when making your paper pattern and once the paper becomes wider than the 95cm (37½in) width roll of brown paper, the paper becomes difficult to manoeuvre.

If your blind is wider I suggest you use just one width of brown paper and when you have completed and marked in your folds and the paper pattern is ready to be checked against your window add a strip of paper about 20cm (8in) deep and cut it to the correct width of your blind. Then add this strip to the top of your paper pattern.

Note: Add to this measurement an extra 3mm (⅛in) to the finished width of the blind. The reason for this additional 3mm is to ensure that the ends of the batten are not visible at the sides once the blind is in position. Whenever turning or stitches are put into fabric it will always slightly shrink back from the paper pattern measurements.

The finished width is now:

$$61.5cm + 3mm = 61.8cm$$
$$24\tfrac{1}{4}in + \tfrac{1}{8}in = 24\tfrac{3}{8}in$$

Finished length (drop) of blind is 99cm (39in).

Cutting length of the blind is finished drop plus:

5cm (2in) at the top for the heading;
5cm (2in) at the bottom for the hem.

Note: The 5cm allowance at the top of the blind will later be cut back to 2.5cm (1in). The reason for the extra 2.5cm is to allow the length of the blind to be adjusted when making the final check for the position of the heading and the clearance from the window sill.

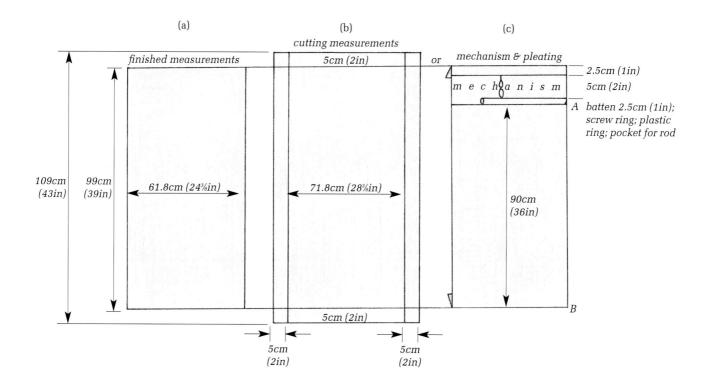

Fig 224b The cutting measurements.

Fig 224 (a) The finished measurements (from your notebook); (b) the cutting measurements; and (c) planning the amount of fabric for the folds.

FACE FABRIC PATTERN AND PLANNING FOLDS

The following measurements are applicable to the worked Roman blind.

Follow these measurements but adapt the patterns and fold calculation to your own measurements.

Look carefully at Fig 224.

The worked Roman blind measurements recorded are:

Fig 224a

Finished width of blind
(i.e. covered width of batten)

plus 3mm (⅛in) ease   61.8cm (24⅜in)

finished length of blind   99cm (39in)

The cutting length

Heading allowance	5cm (2in)
Finished length of blind	99cm (39in)
Hem allowance	5cm (2in)
	109cm (43in)

The cutting width

(sum of two side turnings + width of finished blind)

$$= 5cm + 61.8cm + 5cm = 71.8cm$$

$$= 2in + 24⅜in + 2in = 28⅜in$$

Face Fabric Paper Pattern

Cut a rectangle of brown paper and make a paper pattern to the *cutting length and width* of your material (or width of brown paper).

1 Use your 5cm (2in) measuring card to mark off the heading turning from the top of the paper pattern 5cm and turn down.
2 Mark off the hem turning from the bottom of the pattern 5cm and turn up.
3 Mark off and turn in the two side turnings of 5cm, and mitre the corners of the hem.

You now have your finished size of blind.

After folding over the hem, heading and side turnings, check that this pattern fits your recess from the top of the batten to the sill.

Remember we have allowed a small amount (approximately 3mm or ⅛in 'ease'), which will be taken up in the stitching. Check the clearance at the sides is minimal.

Planning the Folds

♦ The amount of fabric taken up between each fold is really determined by the length of your blind. A larger blind needs a bigger pleat. It is usual to make these folds approximately 10–18cm (4–7in) deep. For the small blind we are making, and looking at the measurements of the finished blind (shown in the diagrams), the folds should be about 10cm (4in) deep. So bearing in mind the length of blind it could work with four folds, so it is assumed that this will be the number of folds.

♦ 20cm (8in) of fabric is needed to give 10cm (4in) folds. For a blind with four full folds, eight half pleats plus an additional half pleat

(behind which the four folded pleats will stack away) are needed.

♦ Place the pattern right side uppermost on your table with the heading, side turnings and hem in place. Mark off from the top the depth of your batten 2.5cm (1in). Now mark off another 5cm (2in). This space will accommodate screw eyes, rings and dowel casings.

♦ From point A measure to point B to give you the length of fabric to be made up into folds. (Fig 224c)

If the pleating drop is 90cm (36in) and there are to be 4 full pleats then there will be a total of eight half pleats plus an additional half pleat at the top into which the folded pleats retract. We must therefore divide the remaining length of material by nine (8+1) equal parts to get the length of a half fold. A full fold will obviously be double.

The example for the worked Roman blind:

♦ 90cm divided by 9 = 10cm (4in) and therefore one full fold will be 20cm (8in).

Mark the pleats out on the paper pattern beginning with the half pleat at the bottom.

Suppose we had assumed three pleats then the figures would have worked out like this:

♦ 90 cm divided by 7 = 12.8cm (5in) and one full pleat will be 25.5cm (10in) (which would be too big for a window of this size and would lose too much light).

♦ Fold the paper pattern into the correct fold lines.

- Check all folds are equal and they fall on top of one another.

- If necessary, allow added extra wide strip of brown paper across the top of the pattern.

- Check this fits your window recess

Set the face fabric paper pattern aside.

The Lining Fabric Paper Pattern

The width of the lining fabric is the FINISHED width of the face fabric. The length of the lining fabric is longer than the face fabric to accommodate the casings for the dowel rods.

Each casing allowance = circumference of rod + 1cm (⅜in) ease for the worked blind, 4cm (1½in) is allowed for each casing.

See Fig 225 for the worked blind and adjust these measurements to your own measurements.

Cutting Length

Finished + heading + case = Total
length   allowance   allowance
of blind
(drop)

99cm + 5cm + 16cm* = 120cm

              or

39in + 2in + 6in• = 47in

(*4 casings × 4cm)
(•4 casings × 1½in)

Cutting Width

Width of finished blind

$$61.5\text{cm} + 3\text{mm ease} = 61.8\text{cm}$$

$$24\tfrac{1}{4}\text{in} + \tfrac{1}{8}\text{in} = 24\tfrac{3}{8}\text{in}$$

Cut a rectangle of brown paper the exact *cutting length* and the FINISHED width of the blind.

The question is often asked, 'Is there no hem allowance?' The hemline on the lining is shorter than the face fabric and is built into this length measurement.

- Cut a paper pattern the correct length.

- Starting at the top, mark in the turning allowance of 5cm (2in) and then the 7.5cm (3in) for the batten and mechanism.

- Mark in pleats and rod pockets, starting your marking from the bottom.

- Fold in a side turning of 2.5cm (1in) at each side. Use card.

Now fold up the hem allowance of 2.5cm (use card). Then leave in the flat, opened out position.

Pin rod folds in lining pattern and check it fits the face fabric pattern by placing the two paper patterns side by side. Note the lining pattern without the hemline in position should be the same length as the finished length of the face fabric pattern.

Face Fabric

CUTTING OUT

1 Straighten fabric. This is most important when making a Roman blind. It *must* be on the straight of grain.
2 Lay on pattern, placing on straight of grain. In the case of a striped fabric, make sure you centralize a stripe. Pin in place.
3 Mark top centre front **V**.
4 Remove paper pattern. Record any necessary information. Set aside for future use.

ORDER OF WORK

1 Using your 5cm (2in) measuring card, iron the two side turnings, iron up hem allowance and tack into place.
2 Mitre corners and ladder stitch.

3 Serge stitch the two side turnings into place leaving the hem unstitched and both sides the measurement of the half pleat from the bottom hemline. It is necessary to leave this open to allow the lath to be placed into the turning of the hemline when you complete your blind.

Marking Out Pleats (Fig 225)

1 Lay the completed, ironed face fabric on the table right side uppermost.
2 Lay the face fabric pattern, hems and side turnings in place.

Mark in the pleats starting at the bottom and carefully pin out each side. This must be accurate and as an added precaution you can always double check using your measuring stick (no tape measures because these stretch).

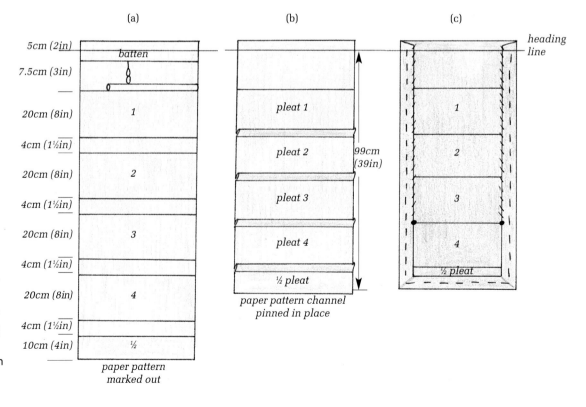

Fig 225 (a) Marking out channels on lining paper pattern; (b) folding channels on lining paper pattern; and (c) checking the pleat line and pleats marked with tailor tack on face fabric.

Once you are sure all measurements are correct, remove each pin and replace with a tailor tack. It is sufficient to use single cotton and loosely tighten the loop onto the side edges of the blind.

Do not iron in folds or top heading turnings.

Set aside.

ORDER OF WORK: LINING THE BLIND

1 Prepare the fabric and cut out following usual procedure with relevant markings, pinning and cutting.

   Note: If necessary, join widths of lining. Remember, equal amounts at each side.
2 Place the lining fabric right side uppermost on the table.
3 Using your lining pattern as a guide, mark out the spaces for your rod channels each side on the right side of the fabric.
4 Using a soft lead pencil, mark only 2.5cm (1in) and do not draw the lines right across the fabric or you will leave marks on the fabric which will be very difficult to remove and will show.
5 Turn the fabric to the wrong side and fold over the two side turnings to the wrong side using your 2.5cm (1in) measuring card.
6 Iron up the hemline using the 2.5cm measuring card.
7 Turn the fabric to the right side.
8 Form the channel's casing using your paper pattern as a visual guide, with the side folds in place, bring each pair of marked lines together, matching the markings (*see* Fig 225).
9 Crease in and iron the line of the channel across the fabric on the right side of lining fabric.

10 Pin and tack in place, making sure the folded edges are exactly matching at both sides. This must be accurate.

You may find it easier to place a marker on your machine to the exact measurement of your casing.

11 Machine casing across the lining. Use reverse mechanism accurately at both ends machining backwards into the last three stitches to strengthen this weak point.
12 Re-check all the machined lines with your paper pattern. It is very important that everything is accurate or you will not be able to marry up the face fabric markings to the lining fabric.

Joining the Lining to the Face Fabric

1 Iron the completed face fabric section and the lining fabric section.
2 Check the lining fabric marks at centre front, top and bottom **V** as pattern.
3 Check the clipped **V** along the top edge is correct and place a pin in the centre of the bottom folded hemline.
4 Place the completed face fabric section of the blind, wrong side uppermost, on the table side by side to the completed lining fabric section, right side uppermost.

Note the following points (*see* Figs 225b and c):

1 The hemline on the lining fabric should be left unfolded. The length of the completed face fabric blind with the hem in place should at this point match the length of the lining.
2 In both cases the turning for the heading remains unfolded and flat.

(Far right) Fig 226 Lining tacked in place plus stabilizing.

3 The tailor tacks on the side edges of the face fabric should exactly match the machined line on the casing of the lining section.

Once you have checked that all is correct, replace the ironed-in hemline on the lining fabric into position.

ORDER OF WORK: LINING THE BLIND (Fig 226)

1 Place the lining fabric wrong side uppermost on the table and using your 2.5cm (1in) marker card, re-check the ironed up 2.5cm turning for the hem.
   Note: This will be 2.5cm shorter than the hemline of the face fabric.
2 Place the wrong side of the lining section to the wrong side of the face fabric blind section, matching the centre markings and pin in place.
3 Run a stabilizing curtain tacking stitch down the centre through both fabrics from top to bottom.

If all is correct you will now have the lining fabric lying in place on the top of the face fabric section with a 2.5cm (1in) border down each side and along the hemline.

4 Check with your 2.5cm card that this is accurate.
   At this stage the heading remains flat and matching on both sections.
5 Pin and tack the sides and bottom edges of the lining in place.
6 Run a stabilizing line across the blind across each line of channel machine stitching through both fabrics.

At this point, with the blind tacked and stabilized, you can make a final check of

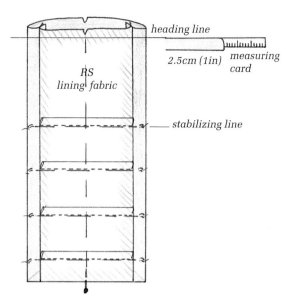

heading line

2.5cm (1in) *measuring card*

RS lining fabric

stabilizing line

the length of your blind. Use your metre stick.

Any adjustment to the final accurate length can now be made at the heading using the same method as marking the final length of your curtain.

7 Trim turning allowance back to 2.5cm (1in) through both face and lining fabrics.
8 Use your 2.5cm measuring card to iron-in a sharp turning along the heading with lining and face fabric together as one.

Attaching the Velcro to the Lining Fabric (Fig 227)

1 Carefully undo the backstitch and take out the tacking stitches from the turning allowance at either side of the blind down to the stabilizing line of the top channel. Secure tacking thread at this point.
2 Peel back the lining fabric from the face fabric.

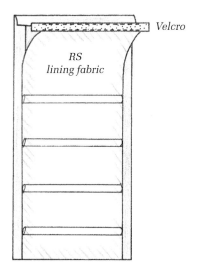

Velcro

RS lining fabric

3 Run the 2.5cm (1in) measuring card along the top of the face fabric heading crease line and sharpen the fold line by re-pressing. Pin and tack into place.

4 Lay the opened out heading marked line of the lining fabric on top of the ironed-in line along the top of the blind to check this is correct.

5 Peel back the lining fabric again and reset the heading line less 2mm (⅟₁₆in). This will now make the turning 2.7cm (1⅟₁₆in) as against the previous 2.5cm (1in).

   There are two reasons for doing this:

   a To ensure the top edge of the lining does not show along the heading line of the face fabric once the Velcro is attached to the strip of Velcro on the batten.

   b At the same time this will slightly lift the length of the blind to a minimal clearance of the window sill ensuring the blind drops in a straight line from top to bottom.

6 The Velcro is now set in this position along the top, folded edge of the lining. This should exactly measure the width of the *finished* lining fabric and extend 2.5cm (1in) either side. There will be about 2.5cm extra at each end. Do not cut this off at this stage.

7 Pin and tack the Velcro along the top edge of the folded heading line of the lining fabric only, through all layers.

8 Pin and tack the bottom edge of the Velcro into place. Tacking in the same direction will ensure the Velcro lies flat.

9 Take the blind to the machine and using a long stitch (3 to 4) machine parallel lines along both long edges of the Velcro in the same direction keeping your stitches straight and as close as possible to the edge of the Velcro. Do not machine the short ends of the Velcro, and leave long ends of thread on both ends of your machine stitching.

Finish off the Ends of the Velcro

The ends of the Velcro are finished off in the following way to ensure the ends do not show at the side edges of the blind and to eliminate bulk.

1 Trim back the two loose ends of the Velcro just short of the side edges of the blind. Before doing this, ensure the loose ends of your machining are pulled through and tied off, so as not to cut the threads when trimming back the Velcro. If you leave long ends they can be tucked under the Velcro.

2 Place the blind on the table with the right side of the lining uppermost and let the Velcro heading of the lining drop into place over the completed face fabric heading line.

3 Pin and tack into place through all thicknesses. The lining is now tacked into place along all edges.

(Far left) Fig 227 Attaching the Velcro to the lining fabric.

4 Slip stitch the lining to the face fabric from the bottom of the blind, starting your stitching at the point 'A' of the bottom channel stabilizing line (Fig 228).

Fig 228 Slip stitching lining into place.

(Far right) Fig 229 Attaching rings into blind and stab stitching lining to face fabric.

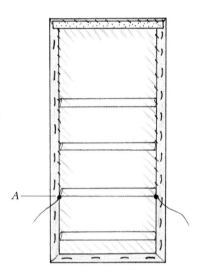

Note: The section of the bottom of the blind is left unstitched but remains tacked until the final assembly of the blind when the lath is placed inside the hemline of the face fabric. Use a small backstitch to finish off the slip stitching and leave the end of the thread loose. This can then be re-threaded to continue the slip stitching once the lath is in place.

ATTACHING THE RINGS TO THE BLIND

It is essential that the rings attached to the channels should be accurate and secure. Lay the completed blind, wrong side uppermost, and check with your paper pattern the exact positioning of the rings.

1 Fold the blind accurately with folds in place. DO NOT PRESS.

It is then possible to mark the position of each ring. Place a vertical pin in each position.

2 Starting from the bottom, prepare to stitch the rings into position.

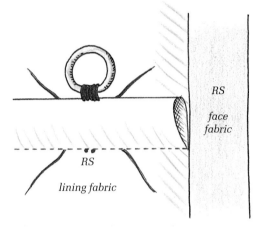

This bottom line of rings will take most of the weight of the blind when it is pulled up plus the fact that it has the added weight of the base lath and the first dowel rod (Fig 229).

Pierce the needle into the edge of the channel 2.5cm (1in) from the marked position of the ring. Leave 5cm (2in) end of thread showing and loose. Bring the needle out just below the marked position for the ring. Secure your thread with a very small backstitch and make four blanket stitches through the ring and the edge of channel.

Keep the stitches close and even. Back-stitch off the last stitch and run the needle 5cm (2in) through the channel and out onto the edge leaving a long end.

3 Stitch the ring at the opposite side of the channel. (If it is necessary to place a ring in the centre, attach this ring last.)

4 Fold the blind to pick up the next channel and check again you have placed the rings in the same position. Repeat on each casing until all the rings are in position.

Securing the lining fabric to the Face Fabric

Although Roman blinds are often machined along the lower edge of each casing, visually you have a line of stitching showing on the right side of your blind. The method described below proves very secure as long as the stitches are done firmly and accurately by using a *stab stitch*. This small stitch, which is barely visible from the right side of the blind, does not spoil the tailored finish of the blind when dropped into its closed position.

These stitches are inserted into the blind immediately underneath the ring now sewn in position into the line of machine stitching holding the channel in place. These small stab stitches are made through the lining and face fabric. Use the same method of attaching your thread as used when sewing on the rings. Use thread, which matches the face fabric.

Run the thread leaving a 5cm (2in) end taking the four machine stitches immediately under the ring. Back stitch into the first machine stitch to secure the thread. Make sure you do not let your needle go through to the face fabric. Using the two machine stitches as a guide, stab stitch into the centre of each machine stitch, making sure you pick up only one thread from the face fabric. You have now done two stab stitches. Do not pull these stitches too tight. Use the fourth machine stitch to backstitch off your thread and making sure you do not go through to the face fabric. Again run the thread through the channel of fabric for 5cm leaving a long end. Repeat at the opposite side.

You must now add another two stab stitches to the centre line. Do this carefully and do not pull the stitches too tight or they will emb a mark from the right side.

When all the rings and stab stitches are complete you can now clip off the long ends of thread from either side of your stab stitches and rings, using the cutting position of your quick unpick, tool.

Preparing and Placing the Dowels into the Channels

◆ Cut the dowels to the correct measurement and sandpaper or file the ends (*see* Definitions, page 235).

◆ Slip the dowels into each casing.

You may find, as you push the dowels into the casings, the lining fabric where the side turning was made may be pushed out of place. This stops the dowel reaching the end of the channel. If this should happen, push the end of your small sharp scissor points into the end of the channel to keep the passage open. Slip stitch to close both ends of the dowel casing using the thread matching the lining.

Inserting the Lath

1 Remove the tacking stitches from the bottom section of the blind. Insert the lath along the bottom hemline.
2 Complete the hem and side turning with the serge stitch.
3 Drop the lining into place and tack into place. Check corners are accurate. Slip stitch into place making sure the corners are accurate using smaller stitches at this point.
4 Remove tacking.

STRINGING THE BLIND

There are several blind cords on the market, which are suitable to string blinds. Do pick a fine cord; these cords are strong as they are made of nylon and can be bought in both natural and white. Once again, consider the appearance from outside the window. A natural-coloured cord blends with a natural lining fabric more easily and is less conspicuous than white cord.

Mounting a Cleat to Receive your Drawstring

Mount the cleat before cutting the length of cord for your blind (*see* Definitions, page 236).

The cleat is mounted on either the window frame or the wall, immediately under the position of the larger screw eye, which will receive the drawstring that should fall into a vertical line under this screw eye.

The nylon cord will be secured to the cleat once the blind is raised. Sufficient

cord should be left on the drawstring to allow the cord to be twisted round the cleat in a figure of eight and still leave sufficient cord to thread all the ends into an acorn or drop weight to finish off the ends of the cord. You will need to leave at least half the length of the drop of your blind, depending where you decide to position your cleat.

Measuring Cords for Stringing up the Blind (Fig 230)

Cut two lengths of cord (three if the blind is over 100cm (40in) and needs the extra middle support).

The length of the first cord 'A' is from the ring on the channel at the base of the blind up and through the reciprocal screw eye 7.5cm (3in) from the edge of the board, across the top of the board through the ring 7.5cm (3in) from the other end of the board, through the larger drawstring screw eye 1.5cm (½in) from the end of the board and down the side of the blind at least half way. Add to this measurement 15cm–20cm (6in–8in) for attaching the cords to the first base ring and finishing off the ends in the acorn or drop weight.

Cut the next cord 'B' the distance from the base ring at either end of the channel to the reciprocal screw eye on the board through the drawstring eye, the same distance down the side of the blind plus the 15–20cm (6–8in).

- Attach the cords to the two batten channel rings with a slip knot (Fig 231).

Thread the nylon cords through the column of plastic rings to the ring on the top channel.

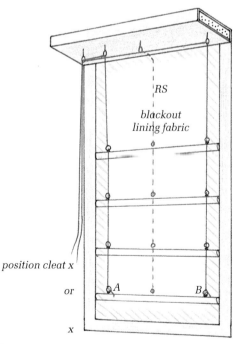

Fig 230 Stringing the blind.

Fig 231 Slip knot.

(a)

(b)

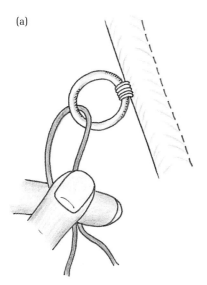

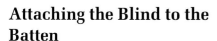

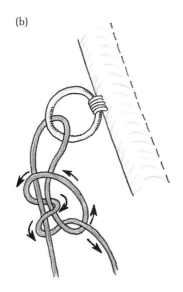

Attaching the Blind to the Batten

The blind is now ready to attach to the board.

1 Position the blind along the top of the board. Make sure it is pushed right up to the soffit allowing the very slight allowance to the width of the blind to lie evenly at each side.
2 Press the Velcro firmly against the Velcro on the batten, running your fingers backwards and forwards pressing firmly. Test it is secure and lift the blind above the board and thread the cords through the first screw eye along the top of the board (if there is a centre screw eye – through the centre) and into the second screw eye and, finally, through the drawstring screw eye. If there is a central cord, follow the centre path. Thread the cord at the operating end into the reciprocal screw eye.
3 Stand back and let the blind drop into place. Do a final check that it is evenly and securely placed on the batten and all the cords are hanging evenly at the chosen drawstring side of the board.

Knot all the cords together at the outside of the screw eye where the cords come through. When all is correct, check that the blind pulls up and down evenly.
4 Even the cords out and let them drop into place down the side of the blind.
5 Cut the cords evenly to the same length and thread the ends through the acorn or drop weight.

MATERIALS AND EQUIPMENT FOR A ROMAN BLIND

1 Face fabric
2 Lining fabric. A cotton lining sateen as an alternative lining you can use blackout or thermal lining fabric.
3 Matching thread to lining and face fabric, plus bold thread.
4 Velcro.
5 Batten to attach blind, screws and Rawlplugs. If mounting blind outside recess you will need angle irons.
6 Timber dowel rods, alternatively, fibreglass dowel rods.

7 Flat wooden lath.

8 Plastic rings, allow two to three per casing.

9 Brass screw eyes (or stainless steel).

10 The same number of rings in one casing plus extra one extra.

11 Nylon or polyester blind cord.

12 Drop weight or acorn.

DEFINITIONS

Batten

A batten is a piece of squared timber 5cm × 2.5cm (2in × 1in) to which to attach a lined, medium-weight fabric Roman blind.

◆ Cut the batten 6mm or ¼in shorter than the recess. This allows for the bulk of the fabric.

◆ The batten is covered with lining fabric if mounting inside the recess of the window and with matching face fabric if mounting on the wall above the recess and must be covered and in position before final measurements can be taken for the blind pattern.

Note: If lined with blackout or with thermal lining, cover the batten with the matching lining sateen in white or natural.

Smooth the ends with sandpaper and drill two holes through the board 12.5cm (5in) from each end and centrally placed, so as not to interfere with the screw eyes, which will be put in the board when it is covered.

FIXING THE COMPLETED BATTEN IN POSITION

If mounting the batten inside the recess it is fixed to the top of the recess (soffit) with screws directly into the soffit.

MOUNTING THE BLIND OUTSIDE THE RECESS

If you mount the blinds on the wall above the window, decide how far you should extend on all sides and measure accordingly.

Note: If mounting your batten outside the window frame you should be careful not to mount it too high, otherwise it will throw out the proportions of your blind. Do not place it any higher than approximately 5cm (2in). This does, however, have the advantage that the mechanism is not seen from outside your window.

◆ The blind should be no more than 5cm (2in) wider than the window at each side.

◆ The blind should drop approximately 5cm (2in) below the sill.

◆ If the blind is face fixed with angle brackets, mark the fixing position of the first bracket.

◆ Drill the fixing holes and screw the bracket in place.

◆ Rest the batten on it and check it is straight. Use a spirit level.

Velcro

The Velcro is placed along the long, narrow edge of the support batten to suspend the Roman blind. Position the Velcro so that the adhesive hook length is to the top of the batten. Staple to reinforce.

Length of Velcro: if mounting the blind in the recess allow sufficient length of Velcro for the length of the board plus returns. If mounting the board on the wall above the recess, allow sufficient Velcro for the length of the board only.

Screw Eyes

- Brass or nickel plated screws are screwed to the underside of the batten to receive the cords.

- The number of rings on the casing plus one.

- Screw the eyes on the underside of the batten, one positioned above every row of rings with one extra screw eye ring on the side of the board you wish to form the drawstring.

- The position of the eye holes corresponding to the position of the rings.

- With a bradawl, mark a hole at each side of the batten to correspond to the rings at each side of the blind.

- Insert a screw eye into each marked hole.

Plastic Rings

Two or three per casing. Sew two 1.5cm (½in) plastic rings to each side of the channel. You will need a ring in the centre of each channel only if the blind is over 132cm (52in).

Mechanism

This is the distance between the last casing at the top of the blind and the bottom of the batten. This allows for the folds to lie neatly on top of one another and provides space for the rod casings and rings, and the screw eyes that accumulate at the top.

Dowel Rods

Pine or fibreglass. Check the circumference and add ease.

Cut the rod 6mm (¼in) shorter than the *finished measurement of the lining.*

Insert the dowels into the casings and slip stitch each end.

Dowel rods are inserted into the casing folds formed when raising the blind.

Lath

- The flat wooden lath is to give extra weight at the bottom of the blind.

- The lath is inserted into the hem at the bottom of the face fabric.

- Cut the lath 1.5cm (½in) shorter than the width of the blind.

- A lath is a piece of split timber in the form of a thin strip about 1in wide.

- A flat wooden lath 1.25cm (½in) thick and 2.5cm (1in) wide, or for a lightweight blind use Ramin wood 5mm (³⁄₁₆in) thick and 3mm (⅛in) wide.

Cord

Nylon or polyester blind cord. The nylon cord is threaded through the plastic rings from bottom to top and through the screw eye and to the side where the drawstring will be.

Cleat

The brass cleat is screwed to the side of the window and is used to secure the cords when the blind is pulled up and down.

◆ Attach the cleat to the wall on the side of the drawstring cord so that the cord can be wound round it when the blind is raised.

◆ Mount the cleat either on the window frame or wall.

Fig 232 Batten in place with stringing attached.

◆ Knot all cords together at the point where they come through the extra screw eye.

◆ Leave an extra 25cm (10in) length of cord for knotting the cords at the bottom ring and for fixing into the acorn.

◆ The ends of the cord can be neatened by putting them in an acorn or drop weight.

WATCHPOINTS:

◆ If a Roman blind is used in conjunction with curtains it must be inside the reveal

◆ If a Roman blind is used in a room where other windows might be dressed with curtaining and the curtain material is patterned, the pattern on your blind material must be lined up with the curtains at the other windows.

◆ Bay windows are divided naturally. Mitre the battens in a bay window.

◆ If you mount the blind on a wall above a window, decide how far you should extend on all sides and measure accurately.

◆ The batten must accommodate the clearance either side of the blind as the blind is made up to fit exactly the width of the covered batten.

◆ Blinds must be dry cleaned.

If you are not aware of all these considerations you will have a disappointing result.

20 Conclusion

For this final project I am going to introduce one of my students, Moira. Apart from the generous support Moira has given me in writing this book she has followed my course with great enthusiasm and has made some excellent soft furnishings for her home. She came to me saying she had visited a show house over the weekend and had seen a very interesting blind. She brought along a quick sketch she had made enabling her to carry the idea to our next meeting. My idea was born that it would be Moira who would close the book using the notes on Roman blinds. It was not difficult to adapt this to the Roman blind she had seen following the same order of work as the basic Roman blind. In addition, from the photographs, you will see only one cord is necessary up the centre of the blind.

Fibreglass rods were used and the lath is Ramin wood which is lighter and thinner. The rods and lath were cut in half to produce the fan shape of the blind.

The following project is Moira's work. I hope that now you have reached the end of this book, you will be familiar with many new and exciting projects that you will have the confidence to undertake for your own homes with your own individuality.

Moira chose a woven silk fabric and lined the blind with a cotton sateen lining. Matching silk thread was used for the silk fabric.

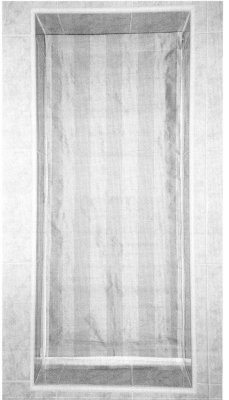
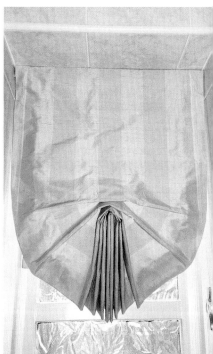

Fig 233 A fan-shaped Roman blind in raised and lowered position, viewed from right and wrong side.

Index